GED® TEST
POWER PRACTICE

Related Titles

GED® Test Flash Review: Mathematical Reasoning
GED® Test Flash Review: Reasoning through Language Arts
GED® Test Flash Review: Science
GED® Test Flash Review: Social Studies
TABE Power Practice

GED® TEST
POWER PRACTICE

Cataloging-in-Publication Data is on file with the Library of Congress.

Printed in the United States of America

9 8 7 6 5 4 3 2 1

ISBN 978-1-57685-995-7

For information on LearningExpress, other LearningExpress products, or bulk sales,
please write to us at:
    80 Broad Street
    4th Floor
    New York, NY 10004

Or visit us at:
    www.learningexpressllc.com

CONTENTS ▶

HOW TO USE THIS BOOK ▶

Welcome to *GED® Test Power Practice*! Congratulations on taking a big step toward preparing for your GED® test and earning a high school equivalency credential. One of your main goals on test day is to be confident that you know the exam inside and out—that's where this book comes in.

This Book's Practice Tests

As you might know, the GED® test is a long exam given on the computer, with four sections and many different types of question formats. You will learn all about the GED® test and its interactive questions in Chapter 1. In this book, you will find two full-length practice exams that look a lot like the actual GED® test. Because the tests in this book are on paper—not on a computer screen—some of the questions can't look exactly like those you will see on test day, but we have made them resemble the computerized versions as closely as they can.

You will have a chance to work with a computerized GED® test and its interactive question types on the free online test you have access to with this book. Visit page 287 to find out how to take this computerized exam.

Taking Your Tests

Try to take the tests in this book under the same conditions you'll have on the actual test day. The beginning of each test tells you how long you have. Sit down in a quiet spot, set your timer, and try to take the exam without any interruptions.

After you finish each section, you will find detailed answer explanations for every question. Not only will these explanations tell you why the correct answer is right, but they will also explain why each of the other choices is wrong.

You will also find scoring information for the short-response and essay questions, along with sample essays to compare yours to.

Scoring Your Best

Practicing with GED®-test-like questions is the best way to prepare for the exam. This book is filled with questions that mirror the ones you will see on test day. Taking these practice tests, especially under the same timing conditions as the real GED® test, will help you get used to pacing yourself. You can see in which subjects you excel and in which you need a bit more study. Use this book as part of your study toolkit, and you will be well on your way to succeeding on the exam!

GED® TEST
POWER PRACTICE

1 ▶ ABOUT THE GED® TEST

The GED® test measures how well you can apply problem solving, analytical reasoning, and critical thinking alongside your understanding of high-school level math, reading, writing, science, and social studies. Passing the GED® test proves you have a high school level education. If you pass, you will be awarded with a GED® test credential, the equivalent of a high school diploma. You should choose to take the GED® test if you would like to receive a high school diploma but are unable or do not want to graduate in the traditional way.

What Are the GED® Tests?

Four separate tests make up the GED® test:

- Mathematical Reasoning
- Reasoning through Language Arts (RLA)
- Social Studies
- Science

To score your best on each test, not only will you need to know the basics of each subject, but you'll also need to use critical thinking, writing, and problem-solving skills.

How Is the Test Delivered?

You will take your GED® test on a computer. Although you absolutely do not need to be a computer expert to take the GED® test, you should be comfortable using a mouse and typing on a keyboard.

How Long Is the Test?

You can choose to take all four GED® tests at once, or you can take each test separately. The entire exam will take about seven hours to complete. The timing for each subject area alone is as follows:

- Mathematical Reasoning—115 minutes
- Reasoning through Language Arts—150 minutes (including a 10-minute break)

- Science—90 minutes
- Social Studies—90 minutes

What Types of Questions Are on the Test?

Most of the questions on the GED® test will be multiple choice, where you have to pick the best answer out of four given choices: A, B, C, D.

Because you'll take the test on a computer, you'll also see some other kinds of questions that will ask you to use your mouse to move images around or use the keyboard to type in your answer.

Drag and Drop

For these questions, you will need to click on the correct object, hold down the mouse, and drag the object to the appropriate place in the problem, diagram, chart, or graph that you're given.

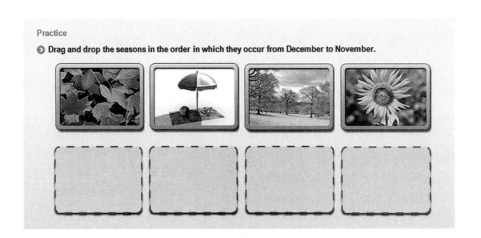

Drag-and-Drop

Drag-and-drop questions have two areas—one area shows all of the answer choices, and the other area is where you will move the correct answers. You will need to drag one or more answer(s) from the first area to the second area.

To answer a drag-and-drop question, click and hold the mouse on an answer and move it (drag it) to the correct area of the screen. Then let go of the mouse (drop it). You can remove an answer and switch it with another answer at any time.

Try the practice question below.

Practice

⊙ Drag and drop the seasons in the order in which they occur from December to November.

Of course, within this book you can't drag and drop items. For the purposes of *GED® Test Power Practice*, you will choose from a list of items, as you would on a typical drag-and-drop question, and write the correct answer(s) in the appropriate spot.

Drop Down

In drop-down questions, you will need to select the answer or phrase to complete a sentence or problem from a menu that drops down with the click of a button.

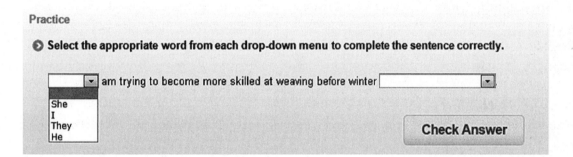

Drop-down questions are very similar to multiple-choice questions, so you will not see them in the two tests within this book.

Fill-in-the-Blank

These questions ask you to manually type in answer(s) to a problem rather than choose from several choices.

Fill-in-the-Blank

A fill-in-the-blank question asks you to type information into one or more blank space(s). There are no answer choices given to you—you must come up with what you think is the correct answer and type it in the blank.

To answer the question, type in what you think is the correct word or phrase for each blank.

Try this practice question.

Henry has $5 more than Oliver, and the same amount of money as Murray. Together, they have $85. How much money does Oliver have?

_____ dollars.

The fill-in-the-blank questions in this book look almost exactly like the ones you'll encounter in the online test, but here you will of course have to write in your answer instead of typing it.

Hot Spot

For hot-spot questions, you will be asked to click on an area of the screen to indicate where the correct answer is located. For instance, you may be asked to plot a point by clicking on the corresponding online graph or to click on a certain area of a map.

Hot Spot

Hot spot questions ask you to choose a certain place on an image.

To answer the question, click on the correct spot of the image provided. You can change your answer by simply clicking on another area.

Now, you try.

Practice

> **Plot the number 2.5 on the number line below.**

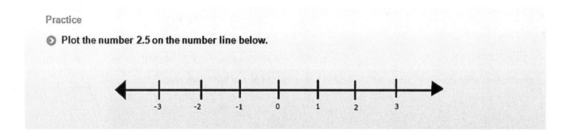

In this book, you will be asked to draw a dot on a specific point or to circle a certain part of a diagram.

Short Answer

Short-answer questions are similar to fill-in-the-blank questions—you must type your response on the provided lines. However, these questions require you to write a paragraph instead of a word or two, usually in response to a passage or an image. Each should take about 10 minutes to answer.

Short Answer and Extended Response

These question types ask you to respond to a question by typing your answer into a box. With short answer and extended response questions, your answer will range from a few sentences to an essay. Like with fill-in-the-blank, there are no answer choices given to you.

You should feel comfortable typing on a keyboard in order to answer these questions, since there is a time limit for each test.

- Short answer questions can be answered with just a few words or sentences—they will probably take about 10 minutes to complete.

- Your extended response question is an essay, and is much longer—it will take 45 minutes to complete.

To answer these question types, enter your response into the text box provided. Here is an example of a response box:

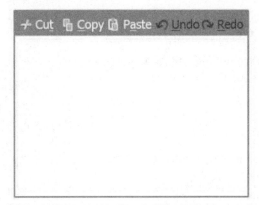

Notice that at the top of the box you will find tools to help you edit your answer if necessary.

Like fill-in-the-blank questions, short-answer questions in this book look as they will online—you will just write in your answer instead of typing it.

Extended Response

For extended response questions on the RLA exam you will be given 45 minutes to read one or two informational articles (a total of 550 to 650 words) and type a response on a computer using a simple word-processing program. This question requires you to read the prompt (the passage provided), create an argument based on it, and write a strong essay with evidence and examples.

When using this book, you can choose to either hand-write your essay or type it on a computer.

When and Where Can I Take the Test?

There are three testing opportunities per year in each subject area. To find a GED® test center, visit the link below, choose your location, and enter your zip code: www.gedtestingservice.com/testers/locate-a-testing-center.

You can sign up for any or all of the GED® tests online at the link above, depending on the availability of spots in your area.

How Much Will the Test Cost?

Each of the four GED® tests costs $30, for a total of $120 for all four tests. You can pay for any or all parts of the test you are ready to take. There may be additional fees, depending on the state in which you take the test. Check the official GED® test website for complete test information.

How Are the Tests Scored?

A minimum score of 150 is required to pass each test. Each question on the GED® test is assigned a different point value depending on its difficulty. You will find out your score or scores on the same day you take the exam.

About the Test Sections

Before you make your way through the tests in this book, let's explore each of the four GED® test sections.

Mathematical Reasoning

On the GED® Mathematical Reasoning test, you will have 115 minutes (just under two hours) to answer 45 questions. These questions will fall under two areas: Quantitative Problem Solving and Algebraic Problem Solving.

Quantitative Problem Solving questions cover basic math concepts like multiples, factors, exponents, absolute value, ratios, averages, and probability.

Algebraic Problem Solving questions cover basic topics in algebra, including linear equations, quadratic equations, functions, linear inequalities, and more.

Calculator

An online calculator, called the **TI-30XS MultiView** (pictured below), will be available to you for most of the questions within the Mathematical Reasoning section.

Your first five questions will be non-calculator questions, but the rest of the test will have this on-screen calculator available for you to use. If you have never used the TI-30XS MultiView or another scientific calculator before, be sure to practice using it before you take the actual test.

The GED® Testing Service has created a calculator reference sheet and tutorial videos on its website to help you practice. The reference sheet will also be available for you to use during the test. However, you should be comfortable with the functions of the calculator BEFORE taking the test. You will not want to take extra time to read through the directions while trying to complete the problems on test day.

The reference sheet can be found at www.gedtestingservice.com

Formulas

A list of formulas will be available for you to use during the test. However, it will NOT include basic formulas, such as the area of a rectangle or triangle, circumference of a circle, or perimeter of geometric figures. You will be expected to know these already.

Visit the Appendix on page 285 to see the list of formulas you will be given on test day.

Reasoning Through Language Arts

The GED® Reasoning through Language Arts (RLA) exam tests your reading, writing, and English-language skills. Questions in this section will ask you to do things like identify the main idea or theme in a reading passage or determine the meanings of words within a passage. The RLA section also tests your knowledge of grammar, sentence structure, and the mechanics of language. Sharpening your reading and writing skills is important for the GED® test, and not only for the RLA section—the GED® Social Studies test and the GED® Science test also measure your ability to understand and communicate ideas through writing.

There are 48 questions and one Extended Response question on the RLA test. You will have 150 minutes to complete the entire exam, with one 10-minute scheduled break.

For most of the questions on the RLA test, you will be given a reading passage, followed by 6 to 8 questions that test your ability to understand and analyze what you have read.

Drop-down items are mostly used on the GED® RLA exam to test grammar and English-language mechanics. Drop-down questions are inserted in the middle of paragraphs. You will be asked to "drop down" a menu with several sentence choices, and choose the one that fits best grammatically in the sentence.

Practice

◉ **Select the appropriate word from each drop-down menu to complete the sentence correctly.**

[▼] am trying to become more skilled at weaving before winter [   ] [▼]

She
I
They
He

Check Answer

Passage Types for Reading Questions

Twenty-five percent of the reading passages on the RLA test will be literature. This includes historical and modern fiction, as well as nonfiction like biographies or essays. You might generally think of literature as fiction (invented stories), but literary texts can also be nonfiction (true stories).

Seventy-five percent of the reading passages will be from informational texts, including workplace documents (like memos or letters). These passages will often cover topics in social studies and science. The RLA test also will feature historical passages that are considered part of the "Great American Conversation." These include documents, essays, and speeches that have helped shaped American history.

There are no poetry or drama passages on the RLA test.

Extended Response Question

As you learned earlier in the chapter, the Extended Response item requires you to find and use information from the reading passage (or passages) to answer the question in a well-thought-out essay. You will be asked to analyze an issue and likely also asked to provide an opinion on what you have read. You will have 45 minutes of your total RLA time to complete this essay—that includes brainstorming, writing a draft, writing a final version, and proofreading your work.

Science

The GED® Science test focuses on scientific reasoning and tests that you can understand and apply science principles in real-world situations. It is made up of 35 questions, which you will have 90 minutes to complete.

The test will include reading passages, graphs, and charts. The majority of the information you need to answer questions will be within the exam itself, whether in a diagram or in a passage. The test does *not* ask you to memorize science facts beforehand.

The science topics covered on the GED® Science test are:

- **Physical science**—40% of the questions
- **Life science**—40% of the questions
- **Earth and space science**—20% of the questions

On the GED® Science test, physical science includes high-school physics and chemistry and covers the structure of atoms, the structure of matter, the properties of matter, chemical reactions, conservation of mass and energy, increase in disorder, the laws of motion, forces, and the interactions of energy and matter.

Life science deals with subjects covered in high-school biology classes, including cell structure, heredity, biological evolution, behavior, and interdependence of organisms.

Earth and space questions will test your knowledge of the Earth and the solar system, the geochemical cycles, the origin and evolution of the Earth and the universe, and energy in the Earth system.

Social Studies

The GED® Social Studies test is made up of 35 questions and one Extended Response item. You will have 65 minutes to answer the questions and 25 minutes to write your essay. The questions on this test are based on information provided to you, such as brief texts, excerpts from speeches, maps, graphics, and tables. As on the GED® Science exam, the information you'll need to answer questions on the GED® Social Studies test will be contained in the passages, political cartoons, maps, and other information presented on the test. You do not have to memorize names, dates, places, and facts beforehand.

As on the GED® RLA test, many of the brief texts featured will be drawn from materials reflecting "the Great American Conversation," which includes documents like the Declaration of Independence and other notable historical texts from U.S. history.

The Social Studies exam will focus on four areas:

- **Civics and government**—approximately 50% of the questions
- **United States History**—20% of the questions
- **Economics**—15% of the questions
- **Geography and the world**—15% of the questions

Good Luck!

Now that you are familiar with the GED® test, you can begin your powerful practice. The exams in this book are designed to be as close as possible to the actual tests you will see on test day. Each question in the exams that come with this book is accompanied by a very detailed answer explanation—you will be able to see not only why the correct answer is right but also why each of the other choices is incorrect. You will also see sample essays at all levels for the Extended Response items.

Best of luck on your GED® test study journey and on your test-taking experience!

2 ▶ GED® MATHEMATICAL REASONING TEST 1

This practice test is modeled on the format, content, and timing of the official GED® Mathematical Reasoning test. Like the official test, the questions focus on your quantitative and algebraic problem-solving skills.

You may refer to the formula sheet in the Appendix on page 285 as you take this exam. Answer questions 1–5 *without* using a calculator. You may use a scientific calculator (or a calculator of any kind) for the remaining exam questions.

Before you begin, it's important to know that you should work carefully but not spend too much time on any one question. Be sure you answer every question.

Set a timer for 115 minutes (1 hour and 55 minutes), and try to take this test uninterrupted, under quiet conditions.

Complete answer explanations for all of the test questions follow the exam. Good luck!

45 Questions
115 Minutes

1. Joseph owns v video games. Harry owns 10 fewer than two times the number of video games that Joseph owns. Which expression represents the number of video games that Harry owns in terms of v?
   a. $10v - 2$
   b. $2v - 10$
   c. $2(v - 10)$
   d. $10(v - 2)$

2. Which of the following is equivalent to $\dfrac{\sqrt[3]{9} \times \sqrt[3]{18}}{3}$?
   a. $\sqrt[3]{2}$
   b. $3\sqrt[3]{2}$
   c. $\sqrt[3]{6}$
   d. $\sqrt[3]{18}$

3. Write your answer on the line below. You may use numbers, symbols, and or text in your response.

   An expression is shown below. Simplify the expression completely. Be sure to leave your answer in radical form.

   $$\frac{\sqrt{72}}{\sqrt{36}}$$

4. Draw a dot on the grid below to plot the point indicated by the ordered pair $(-2,1)$.

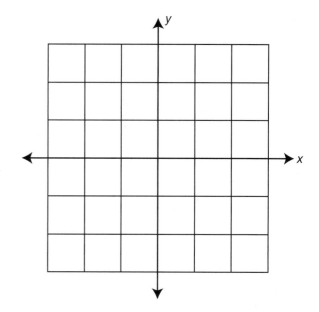

5. As part of a game, Gilbert must take a number and use a special procedure to come up with a new number. To come up with his new number, Gilbert takes the original number, cubes it, adds 5 to it, and finally multiplies it by 2. If the original number is represented by x, which of the following represents Gilbert's new number?
   a. $2(3x + 5)$
   b. $2(x^3 + 5)$
   c. $2x^3 + 5$
   d. $x^6 + 5$

6. The sum of a number n and 4 is less than 5 times the number m. If m is 6, which of the following is true?
   a. n is greater than 6
   b. $n + 4$ is less than 26
   c. n is less than 26
   d. n is equal to 26

7. A company pays its sales employees a base rate of $450 a week plus a 4% commission on any sales the employee makes. If an employee makes $1,020 in sales one week, what will be his total paycheck for that week? Write your answer in the box below.

[ ]

8. The diameter of a circle is 10 meters. In meters, which of the following is the circumference of this circle?

a. 5π

b. 10π

c. 25π

d. 100π

9. Which of the following is equivalent to $(\frac{3}{4})^3$?

a. $\frac{3^3}{4^3}$

b. $\frac{3 \times 3}{4 \times 3}$

c. $\frac{3^3}{4}$

d. $\frac{3}{4 \times 3}$

10. The line n is parallel to the line $y = 3x - 7$ and passes through the point $(5,1)$. At what point does the line n cross the y-axis? Write your answer in the box below.

[ ]

11. A line passes through the point $(4,0)$ and has a slope of $-\frac{1}{2}$. What is the equation of this line?

a. $y = -\frac{1}{2}x + 2$

b. $y = -\frac{1}{2}x - 2$

c. $y = -\frac{1}{2}x + 4$

d. $y = -\frac{1}{2}x - 4$

12. What is the value of $f(-1)$ if $f(x) = 3(x - 1)^2 + 5$?

a. 8

b. 11

c. 15

d. 17

13. What is the equation of the line that passes through the points $(-2,1)$ and $(4,5)$ in the Cartesian coordinate plane?

a. $y = \frac{2}{3}x - \frac{4}{3}$

b. $y = \frac{2}{3}x - \frac{1}{3}$

c. $y = \frac{2}{3}x + \frac{7}{3}$

d. $y = \frac{2}{3}x + 4$

14. A 9-foot-long ladder is placed against the side of a building such that the top of the ladder reaches a window that is 6 feet above the ground. To the nearest 10th of a foot, what is the distance from the bottom of the ladder to the building?

a. 1.7

b. 2.4

c. 6.7

d. 10.8

15. The figure below represents the rate of cooling for a particular material after it was placed in a super-cooled bath.

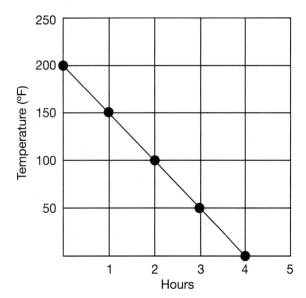

If the temperature, in Fahrenheit, is represented by T and the number of hours elapsed is represented by H, then which of the following would represent a situation where the rate of cooling was faster than the rate indicated in the graph?

a. $T = -25H + 150$
b. $T = -60H + 300$
c. $T = -10H + 200$
d. $T = -50H + 250$

16. In a study of its employees, a company found that about 50% spent more than 2 hours a day composing or reading emails. The overall distribution of time employees spent on these activities was skewed right with a mean time of about 2.5 hours. Complete the box plot below so that is matches the given information.

Draw as many vertical lines as needed on the graph to represent the data.

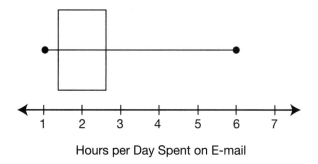

Hours per Day Spent on E-mail

17. What is the equation of the line graphed in the figure below?

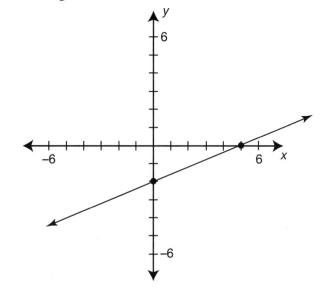

a. $y = \frac{2}{5}x - 2$
b. $y = -\frac{2}{5}x - 2$
c. $y = \frac{2}{5}x + 5$
d. $y = -\frac{2}{5}x - 5$

18. What is a positive solution to the equation $x^2 - 5x = 14$?

 a. 2

 b. 7

 c. 5

 d. 9

19. What is the slope of the line represented by the equation $10x - y = 2$?

 a. 1

 b. 2

 c. 5

 d. 10

20. Which of the following is equivalent to $5^{\frac{1}{2}} \times 5^2$?

 a. $5^{-\frac{3}{2}}$

 b. 5

 c. $5^{\frac{5}{2}}$

 d. $5^{\frac{1}{4}}$

21. A specialized part for a manufacturing process has a thickness of 1.2×10^{-3} inches. To the ten-thousandth of an inch, what would be the thickness of a stack of 10 of these parts?

 a. 0.0001

 b. 0.0012

 c. 0.0120

 d. 0.1200

22. A line is perpendicular to the line $y = \frac{5}{6}x + 1$ and has a y-intercept of $(0,-4)$. What is the equation of this line?

 a. $y = -4x + 1$

 b. $y = \frac{5}{6}x - 4$

 c. $y = -\frac{6}{5}x + 1$

 d. $y = -\frac{6}{5}x - 4$

23. Which of the following expressions is equivalent to $\frac{3}{x} \div \frac{5x}{2}$ for all nonzero x?

 a. $\frac{6}{5x^2}$

 b. $\frac{15x^2}{2}$

 c. $\frac{3}{2}$

 d. $\frac{15}{2}$

24. A factory is able to produce at least 16 items, but no more than 20 items, for every hour the factory is open. If the factory is open for 8 hours a day, which of the following are possibly the numbers of items produced by the factory over a 7-day work period?

Select all of the correct possibilities from this list, and write them in the box below.

 128

 150

 850

 910

 1,115

25. A 32-ounce bag of potato chips has a retail cost of $3.45. To the nearest 10th of a cent, what is the price per ounce of this item (in cents)?

 a. 9.3

 b. 10.8

 c. 28.5

 d. 35.45

26.

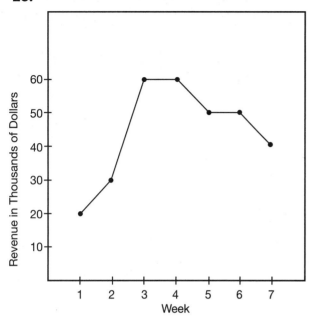

The graph shown here represents the total weekly revenue of a company over several weeks. For which of the following periods has the weekly revenue increased?

a. between weeks 2 and 3

b. between weeks 3 and 4

c. between weeks 4 and 5

d. between weeks 6 and 7

27. Circle the line in the coordinate plane below that represents the graph of the equation $3x - 2y = 1$.

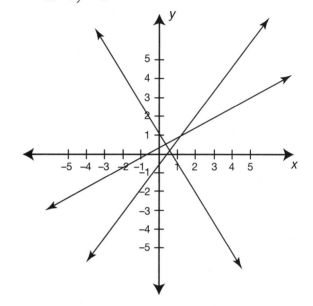

28. A line z is perpendicular to the line $y = -x + 5$. If z passes through the points $(0,-2)$ and $(x,5)$, what is the value of x?

a. 0

b. 3

c. 7

d. 10

29. Which of the following is equivalent to the numerical expression $\sqrt{2}(\sqrt{18} - \sqrt{6})$?

a. $4\sqrt{3}$

b. $5\sqrt{6}$

c. $6 - \sqrt{3}$

d. $6 - \sqrt{6}$

30. A beauty-product manufacturer has been researching the way that people use various beauty products. After several surveys, it has collected the data shown in the scatterplot below, which shows the time that participants spent on their morning beauty routines on a typical morning versus the amount of money the participants spent per month on beauty products.

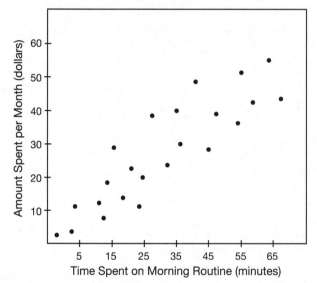

Given this plot, which of the following best describes the relationship between the amount of time spent and the amount of money spent?

a. In general, the longer people spent on their morning beauty routine, the more money they spent per month on beauty products.

b. In general, the longer people spent on their morning beauty routine, the less money they spent per month on beauty products.

c. In general, the amount of time people spent on their morning beauty routine was about the same as the amount of money they spent in dollars on beauty products.

d. In general, there is no clear relationship between the amount of time people spent on their beauty routine and the amount of money they spent per month on beauty products.

31. A walking trail is 11,088 feet long. If a mile is 5,280 feet, how many miles long is the walking trail?
  a. 0.2
  b. 0.5
  c. 1.6
  d. 2.1

32. The product of $x^2 - 6$ and x^4 is
  a. $x^8 - 6$
  b. $x^6 - 6$
  c. $x^6 - 6x^4$
  d. $x^8 - 6x^4$

33. The table below indicates the behavior of the price of one share of a given stock over several weeks.

END OF	CHANGE
Week 1	Increased by $5.00
Week 2	Decreased by 10%
Week 3	Decreased by $1.10
Week 4	Doubled in value

If the stock was worth $10.15 a share at the beginning of week 1, what was the value of one share of this stock at the end of week 4?

  a. $25.07
  b. $29.46
  c. $32.20
  d. $50.12

34. What is the mode of the data set 9, 4, −1, 12, 4, 8, 7?
  a. −1
  b. 4
  c. 7
  d. 13

35. There are 48 total applicants for a job. Of these applicants, 20 have a college degree, 15 have five years of work experience, and 8 have a college degree and five years of work experience. If an applicant is randomly selected, what is the probability, to the nearest tenth of a percent, that he or she has a college degree or has 5 years of work experience?

a. 41.7%

b. 56.3%

c. 72.9%

d. 89.6%

36. A customer uses two coupons to purchase a product at a grocery store, where the original price of the product was $8.30. If the final price paid by the customer was $7.00 and each coupon gave the same discount, what was the value of the discount provided by a single coupon?

a. $0.65

b. $0.90

c. $1.30

d. $2.60

37. Lee is planning to buy a new television and has been watching the price of a particular model for the past month. Last month, the price was $309.99, while this month, the price is $334.99. To the nearest tenth of a percent, by what percent has the price increased over the past month? Write your answer in the box below.

```
                              %
```

38. Which of the following are the two solutions to the equation $x^2 - 2x - 3 = 0$?

a. 3 and −1

b. −3 and 1

c. −3 and −2

d. 2 and 2

39. Which of the following represents the solution set of the inequality $x + 2 > 5$?

a. $\{x: x > 10\}$

b. $\{x: x > 7\}$

c. $\{x: x > 3\}$

d. $\{x: x > 2.5\}$

40. What is the value of $\frac{x - 5}{x^2 - 1}$ when $x = \frac{1}{2}$?

a. −10

b. $\frac{3}{2}$

c. 6

d. 0

41.

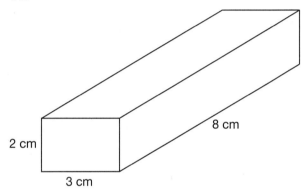

What is the volume of the figure above?

a. 6

b. 24

c. 48

d. 108

42. The bar chart represents the total dollar value of sales for four product versions in July.

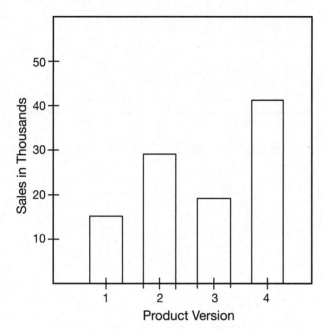

Which two products have combined sales of more than $50,000 in July?
  a. Products 1 and 2
  b. Products 2 and 3
  c. Products 2 and 4
  d. Products 1 and 3

43. The surface area of a sphere is 36π cubic meters. To the nearest meter, what is the diameter of this sphere?
  a. 3
  b. 6
  c. 12
  d. 24

44. What value of x satisfies the system of equations $x - 2y = 8$ and $x + 2y = 14$?
  a. -6
  b. 11
  c. There are infinitely many values of x that satisfy this system.
  d. There are no values of x that satisfy this system.

45. $(x^2 + 5) - (x^2 - x) =$
  a. $5 + x$
  b. $5 - x$
  c. $2x^2 - 5x$
  d. $2x^2 + x + 5$

Answers and Explanations

1. Choice b is correct. "10 fewer than" implies that 10 should be subtracted from the next stated term. That term is "2 times the number of video games that Joseph owns," or $2v$.

Choice **a** is incorrect. This expression represents 2 fewer than 10 times the number of video games Joseph owns.

Choice **c** is incorrect. This expression represents 2 times 10 fewer than the number of video games Joseph owns.

Choice **d** is incorrect. This expression represents 10 times 2 fewer than the number of video games Joseph owns.

2. Choice c is correct. The product in the numerator can be written as $\sqrt[3]{3 \times 3 \times 3 \times 6}$ $= 3\sqrt[3]{6}$. The 3 in the denominator cancels out the 3 in front of the root.

Choice **a** is incorrect. The numerator is made up of a product. The denominator can only cancel one factor of the numerator.

Choice **b** is incorrect. The denominator cannot cancel out a factor within a cube root.

Choice **d** is incorrect. The cube root of 9 is not 3.

3. Correct answer: $\sqrt{2}$

Two factors of 72 are 2 and 36. Further, $\frac{\sqrt{a}}{\sqrt{b}} = \sqrt{\frac{a}{b}}$ for positive numbers a and b. Using these properties, $\frac{\sqrt{72}}{\sqrt{36}} = \frac{\sqrt{2 \times 36}}{36} = \sqrt{2}$.

4.

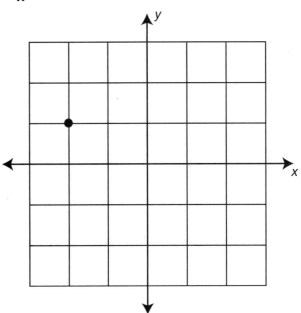

The first term of the ordered pair is the x-coordinate. Since this is negative, the point will be on the left-hand side of the y-axis. The second term is the y-coordinate. This indicates how many units above the x-axis the point is located.

5. Choice b is correct. To cube means to take the number to the third power. Adding 5 to this yields the expression $x^3 + 5$. Finally, multiplying this by 2 yields $2(x^3 + 5)$.

Choice **a** is incorrect. This represents multiplying the number by 3 as the first step. To cube means to take the number to the third power.

Choice **c** is incorrect. This represents multiplying by 2 before adding 5.

Choice **d** is incorrect. Two times x cubed is not equivalent to x to the 6th power.

6. Choice c is correct. The original statement can be written as $n + 4 < 5m$. Given the value of m, $5m = 5 \times 6 = 30$, therefore $n + 4 < 30$. This can be simplified further, to $n < 26$.

Choice **a** is incorrect. The original statement can be written as $n + 4 < 5m$. This statement can be used to show what n is less than, but it can't indicate what n is greater than.

Choice **b** is incorrect. The original statement can be written as $n + 4 < 5m$. Given the value of m, $5m = 5 \times 6 = 30$, therefore $n + 4 < 30$. While $n < 26$, it is not necessarily true that $n + 4 < 26$.

Choice **d** is incorrect. The original statement can be written as $n + 4 < 5m$. This statement can be used to show what n is less than, but it can't indicate what n is equal to.

7. Correct answer: $490.80. The employee is paid a 4% commission on his sales of $1,020. Therefore, he will be paid $0.04 \times \$1{,}020 = \$40.80$ for the sales. This is on top of his regular pay of $450. Therefore, his total paycheck will be $450 + $40.80 = $490.80.

8. Choice b is correct. The radius of the circle is 5, and the circumference is $2 \times \pi \times$ (radius), or 10π. This can also be found simply by multiplying the diameter and π.

Choice **a** is incorrect. The radius of the circle is 5 and must be doubled in order to find the circumference.

Choice **c** is incorrect. This is the area of the circle, which is found by squaring the radius and multiplying by π.

Choice **d** is incorrect. The diameter does not need to be squared in order to find the circumference.

9. Choice a is correct. Applying an exponent to a fraction is equivalent to applying that exponent to the numerator and denominator.

Choice **b** is incorrect. An exponent of 3 is not equivalent to multiplication by 3.

Choice **c** is incorrect. The exponent must be applied to both the numerator and the denominator.

Choice **d** is incorrect. An exponent of 3 is not equivalent to multiplication by 3 and would be applied to both the numerator and the denominator.

10. Correct answer: (0,–14)

Since n is parallel to the given line, it must have the same slope, 3. Given this and the point that n passes through, we can use the point-slope formula to determine the equation for n.

$$y - 1 = 3(x - 5)$$
$$y - 1 = 3x - 15$$
$$y = 3x - 14$$

Now that the equation is in the form $y = mx + b$, we can see that the y-intercept is –14. By definition, this means that the line passes over the y-axis at the point (0,–14).

11. Choice a is correct. The answer choices are in the form $y = mx + b$. Using the given information, when $x = 4$, $y = 0$, and the slope is $m = -\frac{1}{2}$, this gives the equation $0 = -\frac{1}{2}(4) + b$, which has a solution of $b = 2$.

Choice **b** is incorrect. When solving for the y-intercept b, the –2 must be added to both sides of the equation.

Choice **c** is incorrect. The given point (4,0) is not a y-intercept; it's an x-intercept. The equation $y = mx + b$ uses a y-intercept.

Choice **d** is incorrect. If the x-intercept is (4,0) as given, the y-intercept will be –4 only if the slope is 1. Here the slope is $-\frac{1}{2}$.

12. Choice d is correct. Substituting –1 for the x, $f(-1) = 3(-1 - 1)^2 + 5 = 3(-2)^2 + 5 = 3(4) + 5 = 12 + 5 = 17$.

Choice **a** is incorrect. When substituting –1 for x, $x - 1$ represents $-1 - 1 = -2$, not multiplication.

Choice **b** is incorrect. It is not true that $(x - 1)^2 = x^2 + 1$.

Choice **c** is incorrect. By the order of operations, the subtraction within the parentheses as well as the squaring operation must be performed before the multiplication by 3.

13. Choice c is correct. Using the slope formula first, $m = \dfrac{5 - 1}{4 - (-2)} = \dfrac{4}{6} = \dfrac{2}{3}$. Now, applying the point-slope formula we have:

$$y - 1 = \tfrac{2}{3}(x - (-2))$$
$$y - 1 = \tfrac{2}{3}(x + 2)$$
$$y - 1 = \tfrac{2}{3}x + \tfrac{4}{3}$$
$$y = \tfrac{2}{3}x + \tfrac{4}{3} + 1 = \tfrac{2}{3}x + \tfrac{7}{3}$$

Choice **a** is incorrect. In the point-slope formula, the x_1 and y_1 must come from the same point.

Choice **b** is incorrect. When the point $(-2, 1)$ is used in the point-slope formula, the result is $y - 1 = m(x - (-2))$. On the right-hand side of this equation, the 2 ends up being positive.

Choice **d** is incorrect. The slope is found using the change in y on the numerator: $\dfrac{5 - 1}{4 - (-2)} = \dfrac{4}{6} = \dfrac{2}{3}$.

14. Choice c is correct. Using the Pythagorean theorem, the hypotenuse of the right triangle formed by the ladder and the building is 9 while the length of one leg is 6. This yields the equation $6^2 + b^2 = 9^2$ or $b^2 = 81 - 36 = 45$. Therefore, $b = \sqrt{45} \approx 6.7$.

Choice **a** is incorrect. The terms in the Pythagorean theorem are squared.

Choice **b** is incorrect. Applying the Pythagorean theorem to this problem yields the equation $6^2 + b^2 = 9^2$. The exponent of 2 indicates to multiply the term by itself twice, not multiply by 2.

Choice **d** is incorrect. The length of the ladder represents the hypotenuse, or c, in the Pythagorean theorem.

15. Choice b is correct. The rate of cooling indicated in the graph is the slope of the line passing through the points $(0, 200)$ and $(4, 0)$. This slope is –50, which implies the material is losing 50 degrees every hour. The slope of the equation in this answer choice is –60, which implies the material is losing 60 degrees every hour, a faster rate of cooling.

Choice **a** is incorrect. This slope would imply that the material is losing 25 degrees every hour, which is a slower rate of cooling.

Choice **c** is incorrect. This slope would imply that the material is losing 10 degrees every hour, which is a slower rate of cooling.

Choice **d** is incorrect. This slope would indicate the material is losing 50 degrees every hour, which is the same rate of cooling that is given in the graph.

16.

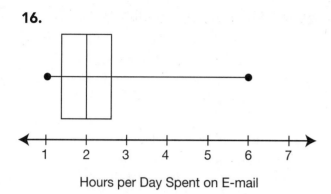

Hours per Day Spent on E-mail

The statement "50% spent more than 2 hours a day composing or reading emails" indicates that the median of this data set is 2. This is typically indicated on a box plot by a vertical line in the center of the box.

17. Choice a is correct. Using the two given points, whenever y increases by 2 units, x increases by 5 units. This means the slope must be $m = \frac{2}{5}$ (the change in y divided by the change in x). Further, the y-intercept is $b = -2$. Using the equation $y = mx + b$, we have $y = \frac{2}{5}x - 2$.

Choice **b** is incorrect. The line rises from left to right; therefore, the slope must be positive.

Choice **c** is incorrect. The x-intercept is not used when writing the equation as $y = mx + b$. In fact, b represents the y-intercept.

Choice **d** is incorrect. The line rises from left to right; therefore, the slope must be positive. Additionally, the y-intercept is -2 and not 5.

18. Choice b is correct. Rewriting the equation by subtracting 14 from both sides yields the quadratic equation $x^2 - 5x - 14 = 0$. The left-hand side of this equation can be factored into $(x - 7)(x + 2)$, indicating that the solutions are 7 and -2.

Choice **a** is incorrect. Once the quadratic equation is rewritten and factored, the zero product rule states that $x - 7 = 0$ or $x + 2 = 0$. Therefore one of the solutions is -2 instead of 2.

Choices **c** and **d** are incorrect. To factor the rewritten quadratic equation, find factors of 14 that sum to -5 instead of numbers that sum to -14.

19. Choice d is correct. To find the slope of the line with this equation, move the y-variable to one side on its own to put the equation in the form $y = mx + b$, where m is the slope. Adding y to both sides and subtracting 2 from both sides gives the equation $y = 10x - 2$, so the slope is 10.

Choice **a** is incorrect. The coefficient of x, not the coefficient of y, represents the slope when the equation is written in the form $y = mx + b$.

Choice **b** is incorrect. The slope cannot be read from the equation in the form it is currently written.

Choice **c** is incorrect. When solving for y to find the slope, 10 will be divided by 1 and not by 2.

20. Choice c is correct. When multiplying terms with the same base, the exponents are added. Therefore $5^{\frac{1}{2}} \times 5^2 = 5^{\frac{1}{2}+2} = 5^{\frac{1}{2}+\frac{4}{2}} = 5^{\frac{5}{2}}$.

Choice **a** is incorrect. When multiplying terms with the same base, the exponents are added, not subtracted.

Choice **b** is incorrect. When multiplying terms with the same base, the exponents are added, not multiplied.

Choice **d** is incorrect. When multiplying terms with the same base, the exponents are added, not divided.

21. Choice c is correct. $1.2 \times 10^{-3} = 0.0012$ and $10 \times 0.0012 = 0.0120$.

Choice **a** is incorrect. It is not possible for the thickness of ten parts to be smaller than the thickness of one part.

Choice **b** is incorrect. This is the thickness of a single part.

Choice **d** is incorrect. This is the thickness of a stack of 100 such parts.

22. Choice d is correct. The slope will be the negative reciprocal of the given slope, and b in the equation $y = mx + b$ is -4.

Choice **a** is incorrect. The slope of a perpendicular line will be the negative reciprocal of the slope of the original line.

Choice **b** is incorrect. Parallel lines have the same slope, while perpendicular lines have negative reciprocal slopes.

Choice **c** is incorrect. The term added to the x-term will be the y-intercept, which is not -1.

23. Choice a is correct. The division is equivalent to $\frac{3}{x} \times \frac{2}{5x} = \frac{6}{5x^2}$.

Choice **b** is incorrect. The division of two fractions is equivalent to multiplying the first fraction by the reciprocal of the second fraction.

Choice **c** is incorrect. This is the result of multiplying and not dividing the fractions if the 5 cancelled out. There are no terms that would cancel with the 5.

Choice **d** is incorrect. This is the result of multiplying the two fractions.

24. Correct Answers: 910 and 1,115

The minimum number of items the factory could produce in this time frame is $16 \times 8 \times 7 = 896$ items while the maximum is $20 \times 8 \times 7 = 1,120$. Any whole number value in between these numbers is a possible number of items the factory could produce over the given time frame.

25. Choice b is correct. The price per ounce is found by dividing 3.45 by 32.

Choice **a** is incorrect. Dividing the number of ounces by the cost will give the number of ounces per cent.

Choice **c** is incorrect. Subtracting terms will not give an interpretable value.

Choice **d** is incorrect. Adding these two terms will not give an interpretable value.

26. Choice a is correct. The revenue is increasing whenever the graph is rising from left to right. This occurs between weeks 2 and 3.

Choice **b** is incorrect. The revenue is increasing whenever the graph is rising from left to right. This does not occur between weeks 3 and 4.

Choice **c** is incorrect. The revenue is increasing whenever the graph is rising from left to right. This does not occur between weeks 4 and 5.

Choice **d** is incorrect. The revenue is increasing whenever the graph is rising from left to right. This does not occur between weeks 6 and 7.

27.

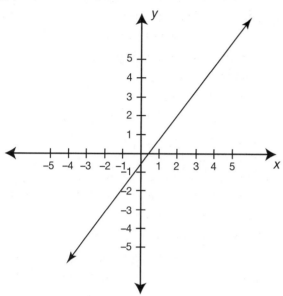

Each of the given lines has a different y-intercept. Solving for y in the given equation will put the equation in $y = mx + b$ form, where b is the y-intercept. In this case, that equation is $y = -\frac{1}{2} + \frac{3}{2}x$. The line given in the image above is the only line with a y-intercept of $-\frac{1}{2}$.

28. Choice c is correct. Since z is perpendicular to $y = -x + 5$, it must have a slope of 1. The given point $(0,-2)$ is a y-intercept since the x-value is 0, so the equation of z must be $y = x - 2$. Plugging in the given y-value of 5 in the point $(x, 5)$ yields the equation $5 = x - 2$, which has the solution $x = 7$.

Choice **a** is incorrect. The y-intercept of the line is -2 and not 5. A perpendicular line does not necessarily have the same y-intercept. Further, the 5 in the point $(x, 5)$ is a y-value and not an x-value.

Choice **b** is incorrect. The 5 in the point $(x, 5)$ is a y-value and not an x-value.

Choice **d** is incorrect. The y-intercept of the line is -2 and not 5. Two perpendicular lines do not necessarily have the same y-intercept.

29. Choice c is correct. Distributing the square root of 2 and simplifying:
$$\sqrt{2}(\sqrt{18} - \sqrt{6}) = \sqrt{36} - \sqrt{12} = 6 - \sqrt{4 \times 3}$$
$$= 6 - 2\sqrt{3}.$$
Choice **a** is incorrect. Radicals and whole numbers are not like terms and therefore cannot be combined.

Choice **b** is incorrect. The square root of 2 must be distributed to both terms. Additionally, the radical and the remaining whole number are not like terms.

Choice **d** is incorrect. The square root of 2 must be distributed to both terms in the parentheses.

30. Choice a is correct. The pattern in the scatterplot has a general upward trend from left to right. This indicates a positive relationship. As one variable increases, the other variable also increases.

Choice **b** is incorrect. A negative relationship would be indicated by a pattern that is generally falling from left to right.

Choice **c** is incorrect. This would be true if, for each point, the x- and y-coordinates were the same. But there are many points where this is not the case.

Choice **d** is incorrect. A general sloping pattern indicates a relationship between the two variables.

31. Choice d is correct. The conversion given can be written as a ratio 1 mile : 5,280 feet. Using this to cancel out units: 11,088 ft $\times$ $\frac{1}{5,280}$ $= \frac{11,088}{5,280} = 2.1$.

Choice **a** is incorrect. There is no need to divide by 12 since the units are not in inches.

Choice **b** is incorrect. Dividing 5,280 by 11,088 leaves the units in terms of $\frac{1}{\text{miles}}$, which doesn't make sense.

Choice **c** is incorrect. Subtracting the two values will not give an interpretable value.

32. Choice c is correct. The two steps are to distribute and add exponents. $x^4(x^2 - 6) = x^{4+2} - 6x^4 = x^6 - 6x^4$.

Choice **a** is incorrect. When two terms with the same base are multiplied, their exponents are added. Further, the term x^4 must be distributed to every term in the given binomial $x^2 - 6$.

Choice **b** is incorrect. The term x^4 must be distributed to every term in the given binomial $x^2 - 6$.

Choice **d** is incorrect. When two terms with the same base are multiplied, their exponents are added.

33. Choice a is correct. After increasing by $5.00, the share was worth $15.15. It then decreased in value by 10% or by $0.1 \times 15.15 = 1.515$. Therefore, at the end of week 2 it was worth $15.15 - \$1.515 = \$13.635$ a share. At the end of week 3, it was worth $13.635 - \$1.10 = \$12.535$. Finally, it doubled in value and was worth $2 \times \$12.535 = \$25.07$ per share.

Choice **b** is incorrect. The stock decreased in value by $1.10 at the end of week 3. This represents subtraction in the problem.

Choice **c** is incorrect. A 10% decrease can be found by multiplying 0.9 and the current value. This answer comes from using 1% or 0.01 as the decrease.

Choice **d** is incorrect. To double means to multiply by 2 and not 4.

34. Choice b is correct. The mode is the most commonly observed value. In this case, 4 occurs the most number of times.

Choice **a** is incorrect. This is the minimum value of the data set.

Choice **c** is incorrect. This is the median of the data set.

Choice **d** is incorrect. This is the range of the data set.

35. Choice b is correct. Given the final question is about an "or" probability, the correct formula to use is:

$$P(A \text{ or } B) = P(A) + P(B) - P(A \text{ and } B),$$

where $P(A)$ stands for the probability of the event A occurring. Applying this here:

$P(\text{degree or five years}) = P(\text{degree}) + P(\text{five years}) - P(\text{degree and five years}) = \frac{20}{48} + \frac{15}{48} - \frac{8}{48} = \frac{27}{48} = 0.5625$

Finally, 0.5625 is equivalent to 56.3%.

Choice **a** is incorrect. Although this is an "or" probability, the numbers for college degree and five years of work experience must be included.

Choices **c** and **d** are incorrect. When finding "or" probabilities, the probability of the "and" event must be subtracted.

36. Choice a is correct. If x represents the discount provided by a single coupon, then $2x$ represents the combined discount provided by both. Given the prices before and after, the following equation can be written and solved:

$$8.3 - 2x = 7$$
$$-2x = -1.3$$
$$x = 0.65$$

Choice **b** is incorrect. If each coupon gave a 90 cent discount, the final price would have been $8.30 - \$1.80 = \$6.50$.

Choice **c** is incorrect. This is the value of both coupons together.

Choice **d** is incorrect. The coupons provide a discount of $1.30 together, so it is not possible that one coupon by itself has a larger discount value.

37. The correct answer is 8.1%.

The percent increase can be found by finding the difference between the two prices and then dividing by the original price:

$$\frac{334.99 - 309.99}{309.99} = 0.0806.$$

Multiplying by 100 to convert this to a percentage yields 8.06%. Rounded, this is 8.1%.

38. Choice a is correct. The equation can be factored and rewritten as $(x-3)(x+1)=0$. Using the zero product rule, this results in the equations $x-3=0$ and $x+1=0$. The solutions to these equations are 3 and –1, respectively. Choice **b** is incorrect. After factoring, the zero product rule must be applied. This will result in the equations $x-3=0$ and $x+1=0$. Choices **c** and **d** are incorrect. The solutions can't be read off the coefficients. Instead, factoring, the quadratic formula, or completing the square should be used to solve a quadratic equation like this.

39. Choice c is correct. Subtracting 2 from both sides yields the solution $x>3$.
Choice **a** is incorrect. In this inequality, the 2 is added to the variable. Therefore, when attempting to isolate the x, both sides should not be multiplied by 2. Instead, 2 should be subtracted from both sides.
Choice **b** is incorrect. In this inequality, the 2 is added to the variable. Therefore when attempting to isolate the x, 2 should be subtracted from both sides instead of being added.
Choice **d** is incorrect. In this inequality, the 2 is added to the variable. Therefore, when attempting to isolate the x, both sides should not be divided by 2. Instead, 2 should be subtracted from both sides.

40. Choice c is correct. After plugging in the given value of x, we must simplify the result using basic operations with fractions:
$$\frac{\frac{1}{2}-5}{\frac{1}{4}-1}=\frac{\frac{1}{2}-\frac{10}{2}}{\frac{1}{4}-\frac{4}{4}}=\frac{-\frac{9}{2}}{-\frac{3}{4}}=\frac{9}{2}\times\frac{4}{3}=\frac{36}{6}=6$$
Choice **a** is incorrect. When plugging in the given value of x, the 5 is subtracted, not multiplied.
Choice **b** is incorrect. When simplifying a fraction over a fraction, the fraction in the numerator is multiplied by the reciprocal of the fraction in the denominator. Dividing the fractions piece by piece is not a valid method.
Choice **d** is incorrect. Taking a value to the power of two is not the same as multiplying it by two. Furthermore, a fraction with a denominator of zero is undefined, not equal to zero.

41. Choice c is correct. The area of the base is $2\times3=6$ square centimeters. Multiplying this by the height of 8 cm gives us the volume in cubic centimeters: $6\times8=48$.
Choice **a** is incorrect. This is the area of one of the smaller faces.
Choice **b** is incorrect. This is the area of one of the larger faces.
Choice **d** is incorrect. This is the surface area of the given shape.

42. Choice c is correct. Since product 2 had almost $30,000 in sales and product 4 had over $40,000 in sales, the total must be more than $50,000.
Choice **a** is incorrect. The total sales in July for these two products was about $45,000.
Choice **b** is incorrect. The total sales in July for these two products was slightly less than $50,000.
Choice **d** is incorrect. The total sales in July for these two products was about $35,000.

43. Choice b is correct. Using the surface area formula:

$$36\pi = 4\pi r^2$$
$$9 = r^2$$
$$r = 3$$

Since the radius is 3, the diameter is $3 \times 2 = 6$.
Choice **a** is incorrect. This is the radius of the sphere. The diameter is twice as large as the radius.
Choice **c** is incorrect. When solving the equation $36\pi = 4\pi r^2$, divide, not multiply, both sides by 4. Additionally, the diameter will be two times as large as the radius.
Choice **d** is incorrect. When solving the equation $36\pi = 4\pi r^2$, divide, not multiply, both sides by 4.

44. Choice b is correct. Using the addition method, adding the two equations yields the equation $2x = 22$, which has a solution of $x = 11$.
Choice **a** is incorrect. Subtracting the two equations will eliminate the x from both equations, making it where y must be found first.
Choice **c** is incorrect. If there were infinitely many solutions, the equations would be multiples of each other.
Choice **d** is incorrect. If there was no solution, the equation would yield an incorrect statement such as $0 = 1$ or $-5 = 3$.

45. Choice a is correct. Distributing the negative and combining like terms yields: $(x^2 + 5) - (x^2 - x) = x^2 + 5 - x^2 - (-x) = 5 + x$.
Choice **b** is incorrect. The negative must be distributed to every term in the parentheses.
Choice **c** is incorrect. Since the second term is being subtracted, the x^2 terms will cancel out. Further, the 5 and the x are not being multiplied.
Choice **d** is incorrect. Since the second term is being subtracted, the x^2 terms will cancel out.

3 ▶ GED® REASONING THROUGH LANGUAGE ARTS TEST 1

This practice test is modeled on the format, content, and timing of the official GED® Reasoning through Language Arts test.

Part I

Like the official exam, this section presents a series of questions that assess your ability to read, write, edit, and understand standard written English. You'll be asked to answer questions based on informational and literary reading passages. Refer to the passages as often as necessary when answering the questions.

Work carefully, but do not spend too much time on any one question. Be sure you answer every question.

Set a timer for 95 minutes (1 hour and 35 minutes), and try to take this test uninterrupted, under quiet conditions.

Part II

The official GED® Reasoning through Language Arts test also includes an essay question, called the Extended Response. Set a timer for 45 minutes, and try to read the given passage and then brainstorm, write, and proofread your essay without interruption, under quiet conditions.

Complete answer explanations for every test question and sample essays at different scoring levels follow the exam. Good luck!

PART I

48 Questions
95 Minutes

Please use the following to answer questions 1–6.

Remarks by the First Lady on a visit to thank USDA employees.

May 3, 2013

1 Thank you for supporting our farmers and our ranchers and working tirelessly to market their products across the globe, which, by the way, helps to create jobs right here at home. Thank you for protecting our environment by promoting renewable energy sources that will power our country for generations to come. So that's an impact on not just us but our children and our grandchildren and their children. Thank you for that work. Thank you for lifting up rural communities. And thank you for keeping our food safe. And I think this is something most of the country doesn't realize—the work that you do here to protect the environment, you keep our food safe, working to end hunger, improve nutrition for families across this country.

2 And the nutrition issue, as Tom mentioned, as you all know, is something near and dear to my heart, not just as First Lady but as a mother. In fact, one of the first things that I did as, you know, as First Lady, was to plant the garden at the White House. And it's really pretty. [*Laughter.*] I hope you guys get a chance to see it—it's beautiful now. It rained a couple of days. Thank you. [*Laughter.*] And the idea with planting the garden wasn't just to encourage kids to eat more vegetables. I also wanted to teach them about where their food comes from.

3 I think you've known this—we see this as we traveled around the country—some kids have never seen what a real tomato looks like off the vine. They don't know where a cucumber comes from. And that really affects the way they view food. So a garden helps them really get their hands dirty, literally, and understand the whole process of where their food comes from. And I wanted them to see just how challenging and rewarding it is to grow your own food, so that they would better understand what our farmers are doing every single day across this country and have an appreciation for that work, that tradition—that American tradition of growing our own food and feeding ourselves.

4 And the garden helped spark a conversation in this country about healthy eating that led us to create Let's Move. As you know, it's a nationwide initiative to end childhood obesity in this country in a generation, so that all of our kids can grow up healthy. And all of you all at USDA, let me just tell you, have been such a critical part of this effort right from the very start. This would not happen—all the conversation, all the movement around health—that's all because of so many of you right here in this room and throughout this building, and in agencies and facilities all over this country. You helped to launch our new MyPlate icon, which is changing the way families serve their meals and gives them a really easy way to understand what a healthy plate looks like.

1. What is the likely overall purpose or intent of the passage?
   a. to discuss the programs Mrs. Obama began with the goal of inspiring kids to eat healthier
   b. to thank farmers for their work
   c. to introduce Mrs. Obama's nutrition initiative
   d. to emphasize the important role of USDA employees in creating good nutrition in the United States

2. Write your response in the box below.

   According to Mrs. Obama, ⬚ mentioned that the nutrition issue is something near and dear to her heart.

3. Based on the passage, Mrs. Obama would most likely
   a. take her children to watch a professional basketball game.
   b. spend an evening teaching her children how to cook dinner.
   c. organize a family game night.
   d. spend an afternoon playing soccer with her husband, the president.

4. Which statement is NOT supporting evidence that the health of United States citizens is important to the First Lady?
   a. "Thank you for protecting our environment by promoting renewable energy sources that will power our country for generations to come."
   b. "And thank you for keeping our food safe."
   c. "And the nutrition issue, as Tom mentioned, as you all know, is something near and dear to my heart not just as a First Lady but as a mother."
   d. "You helped to launch our new MyPlate icon, which is changing the way families serve their meals and gives them a really easy way to understand what a healthy plate looks like."

5. Which of the following is a synonym of the word **initiative** as it's used in this sentence: "It's a nationwide initiative to end childhood obesity in this country in a generation, so that all our kids can grow up healthy"?
   a. program
   b. enthusiasm
   c. disinterest
   d. involvement

6. How does the inclusion of Paragraph 3 affect the overall theme of the passage?
   a. It damages Mrs. Obama's claim.
   b. It strengthens Mrs. Obama's position.
   c. It has no effect on the overall theme.
   d. It intentionally confuses the reader.

Please use the following to answer questions 7–11.

Excerpt from "The Cask of Amontillado," by Edgar Allan Poe

1 He had a weak point—this Fortunato—although in other regards he was a man to be respected and even feared. He prided himself on his connoisseurship in wine. Few Italians have the true virtuoso spirit. For the most part their enthusiasm is adopted to suit the time and opportunity, to practice imposture upon the British and Austrian millionaires. In painting and gemmary, Fortunato, like his countrymen, was a quack, but in the matter of old wines he was sincere. In this respect I did not differ from him materially—I was skillful in the Italian vintages myself, and bought largely whenever I could.

2 It was about dusk, one evening during the supreme madness of the carnival season, that I encountered my friend. He accosted me with excessive warmth, for he had been drinking much. The man wore motley. He had on a tight-fitting parti-striped dress, and his head was surmounted by the conical cap and bells. I was so pleased to see him that I thought I should never have done wringing his hand.

3 I said to him—"My dear Fortunato, you are luckily met. How remarkably well you are looking today. But I have received a pipe of what passes for Amontillado, and I have my doubts."

4 "How?" said he. "Amontillado, a pipe? Impossible! And in the middle of the carnival!"

5 "I have my doubts," I replied, "and I was silly enough to pay the full Amontillado price without consulting you in the matter. You were not to be found, and I was fearful of losing a bargain."

6 "Amontillado!"

7 "I have my doubts."

8 "Amontillado!"

9 "And I must satisfy them."

10 "Amontillado!"

11 "As you are engaged, I am on my way to Luchresi. If anyone has a critical turn it is he. He will tell me—"

12 "Luchresi cannot tell Amontillado from Sherry."

13 "And yet some fools will have it that his taste is a match for your own.

14 "Come, let us go."

15 "Whither?"

16 "To your vaults."

17 "My friend, no; I will not impose upon your good nature. I perceive you have an engagement. Luchresi—"

18 "I have no engagement—come."

19 "My friend, no. It is not the engagement but the severe cold with which I perceive you are afflicted. The vaults are insufferably damp. They are encrusted with nitre."

20 "Let us go, nevertheless. The cold is merely nothing. Amontillado! You have been imposed upon. And as for Luchresi, he cannot distinguish Sherry from Amontillado."

21 Thus speaking, Fortunato possessed himself of my arm; and putting on a mask of black silk and drawing a roquelaire closely about my person, I suffered him to hurry me to my palazzo.

7. Who are Fortunato's "countrymen"?
   a. Italians
   b. Britons
   c. Austrians
   d. Spaniards

8. What do Fortunato and the narrator have in common?
   a. an interest in Italian history
   b. they are wearing the same clothing
   c. a passion for wine
   d. a love of the carnival season

9. Which statement, in context, is NOT supporting evidence that Fortunato has a passion for wine?
   a. "But in the matter of old wines he was sincere."
   b. "I was so pleased to see him that I thought I should never have done wringing his hand."
   c. "Luchresi cannot tell Amontillado from Sherry."
   d. "The cold is merely nothing. Amontillado!"

10. In the context of the story, which of the following is an example of irony?
   a. "He prided himself on his connoisseurship in wine."
   b. "For most part their enthusiasm is adopted to suit the time and opportunity . . ."
   c. "My dear Fortunato, you are luckily met."
   d. "The vaults are insufferably damp."

11. Why does the narrator first insist that he will ask Luchresi's opinion of the Amontillado?
   a. because Luchresi has more expertise in wine than Fortunato does
   b. because Fortunato and the narrator are known enemies
   c. to gain the trust of Fortunato
   d. to prey on Fortunato's pride

Please use the following to answer questions 12–16.

Excerpt from "My First Lie, and How I Got Out of It," by Mark Twain

1   I do not remember my first lie, it is too far back; but I remember my second one very well. I was nine days old at the time, and had noticed that if a pin was sticking in me and I advertised it in the usual fashion, I was lovingly petted and coddled and pitied in a most agreeable way and got a ration between meals besides.

2   It was human nature to want to get these riches, and I fell. I lied about the pin—advertising one when there wasn't any. You would have done it; George Washington did it, anybody would have done it. During the first half of my life I never knew a child that was able to raise above that temptation and keep from telling that lie. Up to 1867 all the civilized children that were ever born into the world were liars—including George. Then the safety pin came in and blocked the game. But is that reform worth anything? No; for it is reform by force and has no virtue in it; it merely stops that form of lying, it doesn't impair the disposition to lie, by a shade. It is the cradle application of conversion by fire and sword, or of the temperance principle through prohibition.

3   To return to that early lie. They found no pin and they realized that another liar had been added to the world's supply. For by grace of a rare inspiration a quite commonplace but seldom noticed

continues

fact was borne in upon their understandings—that almost all lies are acts, and speech has no part in them. Then, if they examined a little further they recognized that all people are liars from the cradle onward, without exception, and that they begin to lie as soon as they wake in the morning, and keep it up without rest or refreshment until they go to sleep at night. If they arrived at that truth it probably grieved them—did, if they had been heedlessly and ignorantly educated by their books and teachers; for why should a person grieve over a thing which by the eternal law of his make he cannot help? He didn't invent the law; it is merely his business to obey it and keep it still; join the universal conspiracy and keep so still that he shall deceive his fellow-conspirators into imagining that he doesn't know that the law exists. It is what we all do—we that know. I am speaking of *the lie of silent assertion*; we can tell it without saying a word, and we all do it—we that know. In the magnitude of its territorial spread it is one of the most majestic lies that the civilizations make it their sacred and anxious care to guard and watch and propagate.

4 For instance. It would not be possible for a humane and intelligent person to invent a rational excuse for slavery; yet you will remember that in the early days of the emancipation agitation in the North the agitators got but small help or countenance from anyone. Argue and plead and pray as they might, they could not break the universal stillness that reigned, from pulpit and press all the way down to the bottom of society—the clammy stillness created and maintained by the lie of silent assertion—the silent assertion that there wasn't anything going on in which humane and intelligent people were interested.

12. Which of the following can be inferred from the first two paragraphs?
   a. The author grew up in the same state as George Washington.
   b. Before 1867, parents punished infants by poking them with pins.
   c. Before 1867, infants wore diapers fastened with straight pins.
   d. Safety pins were critical to eliminating a child's disposition to lie.

13. In the first two paragraphs, which of the following does the author present as evidence that humans are born liars?
   a. scientific data
   b. personal experience
   c. physical evidence
   d. historical documentation

14. Which of the following best expresses the author's position on lying?
   a. It should be forbidden.
   b. It should be forgiven, but only for children.
   c. It should be studied so that its cause can be found and eliminated.
   d. It should be accepted as a fundamental part of human nature.

15. Based on the fourth paragraph, why does the author think that slavery was allowed to continue for so long?
   a. because people acted as though it was not an important issue
   b. because people understood the economic importance of slaves to the South
   c. because slave owners lied to everyone else about how they treated their slaves
   d. because agitators in the North didn't state their case

16. Which of the following details does NOT support the main idea of the passage?
   a. Even babies have a disposition to lie.
   b. The introduction of the safety pin occurred in 1867.
   c. People often lie through acts rather than words.
   d. Early opponents of slavery faced indifference from society.

Please use the following to answer questions 17–20.

Rebecca Garcia, Executive Director
Abacus Childcare
2404 Bellevue Ave
Baton Rouge, LA 70810

(1) I would like to submit an application for the childcare position that was recently posted on your website. I've (2) with children in varying capacities for almost four years, and absolutely love kids of all ages. I have a high energy level and infinite amount of patience that blends well with successfully managing a group of children.

(3), I nannied two preschool-aged twins before they entered kindergarten. During that time, I learned to effectively develop entertaining and educational activities, manage disputes and disruptive behavior in a caring yet firm manner, and maintain a safe environment in the home. I also helped teach the children proper manners, personal cleanliness, and appropriate social skills. I believe the time I spent working with the family allowed me to develop excellent communication skills and management capabilities.

Outside of my work experience, I'm detail-oriented and very organized. I pride myself in (4) problem-solving abilities and love working hard to provide value to my work environment. I am dependable, always on time, and keep the promises that I make.

I would love to speak with you regarding the position if you feel like I would be a good fit on your team. I have attached my resume with contact information and have three references available upon request.

Thank you for your time,

Mallory Holloway

GED® REASONING THROUGH LANGUAGE ARTS TEST 1

17. Which is the correct choice for (1)?

a. Dear Ms. Dyer,

b. dear ms. dyer,

c. dear ms. Dyer,

d. Dear ms. dyer,

18. What is the correct form of the verb "to work" in (2)?

a. to work

b. works

c. worked

d. work

19. Which transitional word fits best in the beginning of (3)?

a. Recently

b. Currently

c. However

d. In addition

20. Which of the following is a correct fit for (4)?

a. your

b. me

c. my

d. mine

Please use the following to answer questions 21–24.

John F. Kennedy's Inaugural Address, 1961

1 Vice President Johnson, Mr. Speaker, Mr. Chief Justice, President Eisenhower, Vice President Nixon, President Truman, Reverend Clergy, fellow citizens:

2 We observe today not a victory of party but a celebration of freedom—symbolizing an end as well as a beginning—signifying renewal as well as change. For I have sworn before you the same solemn oath our forebears prescribed nearly a century and three quarters ago.

3 The world is very different now. For man holds in his mortal hands the power to abolish all forms of human poverty and all forms of human life. And yet the same revolutionary beliefs for which our forebears fought are still at issue around the globe.

4 We dare not forget today that we are the heirs of that first revolution. Let the word go forth from this time and place, to friend and foe alike, that the torch has been passed to a new generation of Americans—born in this century, tempered by war, disciplined by a hard and bitter peace, proud of our ancient heritage—and unwilling to witness or permit the slow undoing of those human rights to which this nation has always been committed, and to which we are committed today at home and around the world.

5 Let every nation know, whether it wishes us well or ill, that we shall pay any price, bear any burden, meet any hardship, support any friend, oppose any foe, to assure the survival and the success of liberty.

6 This much we pledge—and more.

7 To those old allies whose cultural and spiritual origins we share, we pledge the loyalty of faithful friends. United, there is little we cannot do in a host of cooperative ventures. Divided, there is little we can do—for we dare not meet a powerful challenge at odds and split asunder.

GED® REASONING THROUGH LANGUAGE ARTS TEST 1

8 To those new states whom we welcome to the ranks of the free, we pledge our word that one form of colonial control shall not have passed away merely to be replaced by a far more iron tyranny. We shall not always expect to find them supporting our view. But we shall always hope to find them strongly supporting their own freedom—and to remember that, in the past, those who foolishly sought power by riding the back of the tiger ended up inside.

9 To those peoples in the villages of half the globe struggling to break the bonds of mass misery, we pledge our best efforts to help them help themselves, for whatever period is required—not because the communists may be doing it, not because we seek their votes, but because it is right. If a free society cannot help the many who are poor, it cannot save the few who are rich.

10 To our sister republics south of our border, we offer a special pledge—to convert our good words into good deeds—in a new alliance for progress—to assist free men and free governments in casting off the chains of poverty. But this peaceful revolution of hope cannot become the prey of hostile powers. Let all our neighbors know that we shall join with them to oppose aggression or subversion anywhere in the Americas. And let every other power know that this hemisphere intends to remain the master of its own house.

11 To that world assembly of sovereign states, the United Nations, our last best hope in an age where the instruments of war have far outpaced the instruments of peace, we renew our pledge of support—to prevent it from becoming merely a forum for invective—to strengthen its shield of the new and the weak—and to enlarge the area in which its writ may run.

12 Finally, to those nations who would make themselves our adversary, we offer not a pledge but a request: that both sides begin anew the quest for peace, before the dark powers of destruction unleashed by science engulf all humanity in planned or accidental self-destruction.

21. Which sentence best represents the theme of the speech?
  a. "We observe today not a victory of party but a celebration of freedom—symbolizing an end as well as a beginning—signifying renewal as well as change."
  b. "We dare not forget today that we are the heirs of that first revolution."
  c. "But this peaceful revolution of hope cannot become the prey of hostile powers."
  d. "Let all our neighbors know that we shall join with them to oppose aggression or subversion anywhere in the Americas."

22. What word or phrase signifies to the reader the meaning of the word **tyranny** in the following sentence? "To those new states whom we welcome to the ranks of the free, we pledge our word that one form of colonial control shall not have passed away merely to be replaced by a far more iron tyranny."
  a. new states
  b. ranks of the free
  c. colonial control
  d. iron

23. What is the purpose of repeating "little we cannot do" and "little we can do" in the following sentence? "United, there is little we cannot do in a host of cooperative ventures. Divided, there is little we can do—for we dare not meet a powerful challenge at odds and split asunder."

a. to contrast the difference between being united and being divided

b. to highlight the similarity of being united and being divided

c. to stress the United States' role in foreign politics

d. to promise what Kennedy wants to accomplish during his presidency

24. From the list of 5 choices below, circle *all* of the characteristics that Kennedy displays in this speech.

1. fear
2. a strong will
3. compassion
4. morality
5. aggression

Please use the following to answer questions 25–30.

Franklin Delano Roosevelt's Pearl Harbor Address to the Nation, 1941

1 Mr. Vice President, Mr. Speaker, Members of the Senate, and of the House of Representatives:

2 Yesterday, December 7, 1941—a date which will live in infamy—the United States of America was suddenly and deliberately attacked by naval and air forces of the Empire of Japan.

3 The United States was at peace with that nation and, at the solicitation of Japan, was still in conversation with its government and its emperor looking toward the maintenance of peace in the Pacific.

4 Indeed, one hour after Japanese air squadrons had commenced bombing in the American island of Oahu, the Japanese ambassador to the United States and his colleague delivered to our Secretary of State a formal reply to a recent American message. And while this reply stated that it seemed useless to continue the existing diplomatic negotiations, it contained no threat or hint of war or of armed attack.

5 It will be recorded that the distance of Hawaii from Japan makes it obvious that the attack was deliberately planned many days or even weeks ago. During the intervening time, the Japanese government has deliberately sought to deceive the United States by false statements and expressions of hope for continued peace.

6 The attack yesterday on the Hawaiian Islands has caused severe damage to American naval and military forces. I regret to tell you that very many American lives have been lost. In addition, American ships have been reported torpedoed on the high seas between San Francisco and Honolulu.

7 Yesterday, the Japanese government also launched an attack against Malaya.

8 Last night, Japanese forces attacked Hong Kong.

9 Last night, Japanese forces attacked Guam.

10 Last night, Japanese forces attacked the Philippine Islands.

11 Last night, the Japanese attacked Wake Island.

12 And this morning, the Japanese attacked Midway Island.

13 Japan has, therefore, undertaken a surprise offensive extending throughout the Pacific area. The facts of yesterday and today speak for themselves. The people of the United States have already formed their opinions and well understand the implications to the very life and safety of our nation.

14 As Commander in Chief of the Army and Navy, I have directed that all measures be taken for our defense. But always will our whole nation remember the character of the onslaught against us.

15 No matter how long it may take us to overcome this premeditated invasion, the American people in their righteous might will win through to absolute victory.

16 I believe that I interpret the will of the Congress and of the people when I assert that we will not only defend ourselves to the uttermost but will make it very certain that this form of treachery shall never again endanger us.

17 Hostilities exist. There is no blinking at the fact that our people, our territory, and our interests are in grave danger.

18 With confidence in our armed forces, with the unbounding determination of our people, we will gain the inevitable triumph.

19 I ask that the Congress declare that since the unprovoked and dastardly attack by Japan on Sunday, December 7, 1941, a state of war has existed between the United States and the Japanese empire.

25. What is the tone of the address?
   a. shocked but assertive
   b. timid and fearful
   c. surprised and scared
   d. insecure yet aggressive

26. What purpose does the word **indeed** serve in the third paragraph?
   A. to conclude his former idea
   B. to alert the audience of a new premise
   c. to emphasize the surprise of the attack
   d. to introduce a new theme in the speech

27. What can be inferred from the first sentence in paragraph 5?
   a. Japan is close to Hawaii.
   b. Japan and Hawaii are a significant distance apart.
   c. The United States mainland is as close to Hawaii as Japan is.
   d. Japan announced that it was going to attack.

28. What is the purpose of repeating the phrase "Last night, Japanese forces attacked"?
  a. to show that Japanese forces were disorganized
  b. to emphasize that it is cowardly to attack at night
  c. to show how other countries are united against Japan
  d. to emphasize the extent of Japan's attack

29. Which of the following describes "the character of the onslaught against us"?
  a. expected
  b. aggressive
  c. regretful
  d. unintentional

30. Which of the following is NOT evidence that the attack came as a surprise?
  a. "The United States was at peace with that nation."
  b. "One hour after Japanese squadrons had commenced bombing in the American island of Oahu, the Japanese Ambassador to the United States and his colleague delivered to our Secretary of State a formal reply to a recent American message."
  c. "During the intervening time, the Japanese government has deliberately sought to deceive the United States by false statements and expressions of hope for continued peace."
  d. "Hostilities exist."

Please use the following to answer questions 31–34.

Memo to: All Employees
From: Alexandra Chandler
Subject: Work Hours

Hello all!

(1) Beginning next week, we will poll the office in order to receive everyone's input as we modify work hours.

The company (2) they want to change the schedule in order to better fit the needs of the employees. We will have three options to choose from. The first option is to keep the work schedule as it is currently: 9 to 5, Monday through Friday. The second option is to work one more hour per day on Monday through Thursday, but work only half a day on Friday. The third option is to work two extra hours on Monday through Thursday, and have Fridays off.

Although (3) completely open to all three options, the members of the executive board feel that the second option may fit the goals of the company and employees the best. Many of us already stay to work late at the beginning of the week, and the extra hour would not feel unnatural. We have also noticed that on (4). We understand this to be normal behavior and want to alter hours so that we can better serve you.

We think that the second option would fit well with the patterns we have already observed; however, we still want your opinions. We will be sending questionnaires via email for you to fill out within the week. Please take some time to think about your responses before completing the survey as we want the possible change to best reflect the needs of the office.

Please keep a lookout for the questionnaire and return it to us by the end of next week.

Thank you for your time,

Alexandra Chandler

31. Which choice fits correctly in (1)?

   a. We are announcing some really big changes that might really affect us in the next few months.

   b. We would like to announce some potential changes affecting our team in the next few months.

   c. FYI, stuff might be different soon.

   d. PS: Thank you for your cooperation.

32. Choose the correct form of **decide** for (2).

   a. will decide

   b. has decided

   c. decides

   d. decide

33. Which choice fits correctly in (3)?

   a. there

   b. their

   c. they is

   d. they are

34. Which choice fits correctly in (4)?

   a. Friday, afternoons employee activity drops

   b. Friday afternoons employee, activity drops

   c. Friday afternoons, employee activity drops

   d. Friday afternoons employee activity, drops

Please use the following to answer questions 35–42.

Excerpt from Barack Obama's First Inaugural Address, January 20, 2009

1   In reaffirming the greatness of our nation we understand that greatness is never a given. It must be earned. Our journey has never been one of short cuts or settling for less. It has not been the path for the faint-hearted, for those that prefer leisure over work, or seek only the pleasures of riches and fame. Rather, it has been the risk-takers, the doers, the makers of things—some celebrated, but more often men and women obscure in their labor—who have carried us up the long rugged path towards prosperity and freedom.

2   For us, they packed up their few worldly possessions and traveled across oceans in search of a new life. For us, they toiled in sweatshops, and settled the West, endured the lash of the whip, and plowed the hard earth. For us, they fought and died in places like Concord and Gettysburg, Normandy and Khe Sahn.

3   Time and again these men and women struggled and sacrificed and worked till their hands were raw so that we might live a better life. They saw America as bigger than the sum of our individual ambitions, greater than all the differences of birth or wealth or faction.

4   This is the journey we continue today. We remain the most prosperous, powerful nation on Earth. Our workers are no less productive than when this crisis began. Our minds are no less inventive, our goods and services no less needed than they were last week, or last month, or last year. Our capacity remains undiminished. But our time of standing pat, of protecting narrow interests and putting off unpleasant decisions—that time has surely passed. Starting today, we must pick ourselves up, dust ourselves off, and begin again the work of remaking America.

5   For everywhere we look, there is work to be done. The state of our economy calls for action, bold and swift. And we will act, not only to create new jobs but to lay a new foundation for growth. We

continues

will build the roads and bridges, the electric grids and digital lines that feed our commerce and bind us together. We'll restore science to its rightful place and wield technology's wonders to raise health care's quality and lower its cost. We will harness the sun and the winds and the soil to fuel our cars and run our factories. And we will transform our schools and colleges and universities to meet the demands of a new age. All this we can do. All this we will do.

6   Now, there are some who question the scale of our ambitions, who suggest that our system cannot tolerate too many big plans. Their memories are short, for they have forgotten what this country has already done, what free men and women can achieve when imagination is joined to common purpose and necessity to courage. What the cynics fail to understand is that the ground has shifted beneath them, that the stale political arguments that have consumed us for so long no longer apply.

7   The question we ask today is not whether our government is too big or too small, but whether it works—whether it helps families find jobs at a decent wage, care they can afford, a retirement that is dignified. Where the answer is yes, we intend to move forward. Where the answer is no, programs will end. And those of us who manage the public's dollars will be held to account, to spend wisely, reform bad habits, and do our business in the light of day, because only then can we restore the vital trust between a people and their government.

Excerpt from Barack Obama's Second Inaugural Address, January 21, 2013

1   We, the people, still believe that every citizen deserves a basic measure of security and dignity. We must make the hard choices to reduce the cost of health care and the size of our deficit. But we reject the belief that America must choose between caring for the generation that built this country and investing in the generation that will build its future. For we remember the lessons of our past, when twilight years were spent in poverty, and parents of a child with a disability had nowhere to turn. We do not believe that in this country, freedom is reserved for the lucky, or happiness for the few. We recognize that no matter how responsibly we live our lives, any one of us, at any time, may face a job loss, or a sudden illness, or a home swept away in a terrible storm. The commitments we make to each other—through Medicare, and Medicaid, and Social Security—these things do not sap our initiative; they strengthen us. They do not make us a nation of takers; they free us to take the risks that make this country great.

2   We, the people, still believe that our obligations as Americans are not just to ourselves, but to all posterity. We will respond to the threat of climate change, knowing that the failure to do so would betray our children and future generations. Some may still deny the overwhelming judgment of science, but none can avoid the devastating impact of raging fires, and crippling drought, and more powerful storms. The path towards sustainable energy sources will be long and sometimes difficult. But America cannot resist this transition; we must lead it. We cannot cede to other nations the technology that will power new jobs and new industries—we must claim its promise.

continues

That's how we will maintain our economic vitality and our national treasure—our forests and waterways; our croplands and snowcapped peaks. That is how we will preserve our planet, commanded to our care by God. That's what will lend meaning to the creed our fathers once declared.

3 We, the people, still believe that enduring security and lasting peace do not require perpetual war. Our brave men and women in uniform, tempered by the flames of battle, are unmatched in skill and courage. Our citizens, seared by the memory of those we have lost, know too well the price that is paid for liberty. The knowledge of their sacrifice will keep us forever vigilant against those who would do us harm. But we are also heirs to those who won the peace and not just the war, who turned sworn enemies into the surest of friends, and we must carry those lessons into this time as well.

4 We will defend our people and uphold our values through strength of arms and rule of law. We will show the courage to try and resolve our differences with other nations peacefully—not because we are naïve about the dangers we face, but because engagement can more durably lift suspicion and fear. America will remain the anchor of strong alliances in every corner of the globe; and we will renew those institutions that extend our capacity to manage crisis abroad, for no one has a greater stake in a peaceful world than its most powerful nation. We will support democracy from Asia to Africa; from the Americas to the Middle East, because our interests and our conscience compel us to act on behalf of those who long for freedom. And we must be a source of hope to the poor, the sick, the marginalized, the victims of prejudice—not out of mere charity, but because peace in our time requires the constant advance of those principles that our common creed describes: tolerance and opportunity; human dignity and justice.

35. Which best summarizes the main idea expressed in the first paragraph of Obama's First Inaugural Address?
  a. Luck made the United States a successful and great nation.
  b. Those who worked hard and took risks shaped America.
  c. The United States is a great nation and hard work will keep it so.
  d. Obama feels very fortunate to have been elected president.

36. Which sentence's meaning is strengthened by the "men and women [who] sacrificed and struggled" mentioned in the first three paragraphs in Obama's First Inaugural Address?
  a. "Our capacity remains undiminished."
  b. "For everywhere we look, there is work to be done."
  c. "We'll restore science to its rightful place, and wield technology's wonders to raise healthcare's quality and lower its cost."
  d. "Their memories are short, for they have forgotten what this country has already done, what free men and women can achieve when imagination is joined to a common purpose, and necessity to courage."

37. From the list of five choices below, circle *all* of the phrases that support the main idea of Obama's First Inaugural Address.
   1. "Our journey has never been one of shortcuts or settling for less."
   2. "This is the journey we continue today."
   3. "All this we can do. All this we will do."
   4. "We will harness the sun and the winds and the soil to fuel our cars and run our factories."
   5. "What the cynics fail to understand is that the ground has shifted beneath them, that the stale political arguments that have consumed us for so long no longer apply."

38. What is Obama's purpose in beginning each of the first three paragraphs of his second inaugural address with "We, the people"?
a. to show American pride
b. to stress past successes in order to prove the country does not need to change
c. to quote the Preamble
d. to emphasize the theme of betterment in the United States of America

39. What is the effect of repeating the words **generation** and **build** to compare "the generation that built this country" with the "generation that will build the future?"
a. because Obama is talking about the same people
b. to create a connection between the past and the future
c. because he thinks the next generation will be better than the last
d. to emphasize that both generations still have work to do

40. Which of the following does not support Obama's claim in his Second Inaugural Address that Americans feel an obligation to future generations?
a. "For we remember the lessons of our past, when twilight years were spent in poverty, and parents of a child with a disability had nowhere to turn."
b. "We will respond to the threat of climate change, knowing that the failure to do so would betray our children and future generations."
c. "Time and again these men and women struggled and sacrificed and worked till their hands were raw so that we might live a better life."
d. "We will defend our people and uphold our values through strength of arms and rule of law."

41. Where will Obama support democracy, according to his Second Inaugural Address?
a. in the Americas
b. worldwide
c. in Europe
d. in the Middle East

42. Which of the following sentences from the Second Inaugural Address best fits into the theme of the First Inaugural Address?
a. "They do not make us a nation of takers; they free us to take the risks that make this country great."
b. "That's what will lend meaning to the creed our fathers once declared."
c. "We, the people, still believe that enduring security and a lasting peace do not require perpetual war."
d. "We must make the hard choices to reduce the cost of health care and the size of our deficit."

Please use the following to answer questions 43–48.

Remarks upon Signing the Civil Rights Bill (July 2, 1964), Lyndon Baines Johnson

1 My fellow Americans:

2 I am about to sign into law the Civil Rights Act of 1964. I want to take this occasion to talk to you about what that law means to every American.

3 One hundred and eighty-eight years ago this week a small band of valiant men began a long struggle for freedom. They pledged their lives, their fortunes, and their sacred honor not only to found a nation, but to forge an ideal of freedom—not only for political independence, but for personal liberty—not only to eliminate foreign rule, but to establish the rule of justice in the affairs of men.

4 That struggle was a turning point in our history. Today in far corners of distant continents, the ideals of those American patriots still shape the struggles of men who hunger for freedom.

5 This is a proud triumph. Yet those who founded our country knew that freedom would be secure only if each generation fought to renew and enlarge its meaning. From the minutemen at Concord to the soldiers in Viet-Nam, each generation has been equal to that trust.

6 Americans of every race and color have died in battle to protect our freedom. Americans of every race and color have worked to build a nation of widening opportunities. Now our generation of Americans has been called on to continue the unending search for justice within our own borders.

7 We believe that all men are created equal. Yet many are denied equal treatment.

8 We believe that all men have certain unalienable rights. Yet many Americans do not enjoy those rights.

9 We believe that all men are entitled to the blessings of liberty. Yet millions are being deprived of those blessings—not because of their own failures, but because of the color of their skin.

10 The reasons are deeply imbedded in history and tradition and the nature of man. We can understand—without rancor or hatred—how this all happened.

11 But it cannot continue. Our Constitution, the foundation of our Republic, forbids it. The principles of our freedom forbid it. Morality forbids it. And the law I will sign tonight forbids it.

43. Which sentence is NOT an example of an American ideal?
   a. "We believe that all men are created equal."
   b. "The principles of our freedom forbid it."
   c. "Not only for political independence, but for personal liberty."
   d. "Yet many are denied equal treatment."

44. Which sentence expresses the same idea as "Yet many are denied equal treatment"?
   a. Yet many Americans do not enjoy those rights.
   b. We believe that all men are entitled to the blessings of liberty.
   c. We can understand—without rancor or hatred—how this all happened.
   d. Americans of every race and color have died in battle to protect our freedom.

45. Based on Johnson's remarks, which is the best example of the United States' "unending search for justice within our own borders"?
   a. Civil War
   b. The Grand Canyon
   c. Civil Rights Act of 1964
   d. Vietnam War

46. Which answer best summarizes the main idea expressed in the paragraph that begins "One hundred and eighty-eight years ago"?
   a. The United States was formed a long time ago.
   b. The founding fathers worked hard to create a just nation.
   c. The country has always treated everyone fairly.
   d. Men of all races fought for freedom 188 years ago.

47. Which sentence best expresses the theme of President Johnson's remarks?
   a. American ideals include fair treatment for everyone.
   b. The United States is a great country.
   c. Everyone is treated the same in the United States.
   d. Lyndon B. Johnson was one of the best presidents.

48. Which of the following does NOT support Lyndon B. Johnson's stance that the Civil Rights Bill is in line with American values?
   a. "They pledged their lives, their fortunes, and their sacred honor not only to found a nation, but to forge an ideal of freedom."
   b. "Today in far corners of distant continents, the ideals of those American patriots still shape the struggles of men who hunger for freedom."
   c. "Americans of every race and color have died in battle to protect our freedom."
   d. "The reasons are deeply imbedded in history and tradition and the nature of man."

Part II

1 question
45 minutes

This practice allows you to compose your response to the given task and then compare it with examples of responses at the different score levels. You will also get a scoring guide that includes a detailed explanation of how official GED® test graders will score your response. You may use this scoring guide to score your own response.

Before you begin, it is important to note that on the official test this task must be completed in no more than 45 minutes. But don't rush to complete your response; take time to carefully read the passage(s) and the question prompt. Then think about how you would like to respond.

As you write your essay, be sure to:

- Decide which position presented in the passages is better supported by evidence.
- Explain why your chosen position has better support.
- Recognize that the position with better support may not be the position you agree with.
- Present multiple pieces of evidence from the passage to defend your assertions.

- Thoroughly construct your main points, organizing them logically, with strong supporting details.
- Connect your sentences, paragraphs, and ideas with transitional words and phrases.
- Express your ideas clearly and choose your words carefully.
- Use varied sentence structures to increase the clarity of your response.
- Reread and revise your response.

Good luck!

Please use the following to answer the essay question.

An Analysis of Nuclear Energy

1   America runs on energy. As a matter of fact, the United States is the second largest energy consumer in the world, behind China. In recent years, it can be argued that we need to ease our dependence on foreign countries that supply us with oil and develop energy at home. But where can we get the energy we need?

Benefits of Nuclear Energy

2   The U.S. Department of Energy (DOE) promotes the development of safe, domestic nuclear power, and there are many who support the idea that nuclear power is the answer. Compared to fossil fuels such as gas, coal, and oil, nuclear energy is the most efficient way to make electricity. For example, the Idaho National Laboratory reports that "one uranium fuel pellet—roughly the size of the tip of an adult's little finger—contains the same amount of energy as 17,000 cubic feet of natural gas, 1,780 pounds of coal, or 149 gallons of oil."

3   Supporters of nuclear energy cite that nuclear generators don't create the great amounts of poisonous carbon dioxide, nitrogen oxides, and sulfur dioxide like the burning of fossil fuels does. The DOE reports that a nuclear generator produces 30 tons of spent fuel a year compared to the 300,000 tons of coal ash produced by a coal-powered electrical plant.

4   In terms of safety, the Nuclear Regulatory Commission ensures that each and every nuclear reactor maintains strict safety standards. Radioactive waste is contained deep underground behind steel-reinforced, 1.2 meter thick concrete walls. The DOE also points out that "ash from burning coal at a power plant emits 100 times more radiation into the surrounding environment than a nuclear power plant."

continues

Arguments against Nuclear Energy

5 Opponents of nuclear energy argue that nuclear reactors endanger all life on Earth for three basic reasons. First, nuclear radioactivity is deadly and must be contained for thousands of years. Second, no matter how many safety measures are in place, accidents happen, and nuclear meltdowns are global environmental catastrophes. Finally, nuclear fuel used to generate electricity can also be used to build atomic bombs.

6 Nuclear generators used radioactive plutonium and uranium for fuel. Scientists say that exposure to a millionth of an ounce of pluntonium causes cancer. Even nuclear energy proponents agree that life-threatening nuclear waste must be contained for half a million years before it becomes safe to be around. Radioactive dumps last generations.

7 Opponents of nuclear energy also cite that the ever-present threat of meltdowns. Widespread radioactive contamination and death caused by the nuclear accidents at Three Mile Island, Chernobyl, and Fukushima are cautionary lessons. Researchers disagree on how possible it is to safely contain radioactivity, but it's undeniable that nuclear meltdown causes widespread contamination of the air, water, and land with deadly radioactivity. It is also verifiable that nuclear accidents have caused environmental catastrophes that continue to this day.

8 Perhaps even more disturbing than the threat of toxic waste and meltdown is the use of uranium for sinister purposes. On December 7, 2013, Reuters reported that ". . . in news that may concern world powers . . . Iran is moving ahead with testing more efficient uranium enrichment technology. . . ." Indeed, the United Nations and the entire world are worried about Iran's enhancement of uranium for use in nuclear power plants because the same enhanced uranium can be used to build atomic weaponry.

9 Opponents argue that in the same way we learned that fossil fuels are limited and destroy the environment, so must we learn from nuclear disasters. Opponents say the answer is to develop safe, clean, and renewable sources of alternative energy such as solar, wind, tidal, and geothermal power. Why gamble? The future of the world is at stake.

QUESTION:

Nuclear energy proponents argue that it is safe and efficient, while opponents make the case for alternative energy sources, citing the deadly consequences of nuclear disaster.

In your response, analyze both positions presented in the article to determine which one is best supported. Use relevant and specific evidence from both articles to support your response.

You should expect to spend up to 45 minutes planning, drafting, and editing your response.

_____

_____

_____

_____

_____

_____

_____

_____

_____

_____

_____

_____

_____

_____

_____

_____

_____

_____

_____

_____

_____

_____

Answers and Explanations

Part I

1. **Choice d is correct.** This is the only answer that encompasses everything Mrs. Obama speaks on, from thanking the USDA employees to explaining how the healthy initiatives could not succeed without them.
   Choice **a** is incorrect. Although Mrs. Obama discusses different programs she has created with that goal, she uses those examples to demonstrate the greater theme.
   Choice **b** is incorrect. Mrs. Obama shows her appreciation for farmers, but this answer ignores many other ideas and information brought up throughout the passage.
   Choice **c** is incorrect. Mrs. Obama mentions the *Let's Move* initiative, but it is clear from her comments that the initiative is already underway; therefore, the purpose of Mrs. Obama's remarks is not to introduce *Let's Move*.

2. According to Mrs. Obama, a man named **Tom** mentioned that the nutrition issue is something near and dear to her heart. In the second paragraph, Mrs. Obama states: ". . . the nutrition issue, as *Tom* mentioned, as you all know, is something near and dear to my heart . . ."

3. **Choice b is correct.** Selecting this answer choice shows that the reader comprehends the importance Mrs. Obama places on family and healthy habits.
   Choice **a** is incorrect. This answer ignores the main topics of the passage, which include an emphasis on participating in an active lifestyle, not watching one.
   Choice **c** is incorrect. This answer choice only identifies one theme and ignores the focus on nutrition.
   Choice **d** is incorrect. Although this answer incorporates both the themes of family and having healthy habits, it disregards Mrs. Obama's emphasis on teaching children healthy habits.

4. **Choice a is correct.** Even though Mrs. Obama is stating another of the USDA's contributions, this answer does not focus on health or food, but rather renewable resources. Also, the other three answer choices clearly support the question's conclusion.
   Choice **b** is incorrect. This sentence demonstrates Mrs. Obama's concern through her gratitude.
   Choice **c** is incorrect. This statement explicitly states Mrs. Obama's personal interest in health in the United States.
   Choice **d** is incorrect. In this sentence, Mrs. Obama gives a specific example of the ways in which she, along with the USDA, has worked to teach citizens healthy habits.

5. **Choice a is correct.** If you replace the word "initiative" with the word "program," the sentence would retain its meaning.
   Choice **b** is incorrect. The word "enthusiasm" does not fit the context.
   Choice **c** is incorrect. "Disinterest" is an antonym of "initiative."
   Choice **d** is incorrect. Replacing "initiative" with "involvement" loses the meaning of the sentence.

6. Choice b is correct. It demonstrates the necessity of garden programs by highlighting the fact that some children don't know how food is grown or where their food comes from. Choice **a** is incorrect. This response neglects Mrs. Obama's emphasis on why nutritional programs are important.

Choice **c** is incorrect. The paragraph supports the theme of the speech by providing information about why the programs and worker involvement are necessary.

Choice **d** is incorrect. Mrs. Obama is very clear and explicitly states that children not only do not know about nutrition, but do not know where their food comes from. This ties into the overall theme of health and demonstrates why Mrs. Obama believes these programs are needed.

7. Choice a is correct. Two sentences before "countrymen," the narrator says, "Few Italians have the true virtuoso spirit." The next few sentences, including the one that uses "countrymen," are descriptions of traits that Italians do or do not have, according to the narrator.

Choice **b** is incorrect. Two sentences before "countrymen," the narrator says "Few Italians have the true virtuoso spirit." The next few sentences discuss how the enthusiasm of many Italians is often a deception to take advantage of the British or Austrians, according to the narrator.

Choice **c** is incorrect. Two sentences before "countrymen," the narrator says "Few Italians have the true virtuoso spirit." The next few sentences discuss how the enthusiasm of many Italians is often a deception to take advantage of the British or Austrians, according to the narrator.

Choice **d** is incorrect. There is no mention or indication in the passage that Fortunato is a Spaniard.

8. Choice c is correct. The narrator states that Fortunato is "sincere" in his knowledge of "old wines," and that in "This respect I did not differ from him materially."

Choice **a** is incorrect. At no point does the narrator say anything about Italian history.

Choice **b** is incorrect. The narrator describes Fortunato's "parti-striped dress," but does not describe his own clothing.

Choice **d** is incorrect. The narrator states the events happened "one evening during the supreme madness of the carnival season," but makes no declarations about his feelings at the time.

9. Choice b is correct. This describes the narrator's reaction to finding Fortunato, not Fortunato's feelings about wine.

Choice **a** is incorrect. The narrator is clearly stating Fortunato knows wine.

Choice **c** is incorrect. Fortunato is attempting to prove that he knows wines and convince the narrator to take him to the cask of Amontillado instead of to their friend Luchresi.

Choice **d** is incorrect. After the narrator warns Fortunato that his health would be in danger if they went to find the vault because of the cold, Fortunato dismisses the concern in favor of the wine.

10. Choice c is correct. Fortunato is actually quite unlucky as he has just stumbled across a man who wants to, and later does, kill him.

Choice **a** is incorrect. The narrator is being sincere.

Choice **b** is incorrect. This is a follow-up statement used to explain the narrator's claim that "few Italians have the true virtuoso spirit."

Choice **d** is incorrect. Although the narrator does not actually mean to deter Fortunato from the journey to his death, there is no text-based reason to believe that the vaults are not cold and wet.

11. Choice d is correct. Early in the text, the narrator states that Fortunato "had a weak point—this Fortunato—although in other regards he was a man to be respected and even feared. He prided himself on his connoisseurship in wine."
Choice **a** is incorrect. There is nothing in the text that indicates Luchresi has more expertise in wine than Fortunato. As a matter of fact, the narrator himself states that "in the matter of old wines [Fortunato] was sincere."
Choice **b** is incorrect. On the contrary, if the narrator and Fortunato were known enemies, Fortunato would not trust him and follow him down to the vault.
Choice **c** is incorrect. The two men already know and trust each other, which is evidenced in their interactions and dialogue.

12. Choice c is correct. The author suggests that before 1867 many babies were poked by pins, and then the safety pin came along and eliminated the problem. It can be inferred that the reason the earlier babies were being poked was because their diapers were fastened with straight pins.
Choice **a** is incorrect. The only connection the author makes between himself and George Washington is that he, like Washington, was born into the world a liar.
Choice **b** is incorrect. Although the author suggests that before 1867 infants were often poked by pins, he does not imply that pin-poking was a form of parental punishment.
Choice **d** is incorrect. Although the author states that safety pins made children unable to "lie" by crying as if they had been poked by a pin, the author also states that this "doesn't impair the disposition to lie."

13. Choice b is correct. The author states, "During the first half of my life I never knew a child that was able to raise above that temptation and keep from telling that lie."
Choice **a** is incorrect. The author offers no scientific data to support his claim.
Choice **c** is incorrect. The author does not present any physical evidence to support his claim.
Choice **d** is incorrect. Although the author states that George Washington lied as a child, he offers no historical documentation to support this statement.

14. Choice d is correct. The author states that "all people are liars from the cradle onward" and also asks, "[W]hy should a person grieve over a thing which by the eternal law of his make he cannot help?"
Choice **a** is incorrect. The author does not suggest that lying should be forbidden and, in fact, argues that stopping a person from lying does not remove a person's disposition to lie.
Choice **b** is incorrect. The author does not suggest that different rules should be applied to adults and children.
Choice **c** is incorrect. The author does not suggest that eliminating lying is a goal toward which people should strive.

15. Choice a is correct. The author argues that those who didn't speak up about slavery implied "that there wasn't anything going on in which humane and intelligent people were interested," which was a quiet way of countering anti-slavery activists.

Choice **b** is incorrect. The author does not mention economics as an issue related to slavery.

Choice **c** is incorrect. The author does not suggest that slave owners lied to others; the main idea of the paragraph is that people lied to themselves about slavery.

Choice **d** is incorrect. The author says that anti-slavery agitators in the North would "argue and plead and pray," but they didn't get enough support in response.

16. Choice b is correct. While this detail is mentioned in the passage, it does not reflect the main idea of the passage, which is that lying is a part of human nature.

Choices **a**, **b**, and **c** are incorrect. These details support the main idea of the passage, which is that lying is a part of human nature.

17. Choice a is correct. All three words need to be capitalized. Beginning letters of sentences are always capitalized, and people's names and titles are capitalized.

Choice **b** is incorrect. This answer lacks all necessary capitalization. All three words need to be capitalized. Beginning letters of sentences are always capitalized, and people's names and titles are capitalized.

Choices **c** and **d** are incorrect. All three words must be capitalized.

18. Choice c is correct. This is the correct past tense for a singular subject.

Choice **a** is incorrect. "I have to work with children" does not make sense within the context. The author is explaining what she has done in the past.

Choices **b** and **d** are incorrect. These answer choices do not make sense in context.

19. Choice a is correct. This word correctly matches the past-tense verb "nannied."

Choice **b** is incorrect. This does not fit in context with the past-tense verb "nannied."

Choice **c** is incorrect. The word "however" indicates contrast with a previous statement. The ideas in the sentence compliment previous sentences, and do not offer contrast.

Choice **d** is incorrect. This answer choice does not make sense in context. In order to keep with form, "recently" is a better answer.

20. Choice c is correct. "My" is the correct possessive pronoun.

Choice **a** is incorrect. This is not the correct possessive pronoun. The speaker is talking about her abilities.

Choice **b** is incorrect. "Me" is not a possessive pronoun. It is clear that the abilities belong to someone.

Choice **d** is incorrect. Although "mine" is possessive, one uses it to indicate objects that belong to them, and it would be awkward to say "mine abilities."

21. Choice a is correct. This choice summarizes the passage in totality, identifying Kennedy's emphasis on the past and the present as he accepts the presidency.

Choice **b** is incorrect. This choice neglects Kennedy's focus on the future of the nation and the world.

Choice **c** is incorrect. Kennedy stresses hope and good things to come throughout the text; however, this is just a small slice of everything he says and is not the main theme.

Choice **d** is incorrect. Although Kennedy speaks about the United States' and its allies' role in furthering peace and democracy, this choice ignores the weight Kennedy puts on how the past shaped the country.

22. Choice c is correct. The use of "replaced" and "more" signifies that "colonial control" and "tyranny" mean similar things.

Choice **a** is incorrect. The sentence is addressed "to the new states"; this is who the promise of a guard against more tyranny is made.

Choice **b** is incorrect. This phrase represents the opposite of tyranny, the state to which the countries have been "welcomed" to. The second half of the sentence is a promise to protect them and guard against tyranny.

Choice **d** is incorrect. "Iron" is an adjective used to describe tyranny.

23. Choice a is correct. Kennedy is contrasting being united with being divided in order to make a point about why countries should cooperate (because they can accomplish anything "in a host of cooperative ventures").

Choice **b** is incorrect. This is the opposite of Kennedy's intention.

Choice **c** is incorrect. Kennedy is focusing on everyone working together and not on foreign policy.

Choice **d** is incorrect. Although Kennedy says that he is committed to peace and cooperation, this speech focuses on discussing the perils of not working together.

24. Choice **1** is incorrect. Kennedy makes a point of saying that the United States will "pay any price, bear any burden, meet any hardship, support any friend, oppose any foe, in order to assure the survival and the success of liberty." This does not show fear.

Choice 2 is correct. Many times Kennedy emphasizes doing what is necessary to help those in need and that the United States will "pay any price."

Choice 3 is correct. Kennedy stresses that he is committed to showing people who are "struggling" how to "help themselves," and wants to "assist free men and free governments in casting off the chains of poverty."

Choice 4 is correct. Kennedy states he pledges the United States' "best efforts" not for political reasons, "but because it is right." He also says he wants to "convert our good words into good deeds."

Choice **5** is incorrect. In the last paragraph, Kennedy explicitly asks "that both sides begin anew the quest for peace." He does not threaten his opponents but rather warns against the consequences of not working together.

25. Choice a is correct. Roosevelt emphasizes that the attack was a complete surprise because the two nations were not warring, yet states that he has "directed that all measures be taken for our defense." Even though he was not expecting the event, he knows that "hostilities exist" and has handled the situation.

Choice **b** is incorrect. Roosevelt says the United States has "confidence in our armed forces" and "determination of our people" and will "gain the inevitable triumph." These are not words of a timid or fearful person.

Choice **c** is incorrect. Although he asserts many times that the attack came as a surprise, he does not show fear through his words. Rather, he shows confidence in the country.

Choice **d** is incorrect. Some of what Roosevelt says is aggressive, like asking Congress to declare war, but he seems confident in the abilities of the nation rather than insecure.

26. Choice c is correct. Roosevelt is effectively stressing how "the United States was at peace with that nation" by emphatically pointing out that the Japanese ambassador responded to the American message.

Choice **a** is incorrect. The third paragraph is an example that there were "existing diplomatic negotiations," an example of how Japan was "still in conversation," as stated in the previous paragraph.

Choice **b** is incorrect. The third paragraph supports the premise of the second paragraph.

Choice **d** is incorrect. The third paragraph supports the theme of the previous paragraphs.

27. Choice b is correct. Roosevelt is implying that the two islands are far enough apart that the attack had to have been "deliberately planned." Choice **a** is incorrect. The attack wouldn't have had to have been planned "days or even weeks ago" if the island was close and easy for the Japanese to attack.

Choice **c** is incorrect. The United States mainland is not mentioned and is irrelevant in this context.

Choice **d** is incorrect. There is no evidence in the speech to support this answer choice. The opposite is true.

28. Choice d is correct. The drumbeat rhythm of repetition emphasizes the great number of attacks on one country after another.

Choice **a** is incorrect. There is no evidence in the speech that Japan is disorganized. In fact, evidence in the speech supports the conclusion that the opposite is true.

Choice **b** is incorrect. There is no evidence in the speech to support this conclusion.

Choice **c** is incorrect. There is no mention of how the other countries handled or will handle the attack.

29. Choice b is correct. Roosevelt states many times the attack was an intentional move that put "our interests . . . in grave danger."

Choice **a** is incorrect. Contrary to this answer choice, evidence in the speech supports the conclusion that Japan launched a surprise attack on the United States.

Choice **c** is incorrect. There is no evidence in the speech to support this conclusion.

Choice **d** is incorrect. It is clear from the speech that the attack was planned.

30. Choice **d** is correct. This sentence comes after describing how the surprise attack was carried out, acknowledging resulting clear and present danger.

Choice **a** is incorrect. An attack is not expected from a nation in peaceful accord with the United States.

Choice **b** is incorrect. This sentence shows that the nations were working together to find a solution prior to the attack.

Choice **c** is incorrect. This sentence describes how Japan worked to make sure the attack was a surprise by deceiving the U.S.

31. Choice **b** is correct. The tone is appropriate for a work email.

Choice **a** is incorrect. The phrases "some really big" and "that might really affect" are informal and awkward.

Choice **c** is incorrect. The tone is too informal for a work email.

Choice **d** is incorrect. A postscript (PS) comes at the end of a letter, not at the beginning.

32. Choice **b** is correct. This is the past participle verb. The decision "has" already been made.

Choice **a** is incorrect. This is the future tense, and the decision has already been made.

Choice **c** is incorrect. This is the present tense, and the action is not happening now.

Choice **d** is incorrect. This is the present tense of the verb.

33. Choice **d** is correct. The plural pronoun matches the plural form of the verb. The contraction of these two words is "they're" and is a homophone of "there" and "they're."

Choice **a** is incorrect. The word "there" refers to location.

Choice **b** is incorrect. "Their" is a possessive pronoun.

Choice **c** is incorrect. Although this has the correct plural pronoun, "is" is for singular subjects.

34. Choice **c** is correct. This answer correctly closes off the thought from the first part of the sentence before introducing the second part of the sentence. It shows a natural pause.

Choice **a** is incorrect. "Friday" modifies "afternoons," so they cannot be broken up by a comma.

Choice **b** is incorrect. "Employee" serves as an adjective for "activity." They cannot be separated.

Choice **d** is incorrect. "Activity" is the noun and "drops" is the verb. They should not be separated.

35. Choice **b** is correct. Obama remarks that greatness is not a given and must be earned, implying that the United States is not great by luck, but by work and determination.

Choice **a** is incorrect. The future of our great nation is assured.

Choice **c** is incorrect. The future is not mentioned in the first paragraph.

Choice **d** is incorrect. Obama does not discuss his personal feelings about being president in the address.

36. Choice **d** is correct. The sentence later in the passage recalls the men and women mentioned earlier to stress that the cynics are wrong in thinking great things cannot be accomplished.

Choice **a** is incorrect. Although this answer recognizes the theme of the sentence, that the United States has a large and historical "capacity" for greatness, it does not explicitly call on the image of the people working or modify that idea.

Choice **b** is incorrect. This choice neglects the connection Obama makes between the people who worked hard to shape America and the cynics who are ignoring their struggles by doubting change.

Choice **c** is incorrect. This phrase in the question has nothing to do with the cost of healthcare or technology.

37. Choice 1 is correct. The main idea in the Address is that America was formed by hard work, and that attitude needs to and will be continued throughout this presidency. This phrase supports that by firmly stating that taking the easy way out is not what "our journey" has been about.

Choice 2 is correct. This phrase supports the theme of the future of the United States.

Choice 3 is correct. This phrase supports the idea that citizens and the government must work hard and will work hard.

Choice 4 is incorrect. This phrase is about renewable energy, which is used as a detail of what Obama wants to focus on and is not the main focus.

Choice 5 is incorrect. This phrase stresses the negative and opposition to progress; it does not support the idea of ambition.

38. Choice d is correct. Obama draws on the history of the United States, like "the creed our fathers once declared," to stress that citizens have an "obligation" to help "all posterity." **Choice a is incorrect.** Although Obama does carefully praise the country throughout, the point of the passage is to discuss the future challenges and how past successes enable us to face those challenges.

Choice b is incorrect. This answer shows the reader clearly does not comprehend that the main focus of the text is what Obama believes needs to change.

Choice c is incorrect. This is the tool Obama is utilizing, not the effect of utilizing that tool.

39. Choice b is correct. Obama uses words, or rhetoric, to show that he thinks the two are connected and that their interests both matter. **Choice a is incorrect.** This choice neglects the verb tense change of "built" to "will build." This shows he is talking about past people/actions and future people/actions.

Choice c is incorrect. This sentence makes no value judgment on either party, and does not state one is better than the other.

Choice d is incorrect. One generation's actions are in the past, as "built" is the past tense verb; their work is done.

40. Choice b is correct. Obama is looking to the future, arguing that failure to act to halt climate change would "betray our children and future generations."

Choice a is incorrect. In this sentence, Obama looks to the past for solutions to today's problems.

Choice c is incorrect. Here, Obama draws on the past as a reason United States citizens must fight for the future.

Choice d is incorrect. Obama is stressing American might and willingness to use its power, not speaking of obligations to future generations.

41. Choice b is correct. Specifically, Obama says, "We will support democracy from Asia to Africa; from the Americas to the Middle East . . ."

Choices a, b, and c are incorrect. Obama says, "We will support democracy from Asia to Africa; from the Americas to the Middle East . . ."

42. Choice b is correct. This sentence supports the first inaugural's theme of continuing the hard work of the past in order to secure prosperity and freedom for tomorrow.
Choice **a** is incorrect. This sentence refers to healthcare and taking care of the country's citizens; this is mentioned in the first address, but it is not the theme.
Choice **c** is incorrect. Obama's First Inaugural Address did not focus on war.
Choice **d** is incorrect. These details are not the theme of the first address.

43. Choice d is correct. It is not an American ideal to deny freedom. The opposite is true. Freedom is the theme of American ideals.
Choice **a** is incorrect. This American ideal is cited in paragraph 7.
Choice **b** is incorrect. This American ideal is cited in the last paragraph.
Choice **c** is incorrect. This American ideal is cited in paragraph 3.

44. Choice a is correct. People not having the same rights as others means roughly the same thing as the denial of equal treatment.
Choice **b** is incorrect. This means the opposite of the quotation in question.
Choice **c** is incorrect. In this sentence, Johnson is explaining that there were reasons for what happened rather than restating the problem of people being treated differently.
Choice **d** is incorrect. Johnson is affirming that Americans of all races have contributed to their country.

45. Choice c is correct. This is the best answer because one of the main points of the remarks is to explain that the Civil Rights Act will bring the United States closer to achieving its goals and values.
Choice **a** is incorrect. Johnson does not mention the Civil War in the passage.
Choice **b** is incorrect. The Grand Canyon is one of America's natural wonders, unrelated to America's unending search for justice domestically.
Choice **d** is incorrect. Johnson alludes to the Vietnam War in the text and uses it as an example of how American values are spanning the globe, but this is a small detail in the passage rather than a main idea. As well, Vietnam is outside of "our own borders."

46. Choice b is correct. Johnson talks about the values that the forefathers focused on when forming the nation in this paragraph.
Choice **a** is incorrect. This is a detail of the passage, but not the main theme.
Choice **c** is incorrect. This idea is not stated in the paragraph, and it also runs counter to the entire point of the speech.
Choice **d** is incorrect. There is no evidence to support this conclusion in the remarks.

47. Choice a is correct. Johnson expresses many times and in a variety of ways that equality is one of the cornerstones of American values.
Choice **b** is incorrect. Johnson talks about how he believes America is a great country, but this is not the main idea of his remarks.
Choice **c** is incorrect. Johnson's remarks are about America's ideal of ensuring equality, yet to be achieved.
Choice **d** is incorrect. Johnson makes no value judgment about himself.

48. Choice d is correct. This is Johnson's brief explanation of how inequality happened, rather than an explanation of how the law aligns with American values.

Choice **a** is incorrect. Johnson uses history and the vision of the forefathers to illustrate that freedom is a core American value and that freedom includes equality.

Choice **b** is incorrect. Johnson says that because American values are shaping foreign struggles, the United States must continue to make sure that it upholds its own values.

Choice **c** is incorrect. Johnson uses this sentence to say that all kinds of people, regardless of race, have fought for the country.

Part II

Your Extended Response will be scored based on three traits, or elements:

Trait 1: Analysis of arguments and use of evidence

Trait 2: Development of ideas and structure

Trait 3: Clarity and command of standard English conventions

Your essay will be scored on a 6-point scale—each trait is worth up to 2 points. The final score is counted twice, so the maximum number of points you can earn is 12.

Trait 1 tests your ability to write an essay that takes a stance based on the information in the reading passages. To earn the highest score possible, you must carefully read the information and express a clear opinion on what you have read. You will be scored on how well you use the information from the passages to support your argument.

Your response will also be scored on how well you analyze the author's arguments in the passages. To earn the highest score possible, you should discuss whether you think the author is making a good argument, and why or why not.

For your reference, here is a table that readers will use when scoring your essay with a 2, 1, or 0.

	TRAIT 1: CREATION OF ARGUMENTS AND USE OF EVIDENCE
2	• Makes text-based argument(s) and establishes an intent connected to the prompt • Presents specific and related evidence from source text(s) to support argument (may include a few unrelated pieces of evidence or unsupported claims) • Analyzes the topic and/or the strength of the argument within the source text(s) (e.g., distinguishes between supported and unsupported claims, makes valid inferences about underlying assumptions, identifies false reasoning, evaluates the credibility of sources)
1	• Makes an argument with some connection to the prompt • Presents some evidence from source text(s) to support argument (may include a mix of related and unrelated evidence that may or may not cite the text) • Partly analyzes the topic and/or the strength of the argument within the source text(s); may be limited, oversimplified, or inaccurate
0	• May attempt to make an argument OR lacks an intent or connection to the prompt OR attempts neither • Presents little or no evidence from source text(s) (sections of text may be copied from source directly) • Minimally analyzes the topic and/or the strength of the argument within the source text(s); may present no analysis, or little or no understanding of the given argument
Non-scorable	• Response consists only of text copied from the prompt or source text(s) • Response shows that test-taker has not read the prompt or is entirely off-topic • Response is incomprehensible • Response is not in English • No response has been attempted (has been left blank)

Trait 2 tests whether you respond to the writing prompt with a well-structured essay. Support of your thesis must come from evidence in the passages, as well as personal opinions and experiences that build on your central idea. Your ideas must be fully explained and include specific details. Your essay should use words and phrases that allow your details and ideas to flow naturally. Here is a table that outlines what is involved in earning a score of 2, 1, or 0.

TRAIT 2: DEVELOPMENT OF IDEAS AND ORGANIZATIONAL STRUCTURE	
2	• Contains ideas that are generally logical and well-developed; most ideas are expanded upon • Contains a logical sequence of ideas with clear connections between specific details and main ideas • Develops an organizational structure that conveys the message and goal of the response; appropriately uses transitional devices • Develops and maintains an appropriate style and tone that signal awareness of the audience and purpose of the task • Uses appropriate words to express ideas clearly
1	• Contains ideas that are partially developed and/or may demonstrate vague or simplistic logic; only some ideas are expanded upon • Contains some evidence of a sequence of ideas, but specific details may be unconnected to main ideas • Develops an organizational structure that may partially group ideas or is partially effective at conveying the message of the response; inconsistently uses transitional devices • May inconsistently maintain an appropriate style and tone to signal an awareness of the audience and purpose of the task • May contain misused words and/or words that do not express ideas clearly
0	• Contains ideas that are ineffectively or illogically developed, with little or no elaboration of main ideas • Contains an unclear or no sequence of ideas; specific details may be absent or unrelated to main ideas • Develops an ineffective or no organizational structure; inappropriately uses transitional devices, or does not use them at all • Uses an inappropriate style and tone that signals limited or no awareness of audience and purpose • May contain many misused words, overuse of slang, and/or express ideas in an unclear or repetitious manner
Non-scorable	• Response consists only of text copied from the prompt or source text(s) • Response shows that test-taker has not read the prompt or is entirely off-topic • Response is incomprehensible • Response is not in English • No response has been attempted (has been left blank)

Trait 3 tests how you create the sentences that make up your essay. To earn a high score, you will need to write sentences with variety—some short, some long, some simple, some complex. You will also need to prove that you have a good handle on standard English, including correct word choice, grammar, and sentence structure.

Here is a table that outlines what is involved in attaining a score of 2, 1, or 0.

	TRAIT 3: CLARITY AND COMMAND OF STANDARD ENGLISH CONVENTIONS
2	• Demonstrates generally correct sentence structure and an overall fluency that enhances clarity with regard to the following skills: 1) Diverse sentence structure within a paragraph or paragraphs 2) Correct use of subordination, coordination, and parallelism 3) Avoidance of awkward sentence structures and wordiness 4) Use of transitional words, conjunctive adverbs, and other words that enhance clarity and logic 5) Avoidance of run-on sentences, sentence fragments, and fused sentences • Demonstrates proficient use of conventions with regard to the following skills: 1) Subject-verb agreement 2) Placement of modifiers and correct word order 3) Pronoun usage, including pronoun antecedent agreement, unclear pronoun references, and pronoun case 4) Frequently confused words and homonyms, including contractions 5) Use of apostrophes with possessive nouns 6) Use of punctuation (e.g., commas in a series or in appositives and other non-essential elements, end marks, and punctuation for clause separation) 7) Capitalization (e.g., beginnings of sentences, proper nouns, and titles) • May contain some errors in mechanics and conventions that do not impede comprehension; overall usage is at a level suitable for on-demand draft writing
1	• Demonstrates inconsistent sentence structure; may contain some choppy, repetitive, awkward, or run-on sentences that may limit clarity; demonstrates inconsistent use of skills 1–5 as listed under Trait 3, Score Point 2 • Demonstrates inconsistent use of basic conventions with regard to skills 1–7 as listed under Trait 3, Score Point 2 • May contain many errors in mechanics and conventions that occasionally impede comprehension; overall usage is at the minimum level acceptable for on-demand draft writing
0	• Demonstrates improper sentence structure to the extent that meaning may be unclear; demonstrates minimal use of skills 1–5 as listed under Trait 3, Score Point 2 • Demonstrates minimal use of basic conventions with regard to skills 1–7 as listed under Trait 3, Score Point 2 • Contains numerous significant errors in mechanics and conventions that impede comprehension; overall usage is at an unacceptable level for on-demand draft writing OR • Response is insufficient to show level of proficiency involving conventions and usage
Non-scorable	• Response consists only of text copied from the prompt or source text(s) • Response shows that test-taker has not read the prompt or is entirely off-topic • Response is incomprehensible • Response is not in English • No response has been attempted (has been left blank)

Sample Score 6 Essay

Weighing the pro and con arguments presented in the article, I conclude that the case against nuclear energy is more compelling than the case for nuclear energy. While both positions are well reasoned, organized and supported with authoritative quotes and examples, the unimpeachable evidence against nuclear energy, upon reflection, is greater.

Both sides agree that fossil fuels are not healthy for the environment and people. Opponents and proponents also agree that radioactivity is deadly, although the proponents whitewash this fact by only describing the need to keep radioactivity contained by stating in paragraph 4 that "Radioactive waste is contained deep underground behind steel-reinforced, 1.2 meter thick concrete walls." On the other hand, the second essay speaks more plainly, "First, nuclear radioactivity is deadly and must be contained for thousands of years." In fact, the second essay uses evidence found in the first essay to support its premise.

The pro-nuclear position also avoids the topics of meltdown and the construction of atomic weapons from radioactive materials used in nuclear power plants. To not address and gloss over these topics makes the first essay seem more like an advertisement for the nuclear industry rather than an objective assessment of well-known and troubling facts. In paragraph 7, the writer points out what we all know, that "Widespread radioactive contamination and death caused by the nuclear accidents at Three Mile Island, Chernobyl and Fukushima are cautionary lessons." and that "it's undeniable that nuclear meltdown causes widespread contamination of the air, water and land with deadly radioactivity. It is also verifiable that nuclear accidents have caused environmental catastrophes that continue to this day." For me, nothing more needs to be said about the absolute truth about the real danger of nuclear energy, but the author of the second essay indeed provides up-to-date evidence from Reuters regarding international fears of Iran developing atomic weaponry under the guise of building nuclear power plants.

In the end, the opponent position offers a safe and sane solution to fossil fuels and nuclear power.

About this essay:

This essay has earned the maximum number of points in each trait for a total of 6 points.

Trait 1: Creation of Arguments and Use of Evidence

This response evaluates the arguments in the source text, develops an effective position supported by the text, and fulfills the criteria to earn 2 points for Trait 1.

This response establishes its stance in the first sentence (*I conclude that the case against nuclear energy is more compelling than the case for nuclear energy*) and provides a summary of support for that stance (*While both essays are well reasoned, organized and supported with authoritative quotes and examples, the unimpeachable evidence against nuclear energy, upon reflection, is greater*).

He also weighs the validity of evidence (*although the proponents whitewash this fact by only describing the need to keep radioactivity contained*) and critiques omissions (*To not address and gloss over these topics makes the first essay seem more like an advertisement for the nuclear industry rather than an objective assessment of well-known and troubling facts*).

Trait 2: Development of Ideas and Organizational Structure

This response is well developed and fulfills the criteria to earn 2 points for Trait 2. It is well organized, from the writer's clear point of view in the first paragraph to the step-by-step comparison of the pros and cons presented in the source material.

The writer's vocabulary and sentence structures are sophisticated, and the tone shows an urgency of purpose.

Trait 3: Clarity and Command of Standard English Conventions

This response then fulfills the criteria for draft writing and earns 2 points for Trait 3. Besides employing sophisticated sentence structure (*Both sides agree that fossil fuels are not healthy for the environment and people. Opponents and proponents also agree that radioactivity is deadly, although the proponents whitewash this fact by only describing the need to keep radioactivity contained by stating in paragraph 4 that . . .*) this response uses clear transitions in its compare and contrast construction (*On the other hand, the second essay speaks more plainly . . .*)

In addition, the writer adheres to proper grammar and usage.

Sample Score 4 Essay

The supporters of nuclear energy best show how it is superior to other forms of energy. We have only begun to use nuclear energy, and while the opposing position only describes the danger of radioactivity, it is true from another point of view that scientists learn more everyday about how to contain these types of materials. We have only just begun to fulfill the promise of nuclear energy.

In the first paragraph the author states that "The U.S. Department of Energy (DOE) promotes the development of safe, domestic nuclear power…" The United States government and its agencies are powerful and highly-regarded authorities, so if the DOE says that nuclear energy is the way to go, I don't have an argument with that.

The opposing position to nuclear power states that radioactivity is dangerous, that containing the danger is difficult and that evil-doers can create atomic bombs from enriched uranium are scare tactics. First of all, the "Nuclear Regulatory Commission ensures that each and every nuclear reactor maintains strict safety standards." Nuclear accidents are a thing of the past as scientists work hard to be able to control nuclear power plants. Not to mention that so far, there no one has

built a bomb from plutonium stolen used in a nuclear power plant.

All in all, a strong case against nuclear energy was not made and the case for nuclear energy continues to build on the authority of science.

About this essay:

This essay earned 1 point each for Trait 1 and Trait 2, and 2 points for Trait 3.

Trait 1: Creation of Arguments and Use of Evidence

This response makes an argument, supports it with some evidence from the source text, and offers a partial analysis of the opposing argument, earning it 1 point for Trait 1.

The writer makes an issue-based statement of position in the first sentence: *The supporters of nuclear energy best show how it is superior to other forms of energy.* She goes on to cite textual evidence in the second paragraph for support (*The U.S. Department of Energy (DOE) promotes the development of safe, domestic nuclear power . . .*) but then relies on the fallacy of authority to validate this position (*The United States government and its agencies are powerful and highly-regarded authorities, so if the DOE says that nuclear energy is the way to go, I don't have an argument with that*).

The summary of opposing arguments in paragraph 4 is superficial and simplistic: *The opposing position to nuclear power states that radioactivity is dangerous, that containing the danger is difficult and that evil-doers can create atomic bombs from enriched uranium are scare tactics.*

Trait 2: Development of Ideas and Organizational Structure

The response's general conclusion has no support and in general it displays only adequate skill of word choice, though the tone is audience appropriate. The response is fairly organized, but the ideas rely on authority, earning this response 1 point for Trait 2.

The writer establishes a stance in the beginning of the response and roughly organizes material in a compare-and-contrast structure loosely based on speculation not found in the source text: *We have only begun to use nuclear energy, and while the opposing position only describes the danger of radioactivity, it is true from another point of view that scientists learn more everyday about how to contain these types of materials.*

Trait 3: Clarity and Command of Standard English Conventions

Because the response fulfills level criteria for draft writing on-demand, it earns the full 2 points for Trait 3.

Overall, this response displays proper sentence structure and appropriate use of transitional words: *We have only begun to use nuclear energy, and while the opposing position only describes the danger of radioactivity, it is true from another point of view that scientists learn more everyday about how to contain these types of materials.*

In general, the response demonstrates proper use of conventions, including subject-verb agreement, pronoun, and punctuation use.

Sample Score 3 Essay

The benefits of nuclear energy are by far more beneficial to supply America's need for power than fossil, solar or any other kind of alternative energy source. As the introduction states, "it has become clear that we need to ease our dependence on foreign countries that supply us with oil and develop energy at home." That's common sense and pretty much proves the point.

The supporters show how nuclear energy is safe and efficient and gives statistics about how much waste comes from nuclear energy and how much comes from fossil fuels. The opposers suppose nuclear power plants will have meltdowns and contaminate the environment. They also worries about irresponsible people making atom bombs.

After reading both sides though I was convinced that compared to fossil fuels such as gas, coal, and oil nuclear energy is the most efficient way to make electricity, Nuclear energy leaves less waste too.

In conclusion, I agree with the first opinion and hope disasters like Three Mile Island, Chernobyl and Fukishima are a thing of the past.

About this essay:

This essay earned 1 point each for Trait 1, Trait 2, and Trait 3.

Trait 1: Creation of Arguments and Use of Evidence

This draft fulfills the criteria for Trait 1 by generating an argument in the opening sentence that demonstrates a connection to the prompt: *The benefits of nuclear energy are by far more beneficial to supply America's need for power than fossil, solar or any other kind of alternative energy source.*

The argument is then supported by source text (*it has become clear that we need to ease our dependence on foreign countries that supply us with oil and develop energy at home*), but the writer's analysis of the source text and simplistic and limited: *That's common sense and pretty much proves the point.*

Trait 2: Development of Ideas and Organizational Structure

Overall, the writer demonstrates awareness of audience and purpose, earning this response 1 point for Trait 2.

The writer simply summarizes the pro and con arguments without quotation (*The supporters show how nuclear energy is safe and efficient and gives statistics about how much waste comes from nuclear energy and how much comes from fossil fuels. The opposers suppose nuclear power plants will have meltdowns and contaminate the environment. They also worries about irresponsible people making atom bombs*), however demonstrating a logical flow of ideas.

The conclusion in favor of the supporting position is abrupt and unsupported, although the writer's final clause shows attention to the source material and genuine consideration of both sides of the issue: *In conclusion, I agree with the first opinion and hope disasters like Three Mile Island, Chernobyl and Fukushima are a thing of the past.*

Word choice is adequate throughout, and though ideas progress and develop somewhat, thoughts are not fully executed to a supported conclusion.

Trait 3: Clarity and Command of Standard English Conventions

This sample response is comprehensible and maintains an acceptable level of appropriateness to earn it 1 point for Trait 3.

The writer's short response lacks a variety of sentence structures and though most sentences are grammatically correct, there are usage and punctuation errors in the text. For example: *The supporters show how nuclear energy is safe and efficient and gives statistics and They also worries about . . .*

Additionally, source text is cited without quotation marks: *After reading both essays though I was convinced that["] compared to fossil fuels such as gas, coal and oil, nuclear energy is the most efficient way to make electricity, ["]Nuclear energy leaves less waste too.*

Sample Score 0 Essay

The best way to think if solar energy is better then nuclear energy or if fossil fuels is better then wind power are to look at the facts not just listen to opinions of people who don't know what they're talking about or are not scientists which know about energy in the broadest sense of the term... These facts. Most folks got no idea that nuclear power is so much stronger than fossil fuel power because just a tiny bit of uranium can make more energy than barrels of oil or tons of coal. You can take that to the bank.

If you want to know the dangers about nuclear energy, read the second part of the story. People can make bombs from uranium and thereve been lots of accidents too. Some say we should throw the dice with nuclear power though because we have to be independent.

Why we don't want to blow up the Earth. But we need electricity and gas to live our everyday lives. That's why the United States needs to grab the bull by the horn and get scientists to make nuclear energy. Better for future generations.

About this essay:

This essay earned 0 points in Trait 1, Trait 2, and Trait 3.

Trait 1: Creation of Arguments and Use of Evidence

In general, this response provides minimal summary of the source text and lacks insight and topic analysis, earning this response 0 points for Trait 1.

The writer fails to summarize source text in a coherent and organized structure. Though this response addresses the source material, the writer fails to cite evidence to support any arguments.

Trait 2: Development of Ideas and Organizational Structure

Overall, the response is poorly developed, is disorganized, and lacks any clear progression of ideas, earning it 0 points for Trait 2.

The writer uses informal and colloquial language (*You can take that to the bank*) and fails to demonstrate awareness of audience and purpose. The response lacks organizational structure and a clear progression of ideas.

Trait 3: Clarity and Command of Standard English Conventions

Many sentences lack sense and fluency and are incorrect and awkward. The writer misuses and confuses words, punctuation, and usage as well as the conventions of English in general, making the response almost incomprehensible and earning it 0 points for Trait 3.

This short response shows flawed sentence structure, including run-on sentences (*The best way to think if solar energy is better then nuclear energy or if fossil fuels is better then wind power are to look at the facts not just listen to opinions of people who don't know what they're talking about or are not scientists which know about energy in the broadest sense of the term . . .*) and fragments (*These facts* and *Better for future generations*).

4 ▶ GED® SCIENCE TEST 1

This practice test is modeled on the format, content, and timing of the official GED® Science test and, like the official exam, presents a series of questions that focus on the fundamentals of scientific reasoning.

Work carefully, but do not spend too much time on any one question. Be sure you answer every question.

Set a timer for 90 minutes (1 hour and 30 minutes), and try to take this test uninterrupted, under quiet conditions.

Complete answer explanations for every test question follow the exam. Good luck!

PART I

35 total questions
90 minutes to complete

Please use the following to answer questions 1–3.

A non-predatory relationship between two organisms that benefits at least one of the organisms is called a *symbiotic relationship*. These relationships can be categorized further based on the effect of the relationship on the second organism. The table shows the three types of symbiotic relationships and their effects on each organism.

Symbiotic Relationship	Species 1	Species 2
Mutualism	+	+
Commensalism	+	0
Parasitism	+	–

Key
+ benefits
– harmed
0 no effect

Veterinary clinics often treat pets with illnesses resulting from parasitism. Three common parasites diagnosed in dogs are the dog flea, the deer tick, and *Cheyletiella* mites.

Dog fleas and deer ticks both feed on the host animal's (dog's) blood and can transmit diseases to the host animal through their bites. Dog fleas lay their eggs on the host animal's body and can survive on the host animal or on surfaces the animal comes in contact with, such as bedding. Deer ticks lay their eggs on the ground and attach to the host animal only while feeding.

Cheyletiella mites live within and feed on the keratin layer of the host animal's skin. *Cheyletiella* mites reproduce on the host animal and can survive away from the host animal only for short periods of time.

---

1. Read the two descriptions of symbiotic relationships below, and select the correct term for each relationship from the following list. Write the correct answer in the box after each description.

commensalism
mutualism
parasitism

Mistletoe attaches to spruce trees. Using specialized structures, mistletoe penetrates into and extracts water and nutrients from the tree's branches.

```
[                                    ]
```

E. coli bacteria live within the intestinal tract of humans, obtaining nutrients from the food particles that pass through the intestines. Vitamin K produced by the E. coli *is absorbed through the intestinal walls for use in the human body.*

```
[                                    ]
```

2. According to the passage, all of the dog parasites gain which benefit from their symbiotic relationships with the host dogs?
   a. a habitat for living
   b. a vector for disease
   c. a source of nutrients
   d. a site for reproduction

3. A veterinary technician is preparing to examine a dog suspected of having *Cheyletiella* mites. Based on the information in the passage, which precaution would most effectively prevent the transmission of mites to other animals in the clinic?
   a. administering a vaccine to the infected dog
   b. wearing disposable gloves while examining the dog
   c. avoiding contact with open wounds on the dog
   d. sterilizing the exam room before examining the dog

4. The passing of one object in space through the shadow of another object is called an eclipse. The orbits of the moon and Earth in relation to the sun cause both solar and lunar eclipses to occur. During a solar eclipse, the specific alignment of these three objects causes the moon to cast a shadow on the Earth. During a lunar eclipse, the alignment causes the Earth to cast a shadow on the moon.

The following diagram shows the alignment of the sun, Earth, and moon during a lunar eclipse. Draw an "X" in the correct spot to identify the location of the moon necessary to produce a solar eclipse.

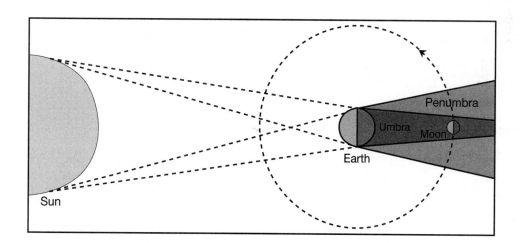

5. The table below compares characteristics for four different groups of plants. A "1" indicates that the characteristic is present, and a "0" indicates that the characteristic is absent.

Plant Type	Vascular Tissue	Seeds	Flowers
Confers	1	1	0
Ferns	1	0	0
Flowering Plants	1	1	1
Mosses	0	0	0

A cladogram illustrates the relatedness of organisms based on shared characteristics. Branches below a given characteristic represent organisms that do not exhibit that characteristic. Branches above a given characteristic represent organisms that do exhibit that characteristic. Each branch represents one plant type.

Use the information in the table to organize the four plant types onto the appropriate branches in the cladogram.

Write the correct plant type into each box. Select from the choices below.

conifers
ferns
flowering plants
mosses

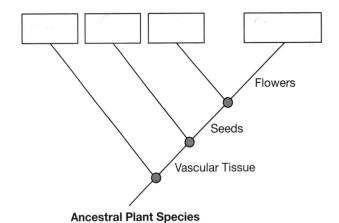

Please use the following to answer questions 6–7.

The amount of oxygen gas dissolved in a body of water can provide information about the health of the aquatic ecosystem. In general, the closer the dissolved oxygen level to the maximum level, the more productive and less polluted the ecosystem can be assumed to be.

The table below shows the maximum amount of oxygen gas that can be dissolved in water at various temperatures.

WATER TEMPERATURE (°C)	MAXIMUM OXYGEN SOLUBILITY (MG/L)
0	14.6
10	11.3
20	9.2
30	7.6
40	6.4
100	0

6. The data in the table support which of the following statements about the relationship between water temperature and oxygen solubility?
   a. Bodies of water with a lower average temperature can support a higher concentration of dissolved oxygen.
   b. Bodies of water with an average temperature higher than 40°C contain no dissolved oxygen.
   c. A 10°C increase in water temperature results in an approximately 3 mg/L change in oxygen solubility.
   d. The oxygen solubility of a body of water is affected by many variables, including water temperature.

7. Researchers find that a body of freshwater with an average temperature of 21 °C has a dissolved oxygen concentration of 7.2 mg/L. What is a reasonable prediction of the water's dissolved oxygen concentration after the population size of freshwater grasses doubles?
   a. 6.3 mg/L
   b. 7.2 mg/L
   c. 8.5 mg/L
   d. 14.4 mg/L

8. The chart below illustrates how the color of the light emitted by a star is dependent on the star's temperature.

CLASS	COLOR	SURFACE TEMP. (K)
O	Blue	>25,000 K
B	Blue-white	11,000–25,000 K
A	White	7,500–11,000 K
F	White	6,000–7,500 K
G	Yellow	5,000–6,000 K
K	Orange	3,500–5,000 K
M	Red	<3,500 K

Which of the following statements is supported by the data in the table?

   a. In general, white stars are hotter than blue-white stars.
   b. A star with a surface temperature of 3,700 K produces red light.
   c. Yellow light is produced by stars within the narrowest temperature range.
   d. The highest known surface temperature of a star is 25,000 K.

9. The diagram below illustrates the structure of an ocean wave.

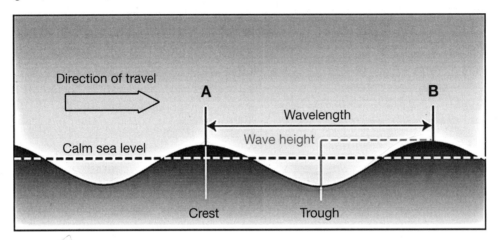

The *period* of a wave is the time required for the wave crest at point A to reach point B. The wave period can also be described as the amount of time required for a wave to do which of the following?

a. reach the shoreline

b. travel one wavelength

c. return to calm sea level

d. travel from crest to trough

Please use the following to answer questions 10–11.

The U.S. Geological Survey (USGS) tracks the annual occurrence and effects of natural hazards in the United States. Based on its data, the USGS has calculated the probability of a natural hazard occurring in any given year that would cause 10 or more fatalities. The table below lists the probabilities for the four most commonly occurring natural hazards.

EVENT	PROBABILITY OF AN ANNUAL EVENT WITH ≥10 FATALITIES IN THE UNITED STATES
Earthquake	0.11
Hurricane	0.39
Flood	0.86
Tornado	0.96

0 = no chance of occurring / 1 = 100% chance of occurring

10. What is the probability of a hurricane and a tornado, each with 10 or more fatalities, both occurring in the same year?

a. 0

b. 0.37

c. 0.96

d. 1.35

11. Write the appropriate natural hazard from the table in the box below.

A boundary between the Pacific and North American tectonic plates lies along the west coast of the continental United States. The probability of a(n) ⬚ with 10 or more fatalities is much higher in this region than the probability for the United States as a whole.

12. A marathon runner consumes foods with a high carbohydrate content before and during a race to prevent muscle fatigue. This practice, called carb loading, supports which of the following energy transformations within the runner's body?

a. chemical to thermal
b. thermal to kinetic
c. kinetic to thermal
d. chemical to kinetic

Please use the following to answer questions 13–15.

Consumers in an ecosystem are classified by feeding level. Primary consumers feed on producers. Secondary consumers feed on primary consumers, and tertiary consumers feed on secondary consumers. Consumers in a food web are classified according to their highest feeding level.

A consumer's population size is determined largely by the complex relationships that exist within the ecosystem's food web. Population size is most obviously limited by the population size of the consumer's food source(s). An increase or decrease in a food source population often leads to a similar change in the consumer population. The availability of a food source may be limited by other consumer populations competing for the same food source. An increase in a competitor population may lead to a decreased availability of the shared food source. Population size is also limited by the population size of the consumer's predator(s). Predation by higher-level consumers keeps the lower consumer population from growing out of control and upsetting the ecosystem's balance.

The food web for a woodland ecosystem bordering an area of farmland is shown below.

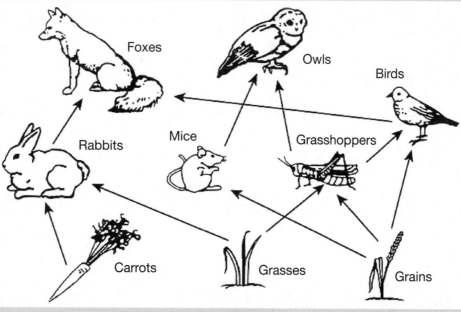

(Not drawn to scale)

13. According to the passage, rabbits are considered primary consumers because they
  a. feed on grasses and carrots
  b. are consumed by foxes only
  c. compete with grasshoppers only
  d. are the only consumer of carrots

14. Which three organisms in the food web obtain energy directly or indirectly from grasshoppers?
  a. owls, birds, and mice
  b. owls, birds, and grains
  c. foxes, rabbits, and mice
  d. foxes, owls, and birds

15. A bacterial disease has destroyed most of the farm's carrot crop for the past two seasons. As a result, the rabbit population has been forced to rely more heavily on grasses for a food source.

Explain how this disruption is likely to affect the rest of the ecosystem's food web. Include multiple pieces of evidence from the text and discuss specific populations (other than carrots and rabbits) as examples to support your answer.

Write your response on the lines below. This task may take approximately 10 minutes to complete.

_____

_____

_____

_____

_____

_____

_____

_____

_____

_____

_____

16. The table below illustrates the range of normal body temperatures in Fahrenheit for different age groups.

NORMAL BODY TEMPERATURE	
AGE GROUP	TEMPERATURE (IN °FAHRENHEIT)
Newborn	97.7 °F–99.5 °F
Infants (1 year or less)	97.0 °F–99.0 °F
Children (1–17 years)	97.5 °F–98.6 °F
Adults (above 18 years)	97.6 °F–99 °F
Elders (above 70 years)	96.8 °F–97.5 °F

The formula for converting Fahrenheit to Celsius is shown below.

$$(°F - 32) \times \frac{5}{9} = °C$$

The normal body temperature range of a newborn baby is ⬜ °C to ⬜ °C. (You may use a calculator to answer this question.)

17. The process of meiosis is depicted in the diagram below.

Meiosis

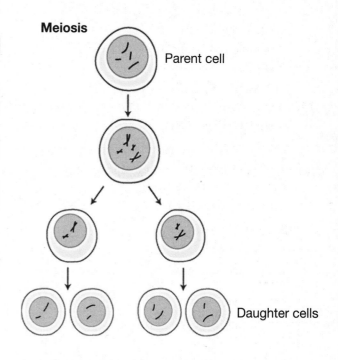

Parent cell

Daughter cells

The daughter cells produced during meiosis are used for what purpose?
a. growth
b. tissue repair
c. differentiation
d. reproduction

18. A highway patrol officer is monitoring the speed of vehicles along a stretch of highway with a speed limit of 55 mph. The results are shown below.

    Vehicle 1: 61 mph
    Vehicle 2: 48 mph
    Vehicle 3: 61 mph
    Vehicle 4: 51 mph
    Vehicle 5: 59 mph

What is the average speed of the five vehicles? (You may use a calculator to answer this question.)

a. 55 miles per hour
b. 56 miles per hour
c. 59 miles per hour
d. 61 miles per hour

19. Meiosis produces cells containing one chromosome from each chromosome pair. The diagram below shows the chromosome combinations that can be produced from a cell containing two pairs of chromosomes.

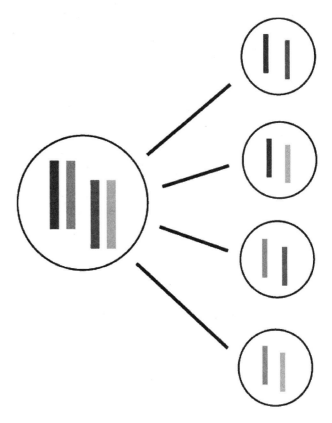

A barley plant has seven pairs of chromosomes. How many unique combinations of chromosomes can result from meiosis in barley?

a. 7
b. 14
c. 49
d. 128

Please use the following to answer questions 20–22.

Respiration is the cellular process used by living things to convert the chemical energy in food to a form that can be used by cells. Adenosine triphosphate (ATP) is the high-energy molecule that all living things use to fuel cellular processes. During respiration, a molecule of glucose is converted to molecules of ATP to be used by the cell.

Depending on the conditions, respiration occurs by two different pathways: aerobic and anaerobic. When a cell has a sufficient supply of oxygen, aerobic respiration occurs. This pathway uses oxygen as a reactant, along with glucose, to produce 36 to 38 molecules of ATP from each molecule of glucose. Aerobic respiration is the preferred pathway in most cells. The general equation for aerobic respiration is shown below.

$$C_6H_{12}O_6 + 6O_2 \rightarrow energy + 6CO_2 + 6H_2O$$

When sufficient oxygen is not available, anaerobic respiration occurs. This pathway produces two molecules of ATP from each molecule of glucose. Anaerobic respiration sometimes occurs in human muscle cells. During exercise, muscle cells use energy faster than the oxygen supply can be replenished, causing the cells to switch temporarily to anaerobic respiration.

20. A student draws the model below to represent the process of aerobic respiration.

Which change would improve the accuracy of the student's model?
   a. connecting all of the circles to each other to show bonds
   b. moving the energy symbol to the left side of the equation
   c. adding five triangles to balance the right side of the equation
   d. making the rectangles smaller to show relative molecular sizes

21. The energy produced by respiration is in what form?
   a. ATP
   b. oxygen
   c. glucose
   d. carbon dioxide

22. Explain the benefit of having two pathways for respiration in the human body.

Include multiple pieces of evidence from the text to support your answer.

Write your response on the lines on the following page. This task may take approximately 10 minutes to complete.

Please use the following to answer questions 23–24.

Matter exists in solid, liquid, and gas states. A substance may change between these three states. State changes can alter the physical properties of a substance, as depicted in the models below.

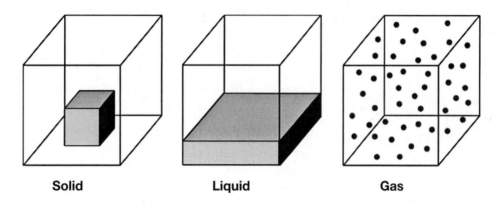

| Solid | Liquid | Gas |

23. Which summary best explains the model of the states of matter?

    a. Liquids have a fixed shape like solids but assume the volume of the container as gases do.

    b. Liquids have a fixed volume and shape like solids. Gases assume the volume and shape of the container.

    c. Liquids have a fixed volume like solids but assume the shape of the container as gases do.

    d. Liquids assume the volume and shape of the container as gases do. Solids have a fixed volume and shape.

24. Based on the model, which state change increases the density of a substance?

    a. gas to liquid

    b. solid to gas

    c. liquid to gas

    d. solid to liquid

Please use the following to answer questions 25–26.

Information about five different fuel sources is listed in the table below.

	ENERGY CONTENT (KJ/G)	CO_2 RELEASED (MOL/10^3KJ)
Hydrogen	120	------
Natural gas	51.6	1.2
Petroleum	43.6	1.6
Coal	39.3	2.0
Ethanol	27.3	1.6

25. Which statement represents a fact supported by the data in the table?

    a. All cars will be fueled by hydrogen cells in the future.

    b. Petroleum is a better fuel source for cars than ethanol is.

    c. Natural gas is too expensive to use as a fuel source for cars.

    d. Ethanol fuel provides a car with less energy per gram than petroleum does.

26. Natural gas, petroleum, and coal are fossil fuels. Ethanol is derived from biomass.

Based on the data in the table, what is the best estimate of the energy content of fossil fuels?
a. 40 kJ/g
b. 42 kJ/g
c. 45 kJ/g
d. 50 kJ/g

27. The term *exothermic* describes a process in which energy is released, usually as thermal energy. The term *endothermic* describes a process in which thermal energy is absorbed.

Which of the following is an example of an exothermic process?
a. a candle burning
b. a snow bank melting
c. a loaf of bread baking
d. a plant making sugar

28. The graph below represents the motion of a remote-controlled car. The car's acceleration, or change in velocity, is indicated by the slope of the graph.

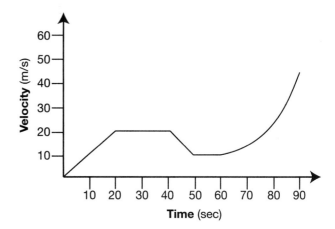

During which period did the car experience a constant positive acceleration?
a. between 0 and 20 seconds
b. between 20 and 40 seconds
c. between 40 and 50 seconds
d. between 50 and 90 seconds

Please use the following to answer questions 29–30.

The mechanical advantage (MA) of a machine is a measure of how much the machine multiplies the input force applied to it.

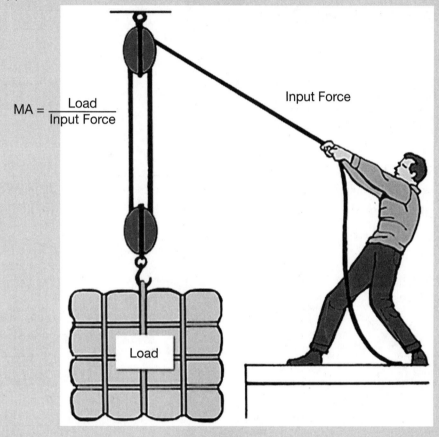

$$MA = \frac{Load}{Input\ Force}$$

The table below shows the input force required to lift different loads using the pulley system shown above.

LOAD (N)	INPUT FORCE (N)
30	10
60	20
90	30
150	50

29. Based on the data in the table, what happens to the mechanical advantage of the pulley system as the load size increases?

a. The mechanical advantage increases at a constant rate.

b. The system's mechanical advantage does not change.

c. The pulley system multiplies the mechanical advantage.

d. The mechanical advantage decreases at a constant rate.

30. A 1 Newton load has a mass of 10 grams. According to the table, what is the maximum mass that can be lifted by the pulley system using an input force of 50 Newtons?

a. 15 grams

b. 50 grams

c. 150 grams

d. 1,500 grams

31. Artificial selection is the process of breeding plants or animals to increase the occurrence of desired traits. Farmers use artificial selection to produce new crop species from existing plant species. The diagram below illustrates six crop species that have been derived from the common wild mustard plant.

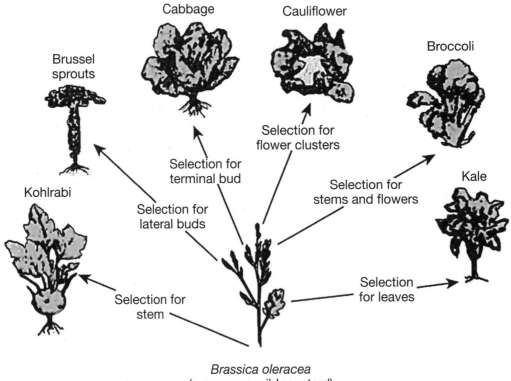

Brassica oleracea
(a common wild mustard)

Based on the information in the passage, how did farmers produce kale?

a. Farmers removed the stems and flowers from mustard plants as they grew.

b. Farmers allowed only wild mustard plants with large leaves to reproduce.

c. Farmers bred small-leafed plants with large-leafed plants to increase leaf size.

d. Farmers prevented wild mustard plants with large leaves from reproducing.

32.

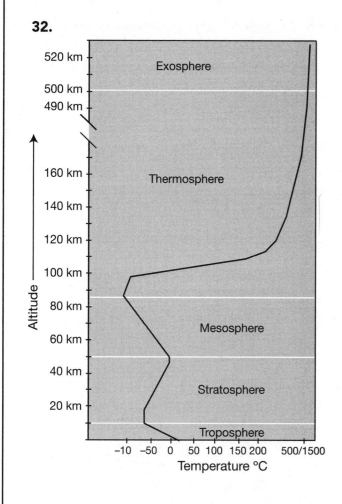

According to the graph, in which atmospheric layers does temperature decrease as altitude increases?

a. mesosphere and exosphere

b. troposphere and thermosphere

c. stratosphere and thermosphere

d. troposphere and mesosphere

33. Surface currents in the ocean are classified as warm or cold currents. In general, warm currents tend to travel from the equator toward the poles along the eastern coast of continents. Cold currents tend to travel from the poles toward the equator along the western coast of continents.

The map below shows the major surface ocean currents of the world.

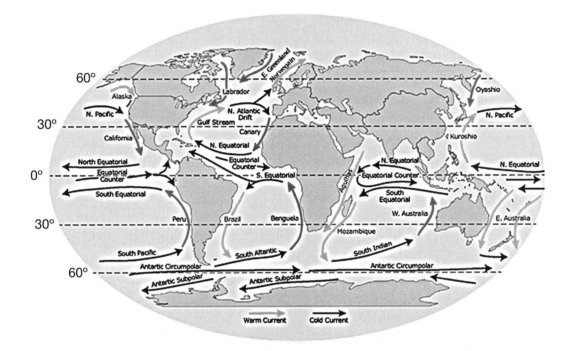

Based on the passage, which of the following statements about the Alaska current is true?
a. The Alaska current is a typical cold current because it travels along the western coast of the continent.
b. The Alaska current is not a true surface current because it does not follow the general pattern of surface currents.
c. The Alaska current is an exception to the general pattern because warm currents typically travel along the eastern coast of continents.
d. The Alaska current transports water from the north pole toward the equator because it travels along the western coast of the continent.

34. Every person has two copies, or alleles, of the ABO blood type gene. A person's ABO blood type is determined by his or her specific combination of alleles. The table below shows the allele combinations that cause the four different ABO blood types.

BLOOD TYPE	GENOTYPE
A	I^AI^A or I^Ai
B	I^BI^B or I^Bi
AB	I^AI^B
O	ii

Suppose that a mother's allele combination is I^Ai, and a father's allele combination is I^AI^B. Which of the following statements is true about the blood type of their first child?

a. The child will have the same blood type as the mother.

b. The child cannot have the father's blood type.

c. The child will have a blood type different from both parents'.

d. The child cannot have blood type O.

35. Blood glucose levels are tightly regulated in the human body by the hormones insulin and glucagon. When glucose levels become too high or low, the pancreas produces the appropriate hormone to return the body to homeostasis. The diagram below shows the feedback mechanism for regulating blood glucose levels.

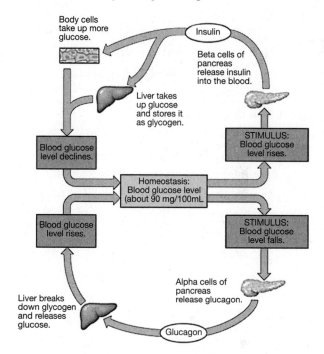

Diabetes mellitus is a disease in which the pancreas is unable to produce the insulin needed to regulate blood glucose levels. What result would occur from providing an insulin injection to a diabetic person with high blood sugar?

a. The insulin travels to the liver, where it binds to and destroys excess glucose in the bloodstream.

b. The insulin signals the pancreas to produce glucagon, which increases the level of glucose in the bloodstream.

c. The insulin causes the liver to convert glucose to glycogen, removing excess glucose from the bloodstream.

d. The insulin breaks down glycogen into glucose, releasing stored glucose into the bloodstream.

Answers and Explanations

1. The symbiotic relationship exhibited by mistletoe and spruce trees is **parasitism**. The mistletoe receives a benefit in the form of a source of nutrients and water. The spruce tree is harmed because it loses nutrients and water, which can eventually lead to the death of the tree. The table indicates that parasitism is occurring when one organism benefits (mistletoe) and the other organism is harmed (spruce tree).

The symbiotic relationship exhibited by *E. coli* and humans is **mutualism**. The *E. coli* receive a benefit in the form of nutrients and a habitat in which to live. The human also receives a benefit because the *E. coli* produce vitamin K, which is then used within the human body. The table indicates that mutualism is occurring when both organisms benefit.

Commensalism is not demonstrated in either of these relationships. The table indicates that commensalism occurs when one organism benefits, but the other organism is neither helped nor harmed.

2. Choice c is correct. The fleas and ticks obtain nutrients from the host animal's blood, and the mites obtain nutrients from the host animal's skin.

Choice **a** is incorrect. Though the fleas and mites may live on the host animal's body, the ticks do not.

Choice **b** is incorrect. Parasites can transmit diseases to the host animal, but this does not provide a benefit to the parasite.

Choice **d** is incorrect. Though the fleas and mites reproduce on the host animal's body, the ticks do not.

3. Choice b is correct. The passage states that *Cheyletiella* mites live within the outermost layer of the dog's skin and have difficulty surviving away from the host animal's body. A technician wearing gloves during examination of the dog and disposing of them afterward helps to prevent mites that may be on the technician's hands from being transmitted to other animals in the clinic.

Choice **a** is incorrect. Vaccines can be administered to uninfected individuals to prevent the transmission of diseases caused by viruses. Mites are arthropods that live on the host animal's body and cannot be eliminated with a vaccine.

Choice **c** is incorrect. Avoiding contact with open wounds would help prevent the transmission of blood-borne pathogens, such as those transmitted by fleas and ticks.

Choice **d** is incorrect. Sterilizing the exam room after, not before, examination of the infected dog could help prevent the transmission of mites to other animals in the clinic.

4. In order for an eclipse to occur, the sun, Earth, and moon must be aligned in a particular way. When the Earth is positioned between the sun and the moon, the Earth will prevent sunlight from reaching the moon. This is a lunar eclipse. When the moon is positioned between the sun and the Earth, the moon will prevent sunlight from reaching a portion of the Earth. This is a solar eclipse.

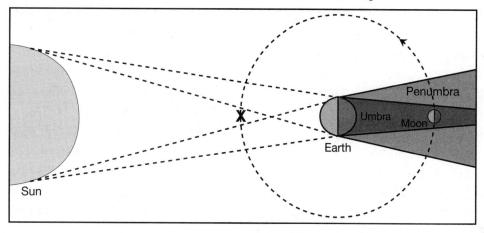

On the diagram, the moon has reached the position in its orbit that is in Earth's shadow, resulting in a lunar eclipse. From its current position on the diagram, the moon would need to travel 180° (or halfway) around its orbit to produce a solar eclipse. In this new position, the moon would cast a shadow on the Earth.

5. In a cladogram, the group that exhibits the fewest characteristics is listed on the bottom left branch, and the group exhibiting the most characteristics is listed on the top right branch.

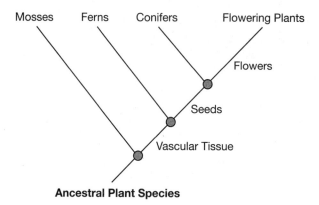

Mosses are placed on the first (lower left) branch because they exhibited none of the characteristics listed in the table. Ferns contain vascular tissue, so are listed on the second branch. Confers are the third branch because they contain vascular tissue and produce seeds. Flowering plants exhibit all three characteristics listed in the table, so are the fourth (highest) branch.

6. Choice a is correct. Describing the pattern in the data allows for the relationship between water temperature and oxygen solubility to be identified. As you look down the table, water temperature increases and maximum oxygen solubility decreases. This shows that water temperature and dissolved oxygen concentration have an inverse relationship, with highest dissolved oxygen concentrations occurring at the lowest temperatures.

Choice **b** is incorrect. According to the table, bodies of water with an average temperature of 40°C have a maximum oxygen solubility of 6.4 mg/L, and bodies of water with an average temperature of 100°C contain no dissolved oxygen. Temperatures between these two should support oxygen concentrations between 6.4 and 0 mg/L.

Choice **c** is incorrect. Though an increase from 0 to 10°C results in a 3 mg/L increase in oxygen solubility, oxygen solubility does not continue to increase by the same increment with each additional 10°C increase in temperature.

Choice **d** is incorrect. Though many variables can affect oxygen solubility, the table focuses only on the relationship between oxygen solubility and water temperature.

7. Choice c is correct. Grasses release oxygen into the environment as a byproduct of photosynthesis. Using this reasoning, it can be predicted that an increase in freshwater grasses will increase the dissolved oxygen concentration. Based on the data in the table, an increase to 8.5 mg/L brings the dissolved oxygen concentration closer to the maximum oxygen solubility for a body of water with an average temperature of 21°C.

Choice **a** is incorrect. Aquatic plants like freshwater grasses release oxygen into the environment. A dissolved oxygen concentration of 6.3 mg/L would result from an event that decreases the amount of dissolved oxygen in the water.

Choice **b** is incorrect. A dissolved oxygen concentration of 7.2 mg/L would indicate no change in the ecosystem. A change in the freshwater grass population would alter the amount of dissolved oxygen in the water.

Choice **d** is incorrect. A doubling of the freshwater grass population would cause an increase in dissolved oxygen concentration but not a doubling. According to the table, a dissolved oxygen concentration of 14.4 mg/L far exceeds the maximum oxygen solubility for a body of water with an average temperature of 21°C.

8. **Choice c is correct.** Range can be determined by calculating the difference between the lowest and highest values in a data set. The table shows that the temperature of a yellow star is between 5,000 K and 6,000 K. This is a range of 1,000 K, which is the smallest (or narrowest) range listed in the table.

Choice **a** is incorrect. White stars have a maximum temperature of 11,000 K. The minimum temperature of blue-white stars is 11,000 K.

Choice **b** is incorrect. Red stars have a maximum temperature of 3,500 K. A star with a temperature of 3,700 K would be within the range of an orange star.

Choice **d** is incorrect. The table does not provide information about the highest surface temperature recorded for a star. The minimum temperature of a blue star is shown to be 25,000 K. This indicates that blue stars can have temperatures higher than 25,000 K.

9. **Choice b is correct.** In the context of this ocean wave diagram, a wavelength is the horizontal distance between two crests (*A* and *B*). Using the given definition of wave period, it can be determined that the wave period is the amount of time required to travel one wavelength.

Choice **a** is incorrect. A shoreline is not shown or mentioned in the diagram.

Choice **c** is incorrect. Wave period relates to the horizontal movement of a wave, while calm sea level is a reference point used to measure the vertical movement of a wave.

Choice **d** is incorrect. In the diagram, points *A* and *B* used to measure wave period are both crests. The time required to travel from crest to trough would be half of a wave period.

10. **Choice b is correct.** A hurricane and tornado occurring in the same year would be considered a compound event because two events are occurring together. The probability of a compound event can be determined by multiplying the probabilities of each event occurring individually. The probability of a hurricane (0.39) multiplied by the probability of a tornado (0.96) provides a compound probability of 0.3744.

Choice **a** is incorrect. A probability of 0 indicates that there is no chance of an event occurring. Since there is a possibility of a hurricane and a possibility of a tornado occurring individually, there is also a possibility of both events occurring in the same year.

Choice **c** is incorrect. This is the probability of a tornado alone occurring during any given year. The probability of both a tornado and a hurricane occurring in the same year would be much lower because the probability of a hurricane is much lower (0.39) than the probability of a tornado (0.96).

Choice **d** is incorrect. A probability greater than 1 indicates that an event is guaranteed to occur. Since the individual probabilities of a hurricane or tornado occurring are both less than 1, the probability of both events occurring in the same year would also be less than 1.

11. The natural hazard that best completes this statement is **earthquake**. The Earth's crust is made up of tectonic plates. The location where two or more tectonic plates meet is called a plate boundary. When the pressure built up at a plate boundary becomes too great, energy is released in the form of an earthquake. Earthquakes can be expected to occur most frequently along plate boundaries. Since the west coast of the continental United States lies on a plate boundary, the probability of an earthquake occurring in this region can be predicted to be much higher than the probability for the United States as a whole, most of which does not lie on plate boundaries.

The occurrence of hurricanes, floods, and tornadoes is not specifically tied to the activity of tectonic plates. An increase in the probability of any of these natural hazards along a plate boundary as compared to the United States as a whole is not a reasonable prediction.

12. **Choice d is correct.** The runner takes in chemical energy in the form of carbohydrates. This chemical energy is transformed into kinetic energy as the runner's muscles contract and relax, causing the runner to move. Runners carb load to ensure that their bodies have enough chemical energy to be transformed into the kinetic energy required to run a marathon. Choice **a** is incorrect. The runner does take in chemical energy in the form of carbohydrates. Though some of this chemical energy is transformed into thermal energy in the form of body heat, the purpose of carb loading is to improve muscle performance, not increase body heat.

Choice **b** is incorrect. The purpose of carb loading is to increase the amount of energy available for transformation into kinetic energy (motion). Carb loading increases the availability of chemical energy, though, not thermal energy. Carbohydrates contain energy stored in their chemical bonds, not as heat.

Choice **c** is incorrect. The goal of carb loading is to improve muscle performance (motion), not increase body heat. Muscle performance is improved by increasing the chemical energy available for transformation into kinetic energy.

13. Choice a is correct. A primary-level consumer feeds on producers. Producers, such as plants, make their own food using energy from sunlight. Rabbits feed on two producers, carrots and grasses, making rabbits a primary-level consumer.

Choice **b** is incorrect. An organism's feeding level is determined by how it obtains its food, not by the organisms that it provides food for. Though the rabbits in the food web are consumed by foxes, this does not determine the rabbits' feeding level.

Choice **c** is incorrect. Competition with other organisms does not affect how an organism's feeding level is classified.

Choice **d** is incorrect. The presence of other organisms that consume the same food source does not affect how an organism's feeding level is classified.

14. Choice d is correct. An organism provides energy to all organisms above it in the food web. In this food web, the grasshoppers provide energy to the birds, owls, and foxes. The birds and owls obtain energy directly when they consume the grasshoppers. The foxes obtain energy indirectly when they consume birds that previously consumed grasshoppers.

Choice **a** is incorrect. Although owls and birds obtain energy from grasshoppers, mice do not obtain energy from grasshoppers.

Choice **b** is incorrect. Grains provide energy to grasshoppers but do not obtain energy from grasshoppers.

Choice **c** is incorrect. Rabbits and mice do not obtain energy from grasshoppers either directly or indirectly.

15.

The highest number of points you can earn on this short-response essay is 3.

A **3-point essay** contains:
- a clear and well-developed explanation of how a change in one population effects change in other populations within the food web
- well-developed examples from the given food web describing the likely effects of change in the rabbit population on other specific populations
- complete support from the passage

Sample 3-point response:

The interrelatedness of populations in the food web makes it likely that all populations will be affected in some way by the shift in the rabbits' feeding habits. The rabbits' increased reliance on grasses will cause a domino effect on the availability of food for all primary consumers. Since grasshoppers directly compete with rabbits for grasses, the availability of grasses for grasshoppers may be limited. As a result, grasshoppers would likely increase their dependence on grains, decreasing the availability of this food source for birds and mice. The overall increase in competition among primary consumers may cause some decreases in population sizes, which would also limit the population sizes of higher-level consumers.

A **2-point essay** contains:
- an adequate or partially articulated explanation of how a change in one population effects change in other populations within the food web
- partial examples from the given food web describing the likely effects of change in the rabbit population on other specific populations
- partial support from the passage

Sample 2-point response:

When the rabbits start eating more grasses, the grasshoppers will have less food because they eat grasses too. This means that the grasshopper population might get smaller, so the owls and birds would have less food. Foxes eat birds, so they would have less food too.

A **1-point essay** contains:

- a minimal or implied explanation of how a change in one population effects change in other populations within the food web
- one or incomplete examples from the given food web describing the likely effects of change in the rabbit population on other specific populations
- minimal or implied support from the passage

Sample 1-point response:

The rabbits will eat more grass. Grasshoppers will not have as much grass to eat. Some grasshoppers will die because they don't have enough food.

A **0-point essay** contains:

- no explanation of how a change in one population effects change in other populations within the food web
- no examples from the given food web describing the likely effects of change in the rabbit population on other specific populations
- no support from the passage

16.

Blank 1:

The appropriate value to complete this statement is **36.5**.

The formula for converting temperature from Fahrenheit to Celsius is given as $(°F - 32) \times \frac{5}{9} = °C$. Replacing the lower variable °F with 97.7 and solving gives $(97.7 - 32) \times \frac{5}{9} = 36.5$.

Blank 2:

The appropriate value to complete this statement is **37.5**.

The formula for converting temperature from Fahrenheit to Celsius is given as $(°F - 32) \times \frac{5}{9} = °C$. Replacing the lower variable °F with 99.5 and solving gives $(99.5 - 32) \times \frac{5}{9} = 37.5$.

17. Choice d is correct. As indicated in the diagram, the daughter cells produced during meiosis each have half the total number of chromosomes as the parent cell does. These daughter cells, called gametes, are used for reproduction. When reproduction occurs, two gametes (egg and sperm) unite to create a cell with a full set of chromosomes.

Choice **a** is incorrect. To allow an organism to grow larger, the daughter cells produced must be identical to the parent cell. Cells used for growth are produced by the process of mitosis.

Choice **b** is incorrect. To allow an organism to repair tissues, the daughter cells produced must be identical to the parent cell. The cells used for tissue repair are produced by the process of mitosis.

Choice **c** is incorrect. Cell differentiation occurs when a single, non-specialized cell is converted to a specialized cell type, like a blood cell or skin cell. No daughter cells are produced during the differentiation process.

18. Choice b is correct. The average speed can be determined by adding the individual vehicle speeds and dividing by the total number of vehicles. This is calculated as $\frac{61 + 48 + 61 + 51 + 59}{5} = 56$ mph.

Choice **a** is incorrect. This is the speed limit for the highway, not the average speed of the five vehicles listed.

Choice **c** is incorrect. This is the median speed of the five vehicles, not the average (mean) speed.

Choice **d** is incorrect. This is the mode for the speed of the five vehicles, not the average (mean) speed.

19. Choice d is correct. Each new cell created by meiosis must contain one chromosome from each of the seven chromosome pairs. As illustrated in the diagram, these single chromosomes can be combined in multiple ways. To determine the total number of unique chromosome combinations, the number of chromosomes in each set (pair) must be multiplied. Seven sets of two chromosomes each means that seven 2's must be multiplied $(2 \times 2 \times 2 \times 2 \times 2 \times 2 \times 2 = 128)$ to determine the total number of unique chromosome combinations possible.

Choice **a** is incorrect. There are seven total chromosomes in a cell produced by meiosis, but the specific chromosome present from each chromosome pair can vary.

Choice **b** is incorrect. Two chromosomes in each of seven pairs provides a total of 14 chromosomes, but the specific chromosome present from each pair can vary.

Choice **c** is incorrect. Multiplying 7×7 does not provide the total number of chromosome combinations possible. To determine this, the number of chromosomes in each pair must be multiplied by the number of chromosomes in each other pair.

20. Choice c is correct. The products of respiration are six molecules of carbon dioxide, six molecules of water, and energy. On the right side of the model, six rectangles are present but only one triangle. To accurately represent a balanced equation, all molecules must be represented in the model.

Choice **a** is incorrect. The circles represent the six molecules of the reactant oxygen. Connecting the circles would not improve the model's accuracy because separate molecules are not bound to each other.

Choice **b** is incorrect. Energy is a product of the respiration reaction and is therefore appropriately placed on the right side of the equation. Moving the energy symbol to the left side of the equation would indicate that energy is a reactant.

Choice **d** is incorrect. Reducing the size of the rectangles is not the most needed change, since the other molecules are not represented to scale.

21. Choice a is correct. The purpose of respiration is to convert energy into a form that is useable by cells. Respiration produces ATP, a high-energy molecule, which the cell can use to carry out cellular functions.

Choice **b** is incorrect. Oxygen is a reactant—not a product—of aerobic respiration and does not provide energy for the cell.

Choice **c** is incorrect. Respiration uses the glucose in food to produce ATP. Respiration does not produce glucose.

Choice **d** is incorrect. Though respiration does produce carbon dioxide, this molecule does not provide energy for the cell.

22. The highest number of points you can earn on this short-response essay is 3.

A **3-point essay** contains:
- a clear and well-developed explanation of the benefits of the aerobic respiration pathway in the human body
- a clear and well-developed explanation of the benefits of the anaerobic respiration pathway in the human body
- complete support from the passage

Sample 3-point response:
The human body may use two different pathways to carry out respiration. The presence of two different pathways is valuable because it allows a cell to choose the pathway that best meets its current energy needs. Aerobic respiration produces the greatest amount of ATP per glucose molecule. Under normal conditions with adequate oxygen, this pathway provides the greatest possible amount of energy to the cell. Anaerobic respiration produces much less ATP per glucose molecule but does not require oxygen. Under strenuous conditions when the cell demands energy faster than the oxygen supply can be replenished, this pathway provides enough energy to maintain cell functions. The ability to switch between aerobic and anaerobic pathways allows the human body to function properly under varying conditions.

A **2-point essay** contains:
- an adequate or partially articulated explanation of the benefits of the aerobic respiration pathway in the human body
- an adequate or partially articulated explanation of the benefits of the anaerobic respiration pathway in the human body
- partial support from the passage

Sample 2-point response:
Aerobic respiration produces the most ATP, but requires oxygen. Anaerobic respiration produces much less ATP, but does not require oxygen. Having two pathways is important because sometimes oxygen is available, and sometimes it is not.

A **1-point essay** contains:
- a minimal or implied explanation of the benefits of the aerobic respiration pathway in the human body
- a minimal or implied explanation of the benefits of the anaerobic respiration pathway in the human body
- minimal or implied support from the passage

Sample 1-point response:
Cells use aerobic respiration most of the time. Muscle cells use anaerobic respiration when a person is exercising. Both types of respiration are important.

A **0-point essay** contains:
- no explanation of the benefits of the aerobic respiration pathway in the human body
- no explanation of the benefits of the anaerobic respiration pathway in the human body
- no support from the passage

23. Choice c is correct. As shown in the model, a solid has a fixed volume and shape. A liquid has a fixed volume but assumes the shape of the container. A gas assumes the volume and shape of the container. A liquid has one property in common with solids, and one property in common with gases.

Choice **a** is incorrect. In this summary, the properties of a liquid are reversed. Liquids have a fixed volume and assume the shape of the container.

Choice **b** is incorrect. Liquids have a fixed volume as solids do, but not a fixed shape.

Choice **d** is incorrect. Liquids assume the shape of the container as gases do, but not the volume.

24. Choice a is correct. The density of a substance describes how tightly packed the substance's molecules are. As shown in the model, a substance's molecules are most spread out when in the gas state. This means that a substance's density is lowest when in the gas state. The substance's density increases when going from gas to liquid state because the molecules become more tightly packed.

Choice **b** is incorrect. A substance's molecules become more spread out when changing from solid to gas state. This causes the substance's density to decrease.

Choice **c** is incorrect. A substance's molecules become more spread out when changing from liquid to gas state. This causes the substance's density to decrease.

Choice **d** is incorrect. A substance's molecules may become slightly more spread out, or less dense, when changing from solid to liquid state. However, the density of a substance does not change much during this state change.

25. Choice d is correct. Based on the data in the table, this statement can be identified as a fact. The energy content of ethanol is 27.3 kJ/g, about 16 kJ/g less than the energy content of petroleum (43.6 kJ/g).

Choice **a** is incorrect. This statement is speculation based on data from the table. According to the table, hydrogen has the greatest energy content and releases no carbon dioxide. Although this data supports the speculation that cars may be fueled by hydrogen cells in the future, this statement is no guarantee.

Choice **b** is incorrect. This statement is a judgment based on data from the table. According to the table, petroleum has a higher energy content than ethanol. Although this data can be used to support the judgment that petroleum is the better fuel source, this statement is an opinion rather than a fact.

Choice **c** is incorrect. This statement is speculation based on data from the table. Although the data in the table suggests that natural gas is a relatively efficient and clean fuel source, the statement is speculation because no information is provided about the cost of natural gas.

26. Choice c is correct. The passage identifies natural gas, petroleum, and coal as fossil fuels, because each is derived from the fossil remains of organisms. The energy content of each fossil fuel can be approximated to 50 kJ/g, 45 kJ/g, and 40 kJ/g, respectively. This provides an estimated average energy content of 45 kJ/g. Choice **a** is incorrect. This would be an appropriate estimate for the energy content of coal, not for the energy content of all three fossil fuels.

Choice **b** is incorrect. This would be an appropriate estimate for the energy content of petroleum and coal, but natural gas is also a fossil fuel.

Choice **d** is incorrect. This would be an appropriate estimate for the energy content of natural gas, not for the energy content of all three fossil fuels.

27. Choice a is correct. Burning a candle is an exothermic process because thermal energy, or heat, is released as a result of the process. Choice **b** is incorrect. Melting a snow bank is an endothermic process because the input of heat is required to melt the snow. This means that thermal energy is absorbed during the process, not released.

Choice **c** is incorrect. Baking a loaf of bread is an endothermic process because the input of heat is required to convert the ingredients to bread. This means that thermal energy is absorbed during the process, not released.

Choice **d** is incorrect. Photosynthesis is an endothermic process because the input of energy (sunlight) is required for plants to make sugar. This means that energy is absorbed during the process, not released.

28. Choice a is correct. The car has a constant positive acceleration when the car's velocity is increasing at a steady, or constant, rate. Between 0 and 20 seconds, the graph moves upward in a straight diagonal line, indicating that the velocity is increasing at a constant rate. Choice **b** is incorrect. Between 20 and 40 seconds, the car is maintaining a constant velocity of 20 m/s. Since the velocity is constant within this time period, the car is not accelerating (has an acceleration of 0 m/s^2). Choice **c** is incorrect. Between 40 and 50 seconds, the car's velocity is decreasing at a constant rate. This indicates a constant negative acceleration.

Choice **d** is incorrect. Between 50 and 90 seconds, the car's velocity is increasing but not at a constant rate. The graph moves upward in a curved line within this time period, indicating that the velocity is increasing at a variable rate.

29. Choice b is correct. The mechanical advantage of a pulley system does not change with the load. Mechanical advantage is calculated as load divided by input force. In the data table, dividing each load by its corresponding input force produces a mechanical advantage of three. Choice **a** is incorrect. As the load size increases, the input force required to lift the load increases at a constant rate. The mechanical advantage of the pulley system does not change.

Choice **c** is incorrect. A pulley system multiplies the input force, not the mechanical advantage, applied to a load.

Choice **d** is incorrect. No decrease in mechanical advantage occurs with an increase in load. The mechanical advantage of a pulley system is constant regardless of the size of the load.

30. Choice d is correct. According to the table, an input force of 50 N can lift a 150 N load. If a 1 N load has a mass of 10 grams, the mass of a load can be determined by multiplying the force of the load by 10. A 150 N load therefore has a mass of 1,500 grams.

Choice **a** is incorrect. This value is the result of dividing the force of the load (150 N) by 10. The mass of the load is determined by multiplying, not dividing, the force of the load by 10.

Choice **b** is incorrect. This is the value of the input force, not the mass of the load.

Choice **c** is incorrect. This is the value of the force of the load in Newtons, not the mass of the load in grams.

31. Choice b is correct. Kale is a leafy crop species. According to the diagram, wild mustard plants were selected for leaves to produce kale. This means that wild mustard plants that had large leaves were specifically bred together to increase leaf size. This selective breeding over multiple generations led to a new species (kale) characterized by large leaves.

Choice **a** is incorrect. Plants with desired characteristics (large leaves for kale) must be bred together to produce offspring plants with those characteristics. Removing stems and flowers from existing mustard plants will not increase leaf size in subsequent generations.

Choice **c** is incorrect. Breeding small-leafed plants and large-leafed plants allows the possibility that offspring will have either small or large leaves. To ensure offspring have the best chances of large leaves, large-leafed plants should be bred together.

Choice **d** is incorrect. Preventing plants with large leaves from growing works to remove the large-leaf trait from subsequent generations rather than increase its appearance.

32. Choice d is correct. In the graph, temperature increases to the right and altitude increases upward. Any portion of the graph that has a negative slope, or slopes to the left, indicates a decrease in temperature. The graph has a negative slope in the troposphere and mesosphere layers.

Choice **a** is incorrect. The graph has a negative slope within the mesosphere but a slight positive slope in the exosphere. This means that temperature decreases as altitude increases in the mesosphere but increases with altitude in the exosphere.

Choice **b** is incorrect. The graph has a negative slope within the troposphere but a positive slope in the thermosphere. Even though the slope is not constant within the thermosphere, the slope remains positive within this layer. This means that temperature decreases in the troposphere but increases in the thermosphere.

Choice **c** is incorrect. The graph has a positive slope within both the stratosphere and the thermosphere. This means that temperature increases with altitude in both layers.

33. Choice c is correct. The Alaska current is a warm current. The passage states that warm currents typically travel along the eastern coast of continents, but the Alaska current travels along the western coast of North America.

Choice **a** is incorrect. Although the Alaska current does travel along the western coast of the continent, the map key indicates that it is a warm current.

Choice **b** is incorrect. The Alaska current does not follow the typical pattern for a warm current but is identified as a surface current on the map.

Choice **d** is incorrect. The map key identifies the Alaska current as a warm current. Warm currents transport warm water originating near the equator toward the poles.

34. **Choice d is correct.** The blood type O can be produced only by the allele combination ii. A child receives one allele from each parent. Since the mother has an i but the father does not, the allele combination ii is not possible for their children.

Choice **a** is incorrect. Based on the table, the mother's blood type is A. The child can receive I^A or i from the mother and I^A from the father, resulting in type A blood caused by the possible allele combinations I^AI^A or I^Ai. However, the child could receive I^B from the father, which would result in a blood type different from the mother's.

Choice **b** is incorrect. Based on the table, the father has blood type AB. The child can receive I^A from the mother and I^B from the father, resulting in the possible allele combination I^AI^B. This allele combination will produce the same blood type as the father's.

Choice **c** is incorrect. Based on the table, the mother's blood type is A, and the father's is AB. The child can receive I^A or i from the mother and I^A from the father, resulting in type A blood caused by the possible allele combinations I^AI^A or I^Ai. The child can receive I^A from the mother and I^B from the father, resulting in the blood type AB caused by the possible allele combination I^AI^B. This means it is possible for the child to have the same blood type as one of the parents'.

35. **Choice c is correct.** According to the diagram, when a person's blood glucose level rises, the pancreas secretes insulin. The insulin signals body cells to absorb glucose from the blood and signals the liver to convert excess glucose into the storage molecule glycogen. These processes remove excess glucose from the blood, returning the blood glucose level to homeostasis. Insulin injected into a diabetic person initiates the same pathway as insulin produced in the pancreas of a healthy person.

Choice **a** is incorrect. Insulin signals the liver to convert and store excess glucose to glycogen, not to destroy the glucose.

Choice **b** is incorrect. Insulin and glucagon do not signal each other but perform opposite functions. Insulin works to decrease blood glucose levels, while glucagon works to increase these levels.

Choice **d** is incorrect. Glucagon signals the breakdown of glycogen into glucose when blood glucose levels are low. Insulin signals the conversion of glucose to glycogen when blood glucose levels are high.

5 ▶ GED® SOCIAL STUDIES TEST 1

This practice test is modeled on the format, content, and timing of the official GED® Social Studies test and, like the official exam, presents a series of questions that focus on the fundamentals of social studies reasoning.

Part I

You'll be asked to answer questions based on brief texts, maps, graphics, and tables. Refer to the information provided as often as necessary when answering the questions.

Work carefully, but do not spend too much time on any one question. Be sure to answer every question.

Set a timer for 65 minutes (1 hour and 5 minutes), and try to take this test uninterrupted, under quiet conditions.

Part II

The official GED® Social Studies test also includes an Extended Response question—an essay question. Set a timer for 25 minutes and try to read the given passage, brainstorm, write, and proofread your essay uninterrupted, under quiet conditions.

Complete answer explanations for every test question and sample essays at different scoring levels follow the exam. Good luck!

PART I

35 total questions
65 minutes to complete

Please use the following passage to answer questions 1–3.

This excerpt is from a speech by George W. Bush given on March 19, 2008.

Operation Iraqi Freedom was a remarkable display of military effectiveness. Forces from the U.K., Australia, Poland, and other allies joined our troops in the initial operations. As they advanced, our troops fought their way through sandstorms so intense that they blackened the daytime sky. Our troops engaged in pitched battles with Fedayeen Saddam, death squads acting on the orders of Saddam Hussein that obeyed neither the conventions of war nor the dictates of conscience. These death squads hid in schools, and they hid in hospitals, hoping to draw fire against Iraqi civilians. They used women and children as human shields. They stopped at nothing in their efforts to prevent us from prevailing, but they couldn't stop the coalition advance.

Aided by the most effective and precise air campaign in history, coalition forces raced across 350 miles of enemy territory, destroying Republican Guard divisions, pushing through the Karbala Gap, capturing Saddam International Airport, and liberating Baghdad in less than one month.

Because we acted, Saddam Hussein no longer fills fields with the remains of innocent men, women, and children. . . . Because we acted, Saddam's regime is no longer invading its neighbors or attacking them with chemical weapons and ballistic missiles.

1. Based on the primary-source excerpt concerning a central idea of American foreign policy since 9/11, what was President Bush's purpose for launching Operation Iraqi Freedom?
   a. to liberate Baghdad in less than one month by destroying Republican Guard divisions
   b. to liberate Iraqi people from a brutal regime and remove Saddam Hussein from power
   c. to stop Saddam Hussein from invading other nations
   d. to join countries in aiding Saddam Hussein's control of the Iraqi people's natural rights

2. Which of the following statements is an opinion, NOT a fact?
   a. "coalition forces raced across 350 miles of enemy territory, . . . liberating Baghdad in less than one month"
   b. "Forces from the U.K., Australia, Poland, and other allies joined our troops in the initial operations."
   c. "Our troops engaged in pitched battles with Fedayeen Saddam, death squads acting on the orders of Saddam Hussein."
   d. "Operation Iraqi Freedom was a remarkable display of military effectiveness."

3. Based on the primary-source excerpt, what can be concluded about the credibility of Bush's choice to launch Operation Iraqi Freedom?
   a. The operation was not justified and Bush makes this clear in his speech.
   b. Bush feels that the operation was justified, but the realities of Saddam's regime discredit any justification.
   c. The operation was justified in trying to bring down a detrimental and brutal regime.
   d. The actions of Saddam's regime justify the operation, but Bush expresses his concern that the operation may not have been justified in his speech.

Please use the following to answer questions 4–6.

This excerpt is from the U.S. Constitution.

The President shall be Commander in Chief of the Army and Navy of the United States, and of the Militia of the several States, when called into the actual Service of the United States . . . He shall have Power, by and with the Advice and Consent of the Senate, to make Treaties, provided two thirds of the Senators present concur.

4. In this portion of the U.S. Constitution, which branch of the government checks the power of which other branch of government by a two-thirds agreement?
   a. the executive checks the power of the legislative
   b. the judicial checks the power of the executive
   c. the legislative checks the power of the executive
   d. the legislative checks the power of the judicial

5. Why is it important for the U.S. Constitution to include rules, such as the one in the excerpt, that allow for power checking between the different branches of government?
   a. to ensure that the legislative branch has power over the executive and judicial branches
   b. to ensure a separation of power that balances the powers of the three branches in order to prevent any one person or group from holding too much or all power
   c. to ensure that the president has the ability to check the power of all other branches
   d. to ensure that the president does not have the power to make treaties without some say from the Senate

6. Based on the excerpt from the U.S. Constitution, what can you infer would be the effect of a failure to receive a two-thirds agreement from the Senate in this instance?
   a. the Senate could not make a treaty but the president could make a treaty
   b. the Senate could make a treaty
   c. the president could not make a treaty because the Senate does not agree
   d. the president could make a treaty

7. What is the difference between a government ruled by popular sovereignty and a government ruled by a dictatorship?

   a. a government ruled by popular sovereignty means that the authority has the consent of the governed to rule, and a government ruled by a dictatorship means that the authority is held by one individual

   b. a government ruled by a dictatorship means that the authority has the consent of the governed to rule, and a government ruled by popular sovereignty does not have consent

   c. popular sovereignty means that the government is ruled by the most popular individual, and a dictatorship means that the government is ruled by the least popular individual

   d. a dictatorship means that the government is ruled by the most popular individual, and popular sovereignty means that the government is ruled by the least popular individual

8. Determine whether each aspect of the federal government listed below is associated with the executive, legislative, or judicial branch of government. Write your answers in the boxes below.

   The Supreme Court
   The House of Representatives
   The Senate
   The president's Cabinet
   The president

Executive Branch	Legislative Branch	Judicial Branch

Please use the following passage to answer questions 9–10.

This excerpt is from a speech by Bill Clinton given on July 19, 1995.

The purpose of affirmative action is to give our Nation a way to finally address the systemic exclusion of individuals of talent on the basis of their gender or race from opportunities to develop, perform, achieve, and contribute. Affirmative action is an effort to develop a systematic approach to open the doors of education, employment, and business development opportunities to qualified individuals who happen to be members of groups that have experienced longstanding and persistent discrimination.

It is a policy that grew out of many years of trying to navigate between two unacceptable pasts. One was to say simply that we declared discrimination illegal and that's enough. We saw that that way still relegated blacks with college degrees to jobs as railroad porters and kept women with degrees under a glass ceiling with a lower paycheck.

The other path was simply to try to impose change by leveling draconian penalties on employers who didn't meet certain imposed, ultimately arbitrary, and sometimes unachievable quotas. That, too, was rejected out of a sense of fairness.

So a middle ground was developed that would change an inequitable status quo gradually but firmly, by building the pool of qualified applicants for college, for contracts, for jobs, and giving more people the chance to learn, work, and earn. When affirmative action is done right, it is flexible, it is fair, and it works.

9. According to the excerpt from Clinton's speech, in which he speaks out against this, affirmative action is a partial solution to which long-standing societal problem that has affected history?
   a. slavery
   b. discrimination
   c. unemployment
   d. poverty

10. According to the excerpt, what changes would affirmative action cause to come about for minority groups that suffer from discrimination?

    a. It will give more people in these minority groups the chance to work, learn, and earn a living by increasing the number of qualified applicants from these groups who are accepted for job positions and places in college.

    b. It will give fewer people in these minority groups the chance to work, learn, and earn a living by decreasing the number of qualified applicants from these groups who are accepted for job positions and places in college.

    c. It will change nothing for minority groups and will instead only reduce penalties on employers who do not meet a certain quota of minority workers in their workplaces.

    d. It will reduce the pay of women in the workplace and decrease the number of minority groups in universities.

Please use the following two documents to answer questions 11–12.

This excerpt is from the Declaration of Independence.

> We hold these truths to be self-evident, that all men are created equal, that they are endowed by their Creator with certain unalienable Rights that among these are Life, Liberty and the pursuit of Happiness. That to secure these rights, Governments are instituted among Men, deriving their just powers from the consent of the governed. That whenever any Form of Government becomes destructive of these ends, it is the Right of the People to alter or to abolish it, and to institute new Government, laying its foundation on such principles and organizing its powers in such form, as to them shall seem most likely to effect their Safety and Happiness.

This excerpt is from the U.S. Constitution.

> We the People of the United States, in Order to form a more perfect Union, establish Justice, insure domestic Tranquility, provide for the common defence, promote the general Welfare, and secure the Blessings of Liberty to ourselves and our Posterity, do ordain and establish this Constitution for the United States of America.

11. Analyze the two excerpts taken from key historical documents that have shaped American constitutional government. Based on these excerpts, which of the following ideas is incorporated into both documents?
    a. the equality of men
    b. the right to abolish destructive government
    c. the abolition of slavery
    d. the right to liberty

12. In the excerpt from the Declaration of Independence, what concept is being described in the following sentences?

"That to secure these rights, Governments are instituted among Men, deriving their just powers from the consent of the governed. That whenever any Form of Government becomes destructive of these ends, it is the Right of the People to alter or to abolish it, and to institute new Government, laying its foundation on such principles and organizing its powers in such form, as to them shall seem most likely to effect their Safety and Happiness."
    a. federalism
    b. popular sovereignty
    c. popular socialism
    d. capitalism

13. The table below displays the number of men killed, wounded, and captured during two battles of the Revolutionary War on both the American and British sides.

Date	Engagement	Commander	Troops	Killed	Wounded	Captured
Apr. 19, 1775	Lexington/Concord	American: Capt. John Parker, et al.	3,763	49	41	0
		British: Lt. Col. Francis Smith	1,800	73	174	7
June 17, 1775	Bunker (Breed's) Hill	American: Gens. Putnam & Ward	2,000	140	271	30
		British: General William Howe	2,400	226	826	0

Based on this information, what was the mean value of men killed in both engagements? Write your answer in the box below. (You may use a calculator to answer this question.)

14. The graph shows the changes in unemployment rates for nonfarm workers between 1926 and 1947.

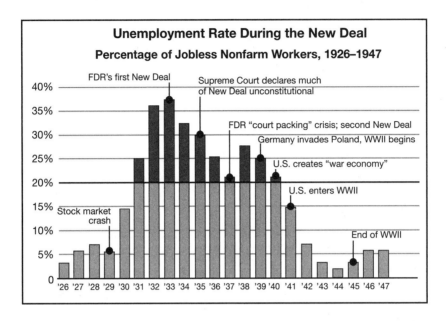

Based on the information shown, select the event that led to the greatest drop in the unemployment rate the following year for nonfarm workers.

a. FDR's first New Deal

b. the United States enters World War II

c. the stock market crash

d. Germany invades Poland, World War II begins

15. Read the following definition of capitalism.

Capitalism is an economic and political system that allows a country's trade and industry to be controlled by private owners for profit.

Based on this definition, write the appropriate word in the box that makes the following statement true.

Capitalism gives [   ] owners the freedom to make a profit from control of the country's trade and industry.

16. The graph shows the percentage of citizens affiliated with each U.S. political party.

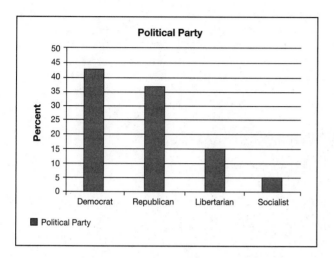

Political Party

Which political party has the most members, and how does the graph show that?

a. The Democratic Party has the most members. Political parties are labeled on the *x*-axis, and the percent of members in those parties is labeled on the *y*-axis. The bar for percentage of Democrats is highest.

b. The Democratic Party has the most members. Political parties are labeled on the *y*-axis, and the percent of members in those parties is labeled on the *x*-axis. The bar for percentage of Democrats is highest.

c. The Libertarian Party has the most members. Political parties are labeled on the *x*-axis, and the percent of members in those parties is labeled on the *y*-axis. The bar for percentage of Libertarians is highest.

d. The Libertarian Party has the most members. Political parties are labeled on the *y*-axis, and the percent of members in those parties is labeled on the *x*-axis. The bar for percentage of Libertarians is highest.

17.

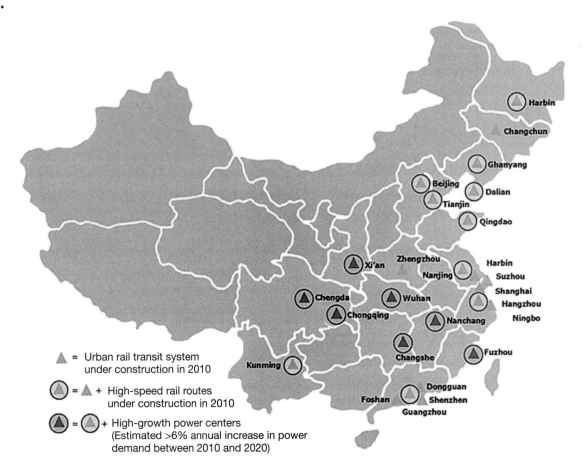

Based on this map of China, select the answer that correlates to a gray triangle surrounded by a circle.

a. urban rail transit system under construction in 2010

b. urban rail transit system and high-speed rail routes under construction in 2010

c. high-speed rail routes under construction in 2010

d. high-growth power centers

18. The graph shows the total campaign expenditures by candidates for the California State Legislature between 1975 and 1998.

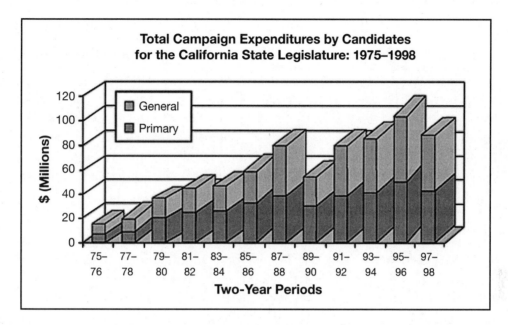

What was the trend in expenditures by candidates for the California State Legislature from 1983 to 1988?

a. decreasing
b. increasing then decreasing
c. decreasing then increasing
d. increasing

Please use the following passage to answer questions 19–20.

This excerpt is from a speech by Barack Obama announcing his candidacy for president in Springfield, Illinois, in 2007.

All of us know what those challenges are today—a war with no end, a dependence on oil that threatens our future, schools where too many children aren't learning, and families struggling paycheck to paycheck despite working as hard as they can. We know the challenges. We've heard them. We've talked about them for years.

What's stopped us from meeting these challenges is not the absence of sound policies and sensible plans. What's stopped us is the failure of leadership, the smallness of our politics—the ease with which we're distracted by the petty and trivial, our chronic avoidance of tough decisions, our preference for scoring cheap political points instead of rolling up our sleeves and building a working consensus to tackle big problems.

For the last six years we've been told that our mounting debts don't matter, we've been told that the anxiety Americans feel about rising health care costs and stagnant wages are an illusion, we've been told that climate change is a hoax, and that tough talk and an ill-conceived war can replace diplomacy, and strategy, and foresight. And when all else fails, when Katrina happens, or the death toll in Iraq mounts, we've been told that our crises are somebody else's fault. We're distracted from our real failures, and told to blame the other party, or gay people, or immigrants.

And as people have looked away in disillusionment and frustration, we know what's filled the void. The cynics, and the lobbyists, and the special interests who've turned our government into a game only they can afford to play. They write the checks and you get stuck with the bills, they get the access while you get to write a letter, they think they own this government, but we're here today to take it back. The time for that politics is over. It's time to turn the page.

19. Based on the excerpt from Obama's speech announcing his candidacy for president, which of the following sets of words represents instances of loaded language?
a. hoax, frustration
b. today, decisions
c. void, lobbyists
d. page, diplomacy

20. The paragraph starting with "For the last six years . . ." could be viewed as an example of which of the following?
a. economic chart
b. campaign speech
c. statistical data
d. campaign promise

Please use the following passage to answer questions 21–22.

This is an excerpt from a speech about health care delivered to Congress by President Obama on September 9, 2009.

Then there's the problem of rising cost. We spend one and a half times more per person on health care than any other country, but we aren't any healthier for it. This is one of the reasons that insurance premiums have gone up three times faster than wages. It's why so many employers, especially small businesses, are forcing their employees to pay more for insurance or are dropping their coverage entirely. It's why so many aspiring entrepreneurs cannot afford to open a business in the first place and why American businesses that compete internationally, like our automakers, are at a huge disadvantage. And it's why those of us with health insurance are also paying a hidden and growing tax for those without it, about $1,000 per year that pays for somebody else's emergency room and charitable care.

  Finally, our health care system is placing an unsustainable burden on taxpayers. When health care costs grow at the rate they have, it puts greater pressure on programs like Medicare and Medicaid. If we do nothing to slow these skyrocketing costs, we will eventually be spending more on Medicare and Medicaid than every other government program combined. Put simply, our health care problem is our deficit problem. Nothing else even comes close. Nothing else.

21. In the excerpt from Obama's speech on health care, what type of statement is "we aren't any healthier for it"?
 a. supported fact
 b. statistic
 c. warning
 d. opinion

22. According to the excerpt from Obama's speech on health care, what does he think will be the eventual effect of unchecked added pressure being put on Medicare and Medicaid from rapidly increasing health-care costs?
 a. the government spending less on Medicare and Medicaid than every other program combined
 b. the government spending more on Medicare and Medicaid than every other program combined
 c. the shutdown of Medicare and Medicaid instead of other programs
 d. the government no longer spending any money on Medicare and Medicaid

23. Why did Christopher Columbus set sail in 1492 in an expedition that would eventually bring him into contact with the Americas for the first time?

   a. He was attempting to claim new territory in the Americas for Spain.

   b. He was going to the Americas to trade with the native peoples.

   c. He was attempting to find a new route to Asia for trade purposes.

   d. He was going to the Americas in order to start a settlement.

24. Based on the pie chart showing the number of women working in the U.S. military during World War II, fill in the box in the following statement to make it correct.

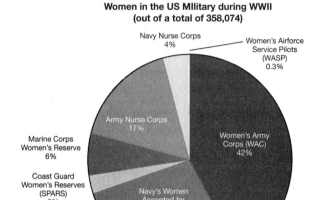

Women in the US Military during WWII
(out of a total of 358,074)

Navy Nurse Corps 4%
Women's Airforce Service Pilots (WASP) 0.3%
Army Nurse Corps 17%
Marine Corps Women's Reserve 6%
Coast Guard Women's Reserves (SPARS) 3%
Women's Army Corps (WAC) 42%
Navy's Women Accepted for Voluntary Emergency Service (WAVES) 28%

During World War II, the number of women who joined ☐ was almost equal to the combined number of women who joined WASP, the Army and Navy Nurse Corps, SPARS, and the Marine Corps Women's Reserve.

25. The map shows the division of European countries according to political alignment during most of the Cold War.

According to the map, how was Turkey aligned in this division?
a. with the Western Bloc
b. with the Eastern Bloc
c. with the Iron Curtain
d. with the United States

26. This excerpt is from a speech by George W. Bush given on March 19, 2008.

To ensure that military progress in Iraq is quickly followed up with real improvements in daily life, we have doubled the number of Provincial Reconstruction Teams in Iraq. These teams of civilian experts are serving all Iraqi—18 Iraqi Provinces, and they're helping to strengthen responsible leaders and build up local economies and bring Iraqis together, so that reconciliation can happen from the ground up. They're very effective. They're helping give ordinary Iraqis confidence that by rejecting the extremists and reconciling with one another, they can claim their place in a free Iraq and build better lives for their families.

Based on the excerpt from Bush's speech, you can infer which of the following is NOT a reason that it was important to have civilian expert teams in Iraq after the military action in the area?
a. to strengthen the local leadership and economy
b. to take control of the local leadership and economy
c. to help give confidence to the people of Iraq
d. to help the Iraqi people build a free Iraq

27. If a company purchases a product for $1 and sells it to consumers for $2.35, the $1.35 that the company receives is an example of what economic concept?
a. monopoly
b. expense
c. profit
d. loss

28. Write the word in the box that completes the following definition.

A [ ] is a tax or duty a government places upon imported or exported goods.

29. This excerpt describes the eligibility requirements for a Stateside Union Bank College Credit Card.

To qualify for a Stateside Union Bank College Credit Card, a student must be at the age of majority in the state of residence, and show proof of enrollment in an accredited college or university.

Applicants must have a minimum income greater than $4,000. Applicants who do not meet this criterion will need a co-applicant with an ability to repay the debt.

Based on the excerpt, in which of the following situations would someone NOT qualify for the card?
a. aged 20, student at the University of Texas, income of $5,000
b. aged 14, high-school student, no income
c. aged 24, graduate student at Rice University, income of $11,000
d. aged 18, student at Baylor University, income of $4,250

30.

Government spending during war that is associated with wartime expenses has short-term positive economic benefits because high levels of spending associated with conflict increase economic growth. However, after the war is over, unintended residual effects of that heightened wartime spending, which is no longer taking place, tend to cause long-term impediments to economic prosperity.

Based on the information above, choose the best description of the economic effects of war.

a. short-term negative effects followed by positive long-term effects

b. wars produce neither positive nor negative economic effects

c. short-term positive effects followed by negative long-term effects

d. wars produce short-term and long-term negative effects

31. The graph below shows the correlation between metal exploration budgets in the United States and the prices of metals between 1989 and 2008.

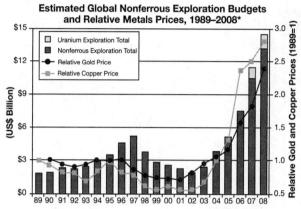

Estimated Global Nonferrous Exploration Budgets and Relative Metals Prices, 1989–2008*

*1989–2006 studies did not include uranium; 2008 relative metals prices are an average through September.

Based on the graph, how did the price of gold and copper correlate to U.S. exploration spending from 2006 to 2008?

a. as the price of gold and copper increased, the amount that the U.S. spent on exploration increased

b. as the price of gold and copper increased, the amount that the U.S. spent on exploration decreased

c. as the price of gold and copper decreased, the amount that the U.S. spent on exploration increased

d. as the price of gold and copper decreased, the amount that the U.S. spent on exploration decreased

32. These two excerpts are taken from separate sources about the Industrial Revolution.

> The era known as the Industrial Revolution was a period in which fundamental changes occurred in agriculture, textile and metal manufacture, transportation, economic policies and the social structure in England . . . The year 1760 is generally accepted as the "eve" of the Industrial Revolution. In reality, this eve began more than two centuries before this date. The late 18th century and the early 19th century brought to fruition the ideas and discoveries of those who had long passed on, such as, Galileo, Bacon, Descartes and others.

> Industrial Revolution, in modern history, is the process of change from an agrarian, handicraft economy to one dominated by industry and machine manufacture. This process began in England in the 18th century and from there spread to other parts of the world.

What is the discrepancy between what is stated in these two passages?
- **a.** the date of the 18th century as the time period
- **b.** defining the time period as a time of fundamental change
- **c.** the real start beginning two centuries before the 18th century
- **d.** the revolution starting and growing in England

33. The map below shows the major ethnic regions of Pacific Asia.

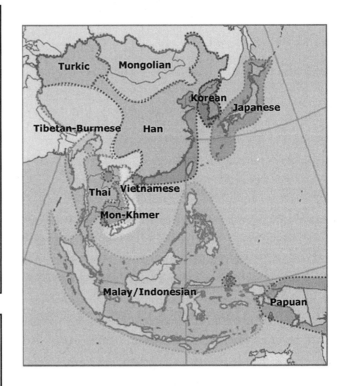

What is the label for the region on the map that covers one island that borders the Korean ethnic region and is located north of the Malay/Indonesian and Papuan ethnic regions?
- **a.** Turkic
- **b.** Thai
- **c.** Han
- **d.** Japanese

Please use the following maps to answer questions 34–35.

These maps are based on information from the U.S. Census Bureau.

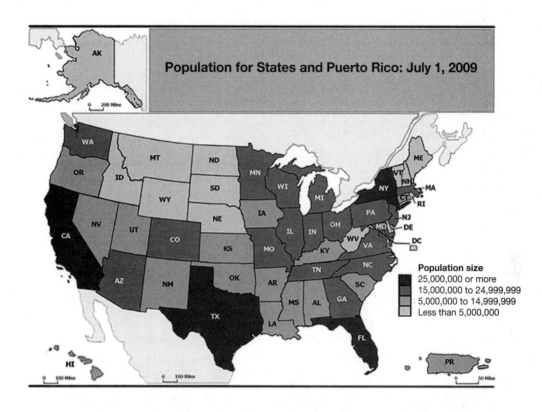

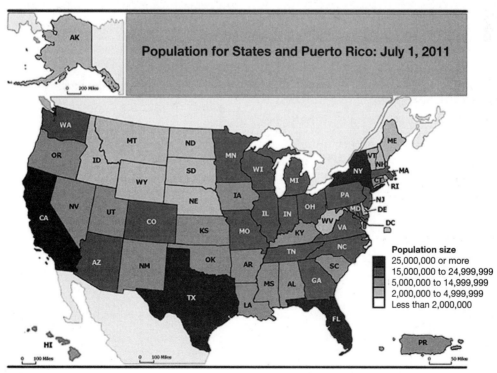

34. Based on the maps showing the population of American states in 2009 and 2011, what has been the population trend between those years for the state of Texas?

a. increased

b. stayed the same

c. decreased

d. increased then decreased

35. Based on the 2011 Census map, how does the population of California relate to the population of Texas?

a. population two categories larger than Texas

b. in the same population category as Tennessee

c. population two categories smaller than Texas

d. in the same population category as Texas

Part II

1 question
25 minutes to complete

This practice test will familiarize you with the Extended Response question found on the GED® Social Studies test.

Before you begin, it is important to note that on the official test, this task must be completed in no more than 25 minutes. But don't rush to complete your response; take time to carefully read the passage(s) and the prompt. Then think about how you would like to respond to the prompt.

As you write your essay, be sure to:

- Develop an argument about how the ideas expressed by President Kennedy are related to the quotation from the Declaration of Independence
- Thoroughly construct your main points, organizing them logically, with strong supporting details
- Present multiple pieces of evidence, using ideas from the quotation and the excerpt
- Connect your sentences, paragraphs, and ideas with transitional words and phrases
- Express your ideas clearly and choose your words carefully
- Use varied sentence structures to increase the clarity of your response
- Reread and revise your response

Good luck!

Please use the following passages to answer the essay question.

This excerpt is from the Declaration of Independence.

> We hold these truths to be self-evident, that all men are created equal, that they are endowed by their Creator with certain unalienable Rights, that among these are Life, Liberty, and the pursuit of Happiness.

This excerpt is from a speech on civil rights given by President John F. Kennedy on June 11, 1963.

This Nation was founded by men of many nations and backgrounds. It was founded on the principle that all men are created equal, and that the rights of every man are diminished when the rights of one man are threatened. Today we are committed to a worldwide struggle to promote and protect the rights of all who wish to be free. And when Americans are sent to Viet-Nam or West Berlin, we do not ask for whites only. It ought to be possible, therefore, for American students of any color to attend any public institution they select without having to be backed up by troops. It ought to be possible for American consumers of any color to receive equal service in places of public accommodation, such as hotels and restaurants and theaters and retail stores, without being forced to resort to demonstrations in the street, and it ought to be possible for American citizens of any color to register and to vote in a free election without interference or fear of reprisal. It ought to be possible, in short, for every American to enjoy the privileges of being American without regard to his race or his color. In short, every American ought to have the right to be treated as he would wish to be treated, as one would wish his children to be treated. But this is not the case. The Negro baby born in America today, regardless of the section of the Nation in which he is born, has about one-half as much chance of completing a high school as a white baby born in the same place on the same day, one-third as much chance of completing college, one-third as much chance of becoming a professional man, twice as much chance of becoming unemployed, about one-seventh as much chance of earning $10,000 a year, a life expectancy which is 7 years shorter, and the prospects of earning only half as much. This is not a sectional issue. Difficulties over segregation and discrimination exist in every city, in every State of the Union, producing in many cities a rising tide of discontent that threatens the public safety. Nor is this a partisan issue. In a time of domestic crisis men of good will and generosity should be able to unite regardless of party or politics. This is not even a legal or legislative issue alone. It is better to settle these matters in the courts than on the streets, and new laws are needed at every level, but law alone cannot make men see right. We are confronted primarily with a moral issue. It is as old as the scriptures and is as clear as the American Constitution.

QUESTION:

In your response, develop an argument about how President Kennedy's stance on the civil-rights issues of the time reflected beliefs that were already built into the section of the Declaration of Independence quoted here, even though the Declaration of Independence was written centuries before civil rights for African Americans became a national focus. Incorporate relevant and specific evidence from the two excerpts and your knowledge of the enduring issue and circumstances surrounding the Civil-rights movement to support your analysis.

_____

_____

_____

_____

_____

_____

_____

_____

_____

_____

_____

_____

_____

_____

Answers and Explanations

Part I

1. **Choice b is correct.** The liberation of the Iraqi people from a brutal ruling regime and the removal of Hussein from power are both goals that would have the ability to bring about all of the changes for Iraq that President Bush mentions came about after the success of the operation. Therefore, it is safe to say that this choice represents the main purpose of the launching of the operation by President Bush.
Choice **a** is incorrect. While the liberation of Baghdad led to Operation Iraqi Freedom's success, it alone was not the purpose of the operation. The capture of this one city would not have been enough to bring about the other changes and freedoms for the Iraqi people that Bush mentions, such as those in the excerpt's final paragraph.
Choice **c** is incorrect. Stopping Hussein from invading nations was an outcome of the operation's success in removing Hussein from power not the actual purpose of the operation. That purpose would be to remove Hussein, which would result in this beneficial outcome.
Choice **d** is incorrect. These nations joined forces for the common cause of the operation to stop Saddam Hussein's control of the Iraqi people's natural rights.

2. **Choice d is correct.** This statement is an opinion held and expressed by Bush. He uses the term "remarkable," which is inherently a term of opinion. Bush may feel that the operation "was a remarkable display of military effectiveness," but this is an opinion, not a fact.
Choice **a** is incorrect. All of these events are facts that are confirmed by the actions and technicalities of the operation. All of these actions were actually carried out during the operation.
Choice **b** is incorrect. This is once again a fact. These forces did all join with the U.S. in the beginning of the operation.
Choice **c** is incorrect. This is another fact of the actions carried out during the operation when troops actually did battle Saddam's death squads.

3. Choice c is correct. All of the atrocities carried out by Saddam that Bush mentions in his speech serve to show the justification for the operation and show just how brutal Saddam's regime was and how detrimental it was to the citizens of that regime who were exposed to atrocities. Bush mentions in the end all the negative things that have been stopped due to the operation, once again bolstering its justification.

Choice **a** is incorrect. Everything that Bush says about the operation in this part of his speech implies that the operation was justified and successful. He mentions on many occasions the brutality of Saddam's regime and gives examples. He then goes on to list atrocities that have been stopped due to the operation.

Choice **b** is incorrect. Everything that Bush says would imply that he feels the operation was justified. However, the realities of Saddam's regime that Bush mentions only lend credit to this justification. Instead of discrediting the operation, the atrocities that Saddam imposed on his people only bolster the idea that it was justified.

Choice **d** is incorrect. While the atrocities of Saddam's regime that Bush mentions justify the operation, Bush does not disagree with that justification. The fact that he mentions all of said atrocities implies that he agrees that the operation was justified, and in the last paragraph he goes on to mention all of the atrocities that have been stopped due to the operation. He never expresses any doubts about the operation's justification.

4. Choice c is correct. The legislative branch involves the Senate and the House of Representatives, and the executive branch consists of the president and his administration. The fact that the Senate must have a two-thirds agreement in order to allow the president to make a treaty means that the legislative branch is checking the power of the executive branch so that the president does not have full and unopposed power to make treaties.

Choice **a** is incorrect. The president is part of the executive branch, and that branch is not checking the powers of any other branches but actually having its own powers checked.

Choice **b** is incorrect. The judicial branch involves the courts, and this branch is not even mentioned in this section of the Constitution.

Choice **d** is incorrect. The judicial branch does not even factor into this section of the Constitution.

5. Choice b is correct. The system of checks and balances in the U.S. government is meant to separate the powers of the branches of government and provide a balance to those powers so that one person or group does not hold all power, which could then be abused and exploited.

Choice **a** is incorrect. The idea behind checks and balances between the branches of government is to keep a balance of power, not to allow the legislative branch to have power over the executive or judicial branches. In the excerpt, this check on the power of the president does not imply that the Senate has power over the president or courts, but rather it is a balance of power.

Choice **c** is incorrect. If the president had the ability to check the power of all the other branches, his power would be more like a dictatorship than a presidency. The system of checks and balances is meant to prevent this. Also, the excerpt shows that the president does not have this power due to the fact that the Senate is actually checking the president's power in this example.

Choice **d** is incorrect. While the example in the excerpt does refer to this check on the power of the president, this is only an example of one instance of checks and balances in the U.S. government and not the actual point of this system. There are many other examples of checks and balances written into the U.S. Constitution.

6. Choice c is correct. Without a two-thirds agreement in the Senate, the president cannot make a treaty. This is part of the system of checks and balances in the U.S. government. It is a check on the power of the executive branch. Choice **a** is incorrect. The president is the one who makes treaties with the consent of the Senate. Therefore, failure to receive a two-thirds agreement would make a treaty impossible, not just in the Senate but for the president as well. Choice **b** is incorrect. The Senate does not make the treaties; the president does. The Senate consults with the president and must agree with the treaty in order for it to be made.

Choice **d** is incorrect. Without a two-thirds agreement in the Senate, the president cannot make a treaty. This is part of the system of checks and balances in the U.S. government. It is a check on the power of the executive branch.

7. Choice a is correct. The concept of popular sovereignty implies that the government holds authority through the consent of the governed, and if the governed fails to approve of said authority, the people can change it. A dictatorship does not take the consent of the governed into account, and one individual rules without consent.

Choice **b** is incorrect. The concept of popular sovereignty implies that the government holds authority through the consent of the governed and if the governed fails to approve of said authority, the government can change it. A dictatorship does not take the consent of the governed into account and one individual rules without consent.

Choice **c** is incorrect. The concept of popular sovereignty does not necessarily mean that the government is run by the most popular person, but rather that the leader of the government has consent of the governed. A dictatorship does not necessarily mean that the government is run by the least popular person, but rather that said person does not take the consent of the governed into account.

Choice **d** is incorrect. A dictatorship does not mean that the government is run by the most popular person, but rather that the leader of the government does not take the consent of the government into account. The concept of popular sovereignty does not mean that the government is run by the least popular person, but rather that said person has the consent of the governed.

8. The executive branch is made up of the **president** and the **president's Cabinet**.

The legislative branch is made up of the **Senate** and the **House of Representatives**, collectively known as Congress.

The judicial branch is made up of the **Supreme Court**.

9. Choice b is correct. Right at the beginning of the excerpt, Clinton references the problems of discrimination from the past and says that it continues to plague the country. He makes it apparent that affirmative action is a way to lessen this discrimination and hopefully solve many problems that it creates for minority groups.

Choice **a** is incorrect. Slavery was a problem that has been abolished by law since the Civil War and Reconstruction. Affirmative action is not addressing slavery or a solution.

Choice **c** is incorrect. While unemployment can be caused by discrimination, affirmative action addresses discrimination, which could then inadvertently help with unemployment as a side effect. Affirmative action is not directly addressing unemployment or providing a direct solution to it.

Choice **d** is incorrect. While poverty can be caused by discrimination, affirmative action addresses discrimination, which could then inadvertently help with unemployment and poverty as a side effect. Affirmative action is not directly addressing poverty or providing a direct solution to it.

10. Choice a is correct. According to Clinton, affirmative action will benefit minority groups "by building the pool of qualified applicants for college, for contracts, for jobs, and giving more people the chance to learn, work, and earn. When affirmative action is done right, it is flexible, it is fair, and it works."

Choice **b** is incorrect. This change is the opposite of the purpose of affirmative action and is the opposite of the correct answer. According to Clinton, affirmative action will benefit minority groups "by building the pool of qualified applicants for college, for contracts, for jobs, and giving more people the chance to learn, work, and earn. When affirmative action is done right, it is flexible, it is fair, and it works."

Choice **c** is incorrect. Clinton mentions that the idea to have penalties for employers who fail to meet high quotas was actually rejected and affirmative action helps to keep this from happening. However, affirmative action has as its main goal the improvement of conditions for minority groups. Therefore, the idea that it would not change anything for minority groups is wrong.

Choice **d** is incorrect. Both of these statements represent things that affirmative action is trying to fix. Affirmative action would increase the amount of minority groups in college, not decrease their numbers. According to Clinton, affirmative action will benefit minority groups "by building the pool of qualified applicants for college, for contracts, for jobs, and giving more people the chance to learn, work, and earn. When affirmative action is done right, it is flexible, it is fair, and it works."

11. Choice d is correct. Both excerpts mention the importance of liberty for all citizens. The Declaration of Independence says all men have the right to liberty, and the Constitution says that the government must "secure the Blessings of Liberty to ourselves and our Posterity."

Choice **a** is incorrect. The concept of all men being equal is mentioned only in the excerpt from the Declaration of Independence.

Choice **b** is incorrect. This idea is mentioned only in the excerpt from the Declaration of Independence.

Choice **c** is incorrect. Neither excerpt mentions anything about slavery or the need to abolish it. Furthermore, the Declaration of Independence was made during a time when slavery was still very prominent.

12. Choice b is correct. Popular sovereignty refers to a government run by the people, where the people have the ability to affect, change, and replace their government as they see fit. This is what the excerpt is essentially describing.

Choice **a** is incorrect. Federalism refers to the concept of a federal government. This excerpt references the ability to replace the government; it doesn't describe a federal system of government.

Choice **c** is incorrect. Socialism deals with a centralized control of wealth in order to make the spread of wealth more equal. This has nothing to do with the ability to replace the government. The term *socialism* is not preceded by the word *popular*.

Choice **d** is incorrect. Capitalism deals with the idea of free markets and private ownership in the economy. This is an economic system, not a system of replacing a destructive form of government.

13. **The correct answer is 122.**

The mean is the average. Therefore, you add up all of the numbers in the column listing the number of men killed: 49 + 73 + 140 + 226 = 488.

Then divide the answer by the number of values given: $\frac{488}{4}$ = 122.

14. **Choice b is correct.** The United States entering World War II took the rate from 14.5% in 1941 to 7% in 1942, or a 7.5% decrease.

Choice **a** is incorrect. FDR's first New Deal took the rate from 37% in 1933 to 33% in 1934, or a 4% drop. This was not the largest decrease.

Choice **c** is incorrect. The stock market crash *increased* the unemployment rate by 9%, from 5.5% in 1929 to 14.5% in 1930.

Choice **d** is incorrect. In the year following the German invasion of Poland, the unemployment rate dropped from 25% to 21%, or a 4% drop. This was not the largest decrease.

15. The answer is **private**, based on an understanding and comprehension of the definition and logical reasoning to understand how it can fit into the statement.

16. **Choice a is correct.** The Democrat bar is the highest and is shown on the graph with political parties being labeled on the *x*-axis (horizontally) and the percentage of members labeled along the *y*-axis (vertically). This allows a viewer to see that the Democratic Party has the highest percentage of members.

Choice **b** is incorrect. While the Democratic Party does have the most members based on the percentages, the political parties are labeled on the *x*-axis, not the *y*-axis. Also, percentages are labeled on the *y*-axis, not the *x*-axis.

Choice **c** is incorrect. While the political parties are labeled on the *x*-axis and percentages are labeled on the *y*-axis, which shows, through the use of bars, which party has the most members, the Libertarian Party does not have the highest bar. Therefore, it does not have the most members.

Choice **d** is incorrect. The Libertarian Party does not have the highest bar representing percentage of members and consequently does not have the most members. Also, political parties are labeled on the *x*-axis, not the *y*-axis, and percentages are labeled on the *y*-axis, not the *x*.

17. **Choice b is correct.** The key indicates that a circle surrounding a gray triangle includes **both** "urban rail transit system under construction in 2010" and "high-speed rail routes under construction in 2010."

Choice **a** is incorrect. The symbol for "urban rail transit system under construction in 2010" is a simple gray triangle.

Choice **c** is incorrect. The key indicates that a circle surrounding a gray triangle includes both "urban rail transit system under construction in 2010" and "high-speed rail routes under construction in 2010."

Choice **d** is incorrect. High-growth power centers are designated by a circle surrounding a black triangle.

18. Choice d is correct. The bars indicating expenditures for that time period are increasing. They increase from around $40 million to $80 million based on the dollar amount labeled on the *y*-axis (vertical) and years labeled on the *x*-axis (horizontal). Choice **a** is incorrect. The bars indicating expenditures for that time period are not decreasing. They increase from around $40 million to $80 million based on the dollar amount labeled on the *y*-axis (vertical) and years labeled on the *x*-axis (horizontal). Choice **b** is incorrect. The bars indicating expenditures for that time period are increasing, but they never decrease during that time. They increase from around $40 million to $80 million based on the dollar amount labeled on the *y*-axis (vertical) and years labeled on the *x*-axis (horizontal). Choice **c** is incorrect. The bars indicating expenditures for that time period are increasing, and they never decrease during that time. They increase from around $40 million to $80 million based on the dollar amount labeled on the *y*-axis (vertical) and years labeled on the *x*-axis (horizontal).

19. Choice a is correct. Loaded language means language that is highly emotive and used to gain support, sway emotions, degrade others, or push an agenda. *Hoax* and *frustration* are words that are being used by Obama to sway voters against the previous political administration in order to win the presidency in the coming election.
Choice **b** is incorrect. Loaded language means language that is highly emotive and used to gain support, sway emotions, degrade others, or push an agenda. *Today* and *decisions* are not words that serve this purpose in this excerpt. Choice **c** is incorrect. Loaded language means language that is highly emotive and used to gain support, sway emotions, degrade others, or push an agenda. *Void* and *lobbyists* are not words that serve this purpose in this excerpt. Choice **d** is incorrect. Loaded language means language that is highly emotive and used to gain support, sway emotions, degrade others, or push an agenda. *Page* and *diplomacy* are not words that serve this purpose in this excerpt.

20. Choice b is correct. Obama is publicizing a point of view or political cause. He does not acknowledge who has been telling Americans this but implies that it is coming from members of the government. Obama wants to replace these members by hopefully winning the presidency. This speech announces his political campaign for president.
Choice **a** is incorrect. Obama is stating his opinions. Obama wants the people hearing him to feel he is right about these issues. He does not present an economic chart.
Choice **c** is incorrect. Obama is stating his opinions. Obama wants the people hearing him to feel he is right about these issues. He does not present statistical facts.
Choice **d** is incorrect. The third paragraph of Obama's speech does not mention anything that he promises to do when he becomes president.

21. Choice d is correct. In the excerpt, Obama does not give any factual evidence to support this statement. Therefore it falls into the category of an opinion or unsupported claim.

Choice **a** is incorrect. In the excerpt, Obama does not give any factual evidence to support this statement.

Choice **b** is incorrect. A statistic is a piece of data that typically comes from a study involving a large amount of numerical data. Obama does not mention any numbers in this statement.

Choice **c** is incorrect. Obama's statement is not a warning that something will happen.

22. Choice b is correct. If Medicare and Medicaid are struggling, then the government would have to spend more on them in order to help the programs. Obama explicitly says, "we will eventually be spending more on Medicare and Medicaid than every other government program combined."

Choice **a** is incorrect. If Medicare and Medicaid are struggling, then the government would have to spend more on them in order to help the programs, not less. Obama explicitly says, "we will eventually be spending more on Medicare and Medicaid than every other government program combined."

Choice **c** is incorrect. While Obama mentions that Medicare and Medicaid are struggling due to rapidly increasing health care costs, he never mentions that this would lead to the shutdown of these programs. As government programs, it is much more likely that the government would spend more money on them instead of shutting them down. Also, due to the fact that so many people rely on these programs, it would take a lot more to actually shut them down.

Choice **d** is incorrect. This is the exact opposite of what Obama implies will happen. As government programs, the government would spend more money on them to help them when they are struggling. If the government stopped spending money on them, their struggles would increase to the point where they could no longer function. Also, Obama explicitly says, "we will eventually be spending more on Medicare and Medicaid than every other government program combined."

23. Choice c is correct. This was the goal of his expedition in 1492. The spice trade was very lucrative at the time, and Columbus had the idea that he could sail in the direction of the Americas and eventually reach Asia, thereby avoiding overland trade routes in the other direction. He did not realize that there was a large landmass in the way, and this is how he discovered the Americas.

Choice **a** is incorrect. Columbus' first expedition in 1492 had nothing to do with finding new territory. He did not know that the Americas existed since this expedition brought him into contact with the land for the first time. While he did eventually make future expeditions to the Americas on behalf of Spain, this was after he knew it existed.

Choice **b** is incorrect. He did not know that the Americas existed since this expedition brought him into contact with the land for the first time. While he did eventually make future expeditions to the Americas for goods on behalf of Spain, he could not be planning an expedition to trade with native peoples who he did not know existed.

Choice **d** is incorrect. Columbus' first expedition in 1492 had nothing to do with creating a new settlement for Spain in the Americas. He did not know that the Americas existed since this expedition brought him into contact with the land for the first time, and he could not be looking to make a settlement in a place he didn't know existed. While he did eventually make future expeditions to the Americas on behalf of Spain, this was after he knew it existed.

24. The correct answer is **Navy's Women Accepted for Voluntary Emergency Service**, or **WAVES**. Based on the pie chart, 0.3% of the women joining the military during World War II were Women's Airforce Service Pilots or WASP, 4% were Navy Nurse Corps, 17% were American Nurse Corps, 6% were Marine Corps Women's Reserves and 3% were Coast Guard Women's Reserves or SPARS. The combination of all of those percentages comes out to 30.3% of women joining the military. This is closest to the 28% of the Navy's Women Accepted for Voluntary Emergency Service rather than the 42% that was the Women's Army Corps.

25. Choice a is correct. The map shows countries in the Eastern Bloc in darker gray and the Western Bloc in lighter gray. Turkey is colored lighter gray and is, therefore, part of the Western Bloc.

Choice **b** is incorrect. The map shows countries in the Eastern Bloc in darker gray and the Western Bloc in lighter gray. Turkey is colored lighter gray and is, therefore, part of the Western Bloc.

Choice **c** is incorrect. The Iron Curtain is a dividing line. Therefore, it is not one of the divisions that countries could be put into during the Cold War. It is shown as a white line, which Turkey only barely touches.

Choice **d** is incorrect. This map does not give any information about Turkey's relationship with the United States. The United States is not depicted on the map.

26. **Choice b is correct.** Bush never mentions that the goal is to control the local leadership and economy in Iraq, but rather the goal is to help the Iraqi people eventually be able to completely control their own government. Therefore, this is not a reason that it was important to have civilian experts in Iraq. Choice **a** is incorrect. Bush explicitly states, "they're helping to strengthen responsible leaders and build up local economies." Therefore, this choice is a reason that it was important to have civilian experts in Iraq. Choice **c** is incorrect. Bush explicitly states, "they're helping give ordinary Iraqis confidence." Therefore, this choice is a reason that it was important to have civilian experts in Iraq. Choice **d** is incorrect. Bush explicitly states, "they can claim their place in a free Iraq." Therefore, this choice is a reason that it was important to have civilian experts in Iraq.

27. **Choice c is correct.** A profit is a financial gain. Since the company only spent $1 on the product and then sold it for $2.35 to consumers, the company makes a financial gain of $1.35 every time that a consumer purchases the product. The company makes a profit of $1.35.
Choice **a** is incorrect. A monopoly is an entity that has exclusive control over a product or service. A dollar amount cannot be an example of something that has complete control over a product or service. Also, the example gives no indication that the company has exclusive control of the product.
Choice **b** is incorrect. The $1.35 would only be a part of the expense for the consumer, not an expense for the company. The company's only expense was the $1 that it spent on the product before selling it.
Choice **d** is incorrect. Since the company only spent $1 on the product and then sold it for $2.35 to consumers, the company makes a financial gain of $1.35 every time that a consumer purchases the product. The company makes a profit of $1.35, not a loss.

28. **The correct answer is tariff.**
A tariff is a tax or duty placed on imports or exports.

29. **Choice b is correct.** The person in this situation would not qualify for the card. He or she is not old enough, is a high school student not a college student, and does not have an income greater than $4,000.
Choices **a**, **b**, and **c** are incorrect. The people in these situations would qualify for the card. They are old enough, are students of an accredited university, and have an income greater than $4,000.

30. Choice c is correct. The excerpt mentions that the economy benefits in the short-term from substantial spending increases during the conflict; however, this leads to negative residual effects that hurt the economy in the long term after the war is over and there is no longer a spending boom related to the conflict.

Choice **a** is incorrect. The excerpt mentions that the economy benefits in the short-term from substantial spending increases during the conflict; however, this leads to negative residual effects that hurt the economy in the long term after the war is over and there is no longer a spending boom related to the conflict.

Choice **b** is incorrect. The excerpt mentions that the economy benefits in the short-term from substantial spending increases during the conflict; however, this leads to negative residual effects that hurt the economy in the long term after the war is over and there is no longer a spending boom related to the conflict. Therefore, wars definitely have economic effects.

Choice **d** is incorrect. The excerpt mentions that the economy benefits in the short-term from substantial spending increases during the conflict; however, this leads to negative residual effects that hurt the economy in the long term after the war is over and there is no longer a spending boom related to the conflict. The effects are not all negative due to the positive short-term effects.

31. Choice a is correct. Dark gray bars represent the amount that the U.S. spent on metal exploration. The two lines represent the price of gold and copper. Based on this information, between the years of 2006 and 2008 the prices of gold and copper along with U.S. spending on metal exploration all increased.

Choices **b**, **c**, and **d** are incorrect. Dark gray bars represent the amount that the U.S. spent on metal exploration. The two lines represent the price of gold and copper. Based on this information, between the years of 2006 and 2008 the prices of gold and copper along with U.S. spending on metal exploration all increased.

32. Choice c is correct. The quote from the first source says, "in reality, this eve began more than two centuries before this date," while the quote from the second source does not mention this idea.

Choice **a** is incorrect. Both quotes mention that the time period of the Industrial Revolution was in the 18th century.

Choice **b** is incorrect. Both quotes define the Industrial revolution as a time of great change. "The era known as the Industrial Revolution was a period in which fundamental changes occurred" and "Industrial Revolution, in modern history, is the process of change from an agrarian, handicraft economy to one dominated by industry and machine manufacture."

Choice **d** is incorrect. Both sources mention that England is where the Industrial Revolution began and grew. "The era known as the Industrial Revolution was a period in which fundamental changes occurred in agriculture, textile and metal manufacture, transportation, economic policies and the social structure in England" and "This process began in England in the 18th century and from there spread to other parts of the world."

33. **Choice d is correct.** The Japanese region covers an island, borders the Korean region, and is north of the Malay/Indonesian and Papuan regions.

Choice **a** is incorrect. The Turkic region is above the Malay/Indonesian and Papuan regions, but it is not covering an island and does not border the Korean region.

Choice **b** is incorrect. The Thai region is above the Malay/Indonesian and Papuan regions, but it is not covering an island and does not border the Korean region.

Choice **c** is incorrect. The Han region is above the Malay/Indonesian and Papuan regions and borders the Korean region, but it is not covering an island.

34. **Choice a is correct.** The map key shows that states labeled with the darkest gray have a population size of 25,000,000 or more, and the states labeled with one shade lighter have a population size of 15,000,000 to 24,999,999. In the 2009 map, Texas is colored the second to darkest shade and in the 2011 map it is colored the darkest shade. Therefore, its population increased from the 15,000,000–24,999,999 range to the 25,000,000 or more range.

35. **Choice d is correct.** Texas and California are both colored the darkest shade of gray, representing a population of 25,000,000 or more. Therefore, the population of California is in the same category as the population of Texas according to the information given in the map. Choice **a** is incorrect. California does not have a larger population than Texas. Both are colored the darkest shade of gray, representing a population of 25,000,000 or more. Therefore the population of California is in the same category as the population of Texas according to the information given in the map. The map does not show exact population numbers, so there is no way to determine which one actually has a slightly larger or smaller population. Choice **b** is incorrect. Texas and California are both colored the darkest shade of gray, representing a population of 25,000,000 or more. Tennessee has a smaller population than either Texas or California.

Choice **c** is incorrect. Texas and California are both colored the darkest shade of gray, representing a population of 25,000,000 or more. Therefore, the population of California is in the same category as the population of Texas according to the information given in the map. The map does not show exact population numbers, so there is no way to determine which one actually has a slightly larger or smaller population.

Part II

Your Extended Response will be scored based on three traits, or elements:

Trait 1: Creation of arguments and use of evidence

Trait 2: Development of ideas and organizational structure

Trait 3: Clarity and command of standard English conventions

Your essay will be scored on a 4-point scale—Trait 1 is worth 0–2 points, and Traits 2 and 3 are worth 0–1 point.

Trait 1 tests your ability to write an essay that takes a stance and makes an argument based on the information in the passages. To earn the highest score possible, you must carefully read the information and express a clear opinion on what you have read. You will be scored on how well you use the information from the passages to support your argument. Your response will also be scored on how well you analyze the information in the passages.

For your reference, here is a table that readers will use when scoring your essay with a 2, 1, or 0.

	TRAIT 1: CREATION OF ARGUMENTS AND USE OF EVIDENCE
2	• Makes a text-based argument that demonstrates a clear understanding of the connections between ideas, figures, and events as presented in the source text(s) and the historical contexts from which they are drawn • Presents specific and related evidence from primary and secondary source text(s) that sufficiently supports an argument • Demonstrates a good connection to both the source text(s) and the prompt
1	• Makes an argument that demonstrates an understanding of the connections between ideas, figures, and events as presented in the source text(s) • Presents some evidence from primary and secondary source texts in support of an argument (may include a mix of related and unrelated textual references) • Demonstrates a connection to both the source text(s) and the prompt
0	• May attempt to make an argument, but demonstrates little or no understanding of the ideas, figures, and events presented in the source text(s) or the contexts from which they are drawn • Presents little or no evidence from the primary and secondary source text(s); may or may not demonstrate an attempt to create an argument • Lacks a connection to either the source text(s) or the prompt
Non-scorable	• Response consists only of text copied from the prompt or source text(s) • Response shows that test taker has not read the prompt or is entirely off-topic • Response is incomprehensible • Response is not in English • No response has been attempted (has been left blank)

Trait 2 tests whether you respond to the writing prompt with a well-structured essay. Support of your thesis must come from evidence in the passages, as well as personal opinions and experiences that build on your central idea. Your ideas must be fully explained and include specific details. Your essay should use words and phrases that allow your details and ideas to flow naturally. Here is a table that outlines what is involved in earning a score of 1 or 0.

	TRAIT 2: DEVELOPMENT OF IDEAS AND ORGANIZATIONAL STRUCTURE
1	• Contains a logical sequence of ideas with clear connections between specific details and main ideas • Contains ideas that are developed and generally logical; multiple ideas are expanded upon • Demonstrates an appropriate understanding of the task
0	• Contains an unclear or indiscernible sequence of ideas • Contains ideas that are inadequately developed or illogical; only one idea is expanded upon • Does not demonstrate an understanding of the task
Non-scorable	• Response consists only of text copied from the prompt or source text(s) • Response shows that test taker has not read the prompt or is entirely off-topic • Response is incomprehensible • Response is not in English • No response has been attempted (has been left blank)

Trait 3 tests how you create the sentences that make up your essay. To earn a high score, you will need to write sentences with variety—some short, some long, some simple, some complex. You will also need to prove that you have a good handle on standard English, including correct word choice, grammar, and sentence structure. Here is a table that outlines what is involved in attaining a score of a 1 or 0.

TRAIT 3: CLARITY AND COMMAND OF STANDARD ENGLISH CONVENTIONS	
1	• Demonstrates adequate use of conventions with regard to the following skills: 1) subject-verb agreement 2) placement of modifiers and correct word order 3) pronoun usage, including pronoun antecedent agreement, unclear pronoun references, and pronoun case 4) frequently confused words and homonyms, including contractions 5) use of apostrophes with possessive nouns 6) use of punctuation (e.g., commas in a series or in appositives and other non-essential elements, end marks, and punctuation for clause separation) 7) capitalization (e.g., beginnings of sentences, proper nouns, and titles) • Demonstrates generally correct sentence structure and sentence variation; demonstrates overall fluency and clarity with regard to the following skills: 1) correct use of subordination, coordination, and parallelism 2) avoidance of awkward sentence structures and wordiness 3) usage of transitional words, conjunctive adverbs, and other words that enhance clarity and logic 4) avoidance of run-on sentences, sentence fragments, and fused sentences 5) standard usage at a level appropriate for on-demand draft writing • May contain some errors in mechanics and conventions that do not impede comprehension
0	• Demonstrates minimal use of basic conventions with regard to skills 1–7 as listed under Trait 3, Score Point 1 • Demonstrates consistently improper sentence structure; little or no variation to the extent that meaning may be unclear; demonstrates minimal use of skills 1–5 as listed under Trait 3, Score Point 1 • Contains numerous significant errors in mechanics and conventions that impede comprehension OR • Response is insufficient to show level of proficiency involving conventions and usage
Non-scorable	• Response consists only of text copied from the prompt or source text(s) • Response shows that test taker has not read the prompt or is entirely off-topic • Response is incomprehensible • Response is not in English • No response has been attempted (has been left blank)

Sample Score 4 Essay

Although equal civil rights for all Americans, regardless of race, were not guaranteed by law until the 1960s, the same ideals that inspired the civil rights movement were part of the basic structure of American government from its creation, nearly two centuries before. While cultural, economic, and political factors may have interfered with the achievement of this goal for many years, its inclusion in the founding documents of the nation underlines the enduring nature of this issue.

The Declaration of Independence is widely regarded as the first formal expression of American democracy. The document states that "all men are created equal," and refers to "certain unalienable rights," meaning that these basic rights cannot be taken away. While the United States was not the first nation to suggest that citizens should be given basic rights, it was undoubtedly one of the first to support the notion of equal rights for all citizens. This extended basic protections to even the lowest classes of society, and also held the higher classes accountable to the same laws as everyone else.

At the time the Declaration of Independence was written, the idea that "all men are created equal" was, in many ways, difficult to implement in its purest form. Slaves were not considered as equals, and were in fact treated by the law as property; women were also excluded from many of the basic protections and rights that men enjoyed. Even among free white men, the application of equality was inconsistent at best. For example, in the nation's first elections, only wealthy, land-owning men were allowed to vote.

The history of the United States is a history of edging ever closer to the ideals expressed in the Declaration of Independence and the U.S. Constitution. The obstacles that have impeded this progress have been economic and social factors such as slavery and prejudice. When slavery ended in the mid-nineteenth century, the U.S. Congress passed constitutional amendments intended to protect the voting rights and citizenship of former slaves. However, as Kennedy stated, "law alone cannot make men see right." These laws, despite their

intent, proved ineffective at preserving the rights of African Americans in many situations. For example, many parts of the country established separate facilities for blacks such as schools, bathrooms, and even drinking fountains. However, these facilities rarely met the same standards as those for whites. This sort of fundamental racial discrimination led to conditions like the ones Kennedy lists in his speech: African Americans were likely to be poorer, less educated, and to die sooner than white Americans. This is why Kennedy supported new civil rights legislation intended to strengthen protections of the rights of all people, regardless of race— bring the United States one step closer to the dream of a nation where, indeed, all men are created equal.

About this essay:

This essay has earned the maximum number of points in each trait for a total of 4 points.

Trait 1: Creation of Arguments and Use of Evidence

The sample response presents an argument about the role of equality in the Civil-rights movement and how it relates to the very beginnings of the founding of the U.S., even though the founding fathers did not yet realize that the idea of equality would be used in this way. The test taker's argument cites multiple ideas from the source texts that bolster his or her position. Additionally, the writer incorporates into the response background knowledge about the importance of equality throughout U.S. history in general, and the role of equality in the Civil-rights movement in particular. Taken as a whole, the response offers an argument that is closely aligned to what is directed by the prompt and is well supported by the source texts.

Trait 2: Development of Ideas and Organizational Structure

This response earns one point in Trait 2 because it makes clear and understandable connections between ideas and establishes a progression in which one idea logically leads into the next, starting from the very beginning *Although equal civil rights for all Americans, regardless of race, were not guaranteed by law until the 1960s, the same ideals that inspired the civil rights movement were part of the basic structure of American government from its creation, nearly two centuries before.*

The main points are fully developed with multiple details given in support of each. Additionally, this response applies the level of formality appropriate for communicating in either workplace or academic settings, while also keeping in mind the purpose of the task, which is to present a well-supported argument.

Trait 3: Clarity and Command of Standard English Conventions

This response earns one point on Trait 3 because it effectively applies standard English language usage and conventions to convey ideas with clarity. In general, the response contains minimal mechanical errors, and the errors that do exist do not impede readers' understanding. The response contains language appropriate for expressing its ideas and thoughtfully composed sentences that generally avoid wordiness and awkwardness. Additionally, clarity and flow of the response are enhanced with varied sentence structure and appropriate application of transitional words and phrases to connect sentences, paragraphs, and ideas.

Remember, however, because the Extended Response question on the GED® Social Studies test asks for a draft written in approximately 25 minutes, there is no expectation that your response be completely free of convention and usage errors.

Sample Score 2 Essay

In Kennedy's speech, he states that "every American ought to have the right to be treated as he would wish to be treated, as one would wish his children to be treated." This idea directly reflects the beliefs held by the Founding Fathers, as evidenced in the statement "all men are created equal" found in the declaration of independence.

For a number or reasons at the time of the signing of the declaration of independence "all men" did not include slaves and women. At the time of Kennedy's speech, Africans Americans still weren't being treated as equals in America, especially in the south. I know this is true because my grandmother lived in Mississippi during that time. Kennedy also states in his speech how African Americans were poorer and did not live as long as white people.

Kennedy argued that the issue of equality is a moral one that goes all the way back to the Constitution. Actually, it goes back to the declaration of independence, which came first and says "all men are created equal." So he supported new laws to make sure that people all other races were all treated fairly. This was exactly what the Founding Fathers argued in favor of, even though they couldn't really do it themselves at the time.

About this essay:

This essay has earned 1 of 2 possible points in Trait 1, 0 points in Trait 2, and 1 point in trait 3, for a total of 2 out of the 4 maximum points.

Trait 1: Creation of Arguments and Use of Evidence

This somewhat brief response offers an argument that demonstrates an understanding of how the enduring issue of equality for all men is presented in both of the excerpts: *[Kennedy's]idea directly reflects the beliefs held by the Founding Fathers, as evidenced in the statement "all men are created equal" found in the declaration of independence.*

The writer also provides some evidence from both excerpts; for example, in the third paragraph: *He argues that the issue of equality is a moral one that goes all the way back to the Constitution. Actually, it goes back to the declaration of independence, which came first and says "all men are created equal."* However, the writer also interjects a personal aside unrelated to the excerpts about his or her grandmother.

Though this brief sample response is connected to the prompt and the excerpts, it does not offer much information beyond what is presented in the excerpts about the enduring issue of equality or the civil-rights movement in the 1960s, so it earns only one point in this trait.

Trait 2: Development of Ideas and Organizational Structure

This response does not earn a point in Trait 2. Though it does demonstrate an understanding of the task, the sequence of ideas is unclear and only limited ideas are developed. For example, the writer begins the second paragraph with: *For a number or reasons at the time of the signing of the declaration of independence "all men" did not include slaves and women.* But he or she does elaborate upon those reasons other than at the closing of the essay: *even though* [the Founding Fathers] *couldn't really do it themselves at the time.*

Trait 3: Clarity and Command of Standard English Conventions

This response earns one point on Trait 3. In general, the response contains minimal mechanical errors (though, glaringly, the writer does not capitalize *Declaration of Independence* throughout), however these errors that do not impede readers' understanding. The response contains appropriate language for expressing its ideas and thoughtfully composed sentences that generally avoid wordiness and awkwardness.

Sample Score 0 Essay

The foundling fathers beleived that all man were created equal and we all have rights. I beleive this too and so does JFK.

JFK said we are committed to a worldwide struggle to promote and protect the rights of all who wish to be free. Laws needed to be passed JFK he passed them and the world is better today.

Difficulties over segregation and discrimination exist in every city, in every State of the Union, producing in many cities a rising tide of discontent that threatens the public safety. Nor is this a partisan issue. In a time of domestic crisis men of good will and generosity should be able to unite regardless of party or politics. This is not even a legal or legislative issue alone.

About this essay:

This essay earns a score of 0 in each of the three traits.

Trait 1: Creation of Arguments and Use of Evidence

This sample response earns a score of 0 in Trait 1. It is extremely brief, is composed mostly of direct quotations or paraphrases from the excerpts, and attempts an argument that is barely connected to the ideas in the excerpts: *The foundling fathers beleived that all man were created equal and we all have rights. I beleive this too and so does JFK.* Therefore, it is not sufficiently connected to the prompt.

Trait 2: Development of Ideas and Organizational Structure

This sample response also earns a score of 0 in Trait 2. The organizational structure is scattered and the progression of the one idea (Kennedy recognized the need to pass laws for equality) is barely discernible.

Trait 3: Clarity and Command of Standard English Conventions

This sample response also earns a score of 0 in Trait 2. The bulk of the response is composed of text lifted directly from the excerpts, with the exceptions of the first paragraph and *Laws needed to be passed JFK he passed them and the world is better today.* This lack of original writing by the writer demonstrates an insufficient level of mastery of conventions and usage. In addition, the original writing does not employ the proper punctuation to mark quotations from the excerpts and contains numerous errors in sentence construction.

6 ▶ GED®
MATHEMATICAL
REASONING TEST 2

This practice test is modeled on the format, content, and timing of the official GED® Mathematical Reasoning test. Like the official exam, the questions focus on your quantitative and algebraic problem-solving skills.

You may refer to the formula sheet in the Appendix on page 285 as you take this exam. Answer questions 1–5 *without* using a calculator. You may use a scientific calculator (or a calculator of any kind) for the remaining exam questions.

Work carefully, but do not spend too much time on any one question. Be sure you answer every question.

Set a timer for 115 minutes (1 hour and 55 minutes), and try to take this test uninterrupted, under quiet conditions.

Complete answer explanations for every test question follow the exam. Good luck!

45 questions
115 minutes

1. The product of two consecutive integers is 42. If the smaller integer is x, which of the following equations must true?
   a. $x + 1 = 42$
   b. $x^2 + x = 42$
   c. $2x + 1 = 42$
   d. $2x^2 + x = 42$

2.

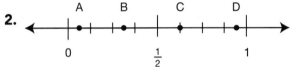

   If x is a rational number such that $\frac{1}{2} < x < \frac{3}{4}$, then which of the points on the number line above may represent x?
   a. Point A
   b. Point B
   c. Point C
   d. Point D

3. A real-estate agent has found that the asking price of a home in his area can be estimated by taking the square footage, multiplying by 84, and adding 1,065. If the square footage is represented by S and the asking price by P, then which of the following formulas represents this estimation?
   a. $P = 1,149S$
   b. $P = 84(S + 1,065)$
   c. $P = 84S + 1,065$
   d. $P = S + 1,149$

4. In the x-y coordinate plane below, draw a dot on the point which is represented by the ordered pair $(4, -2)$.

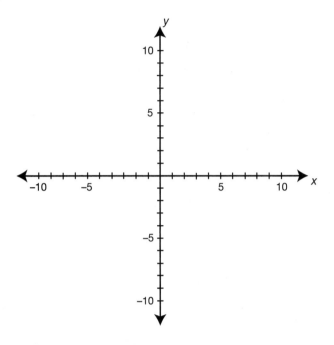

5. Which of the following is equivalent to $\frac{2^5}{2^2}$?
   a. 2
   b. 2^3
   c. 2^7
   d. 2^{10}

6. Which of the following graphs shows n as a function of m?

a. n

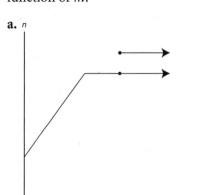

b. n

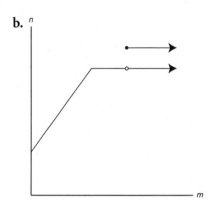

c. n

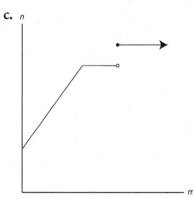

d. n

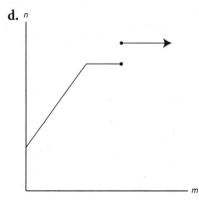

7. As a simplified fraction, $\frac{1}{4}\left(\frac{5}{2} - \frac{1}{6}\right) =$

a. $-\frac{1}{4}$

b. $\frac{1}{6}$

c. $\frac{7}{12}$

d. $\frac{3}{2}$

8. Suppose that for a rational number x, $3(x - 5) = 3$. Select which of the following must be true.

a. $x - 5 = 1$

b. $3x - 15 = 9$

c. $x = 5$

d. $3x = 8$

9. For input a, the function f is defined as $f(a) = -2a^2 + 1$. What is the value of $f(-8)$?

a. -127

b. -34

c. 33

d. 129

10. Which of the following represents the solution set of the inequality $4x - 9 < 3x + 1$?

a. $x < -\frac{8}{7}$

b. $x < -8$

c. $x < 10$

d. $x < \frac{10}{7}$

11. $(x - 5)(2x + 1) =$

a. $2x^2 - 3x + 1$

b. $2x^2 - 9x - 5$

c. $2x^2 - 5$

d. $2x^2 - 10$

12. What is the largest possible value of x if $x^2 - 14x + 35 = -10$? Write your answer in the box below.

13. The figure below shows the graph of a function and all of its turning points.

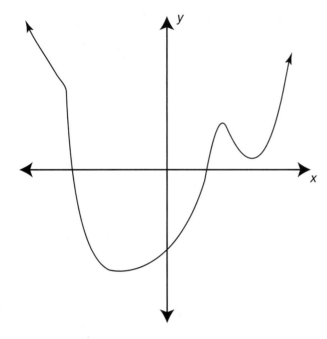

How many *x*-intercepts does the function have?

a. None

b. 1

c. 2

d. infinitely many

14. A website is selling a laptop computer for $375.00 plus 6.5% state sales tax. A student wishes to purchase two of these computers: one for his brother and one for himself. Including tax, what will be the total cost of his order? Write your answer in the box below.

15. A small town has a population of 20,510 and an area of 86.8 square miles. To the nearest tenth, what is the population density as measured by the value "people per square mile"?

a. 2.72

b. 236.3

c. 2,201.4

d. 55,833.1

16. $\dfrac{2}{x(x-1)} + \dfrac{1}{x-1} =$

a. $\dfrac{3}{2x(x-1)}$

b. $\dfrac{2+x}{x(x-1)}$

c. $\dfrac{3}{x(x-1)}$

d. $\dfrac{2}{x-1}$

17.

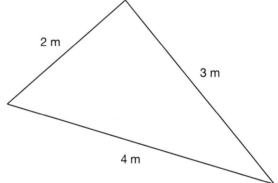

In meters, what is the perimeter of the given triangle?

a. 3

b. 6

c. 7

d. 9

18. Two friends go to a restaurant for lunch and receive a final bill of $24.36. One friend believes they should tip 15%, while the other believes they should tip 20%. To the nearest cent, what is the difference between the two possible tips?
a. $1.22
b. $3.65
c. $4.87
d. $8.52

19. Two high-school biology classes hosted a bird watching day where students kept track of how many different species of birds they observed in a nearby park. The dot plot represents the number of species observed by many of the students.

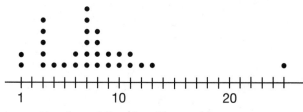

Number of Species Observed

Four of the students have not been included on the plot. The number of species these students observed was:

STUDENT	NUMBER OF SPECIES OBSERVED
Amy	14
Scott	14
Crystal	21
Gilbert	9

Draw as many dots on the graph above as is necessary to add these students' observations to the plot.

20. Which of the following is equivalent to the expression $2x + 3(x - 2)^2$?
a. $3x^2 - 10x + 12$
b. $3x^2 + 3x - 4$
c. $3x^2 - 2x + 4$
d. $3x^2 - 10x + 4$

21. The histogram below represents the data collected through a survey of students at a large commuter college. Each student surveyed provided the one-way distance he or she travels to campus.

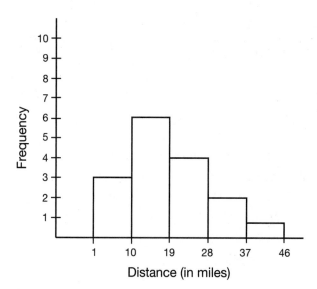

Distance (in miles)

Based on the data, which of the following statements must be true?
a. A total of 46 students were surveyed.
b. There is one student who travels exactly 46 miles to campus, one way.
c. Between 10 and 19 students travel exactly 6 miles to campus, one way.
d. Fewer than 5 students travel less than 10 miles to campus, one way.

22. The figure below represents the cumulative number of packages loaded onto trucks in one day at a small warehouse. When the day began, there were already 50 packages loaded.

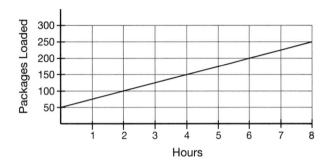

Based on this graph, how many packages were loaded each hour?

a. 25

b. 50

c. 125

d. 250

23. A right triangle has legs of length 7 and 4. To the nearest tenth, what is the length of its hypotenuse?

a. 3.3

b. 5.7

c. 8.1

d. 11.0

24.

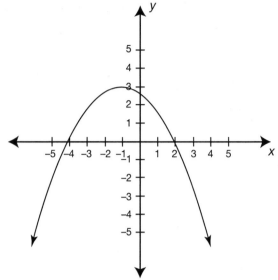

The graph shown here represents a function $y = g(x)$. Select the correct description of the function from the options that follow.

a. The function has a maximum value of −1 when $x = 3$.

b. The function has a maximum value of 3 when $x = -1$.

c. The function has a minimum value of 3 when $x = -1$.

d. The function has a minimum value of −1 when $x = 3$.

25. A map is drawn such that 2.5 inches on the map represents a true distance of 10 miles. If two cities are 7.1 inches apart on the map, then to the nearest tenth of a mile, what is the true distance between the two cities?

a. 14.6

b. 17.8

c. 28.4

d. 71.0

26. Over the last 6 months, a company's monthly revenue has increased by 28%. If the revenue this month is $246,990, then what was the revenue six months ago? Round your answer to the nearest cent. Write your answer in the box below.

$ [   ]

27. The chart below represents the enrollment in an annual professional training program for several nonconsecutive years. Circle the year for which there was the largest difference between the number of men enrolled and the number of women enrolled in the program.

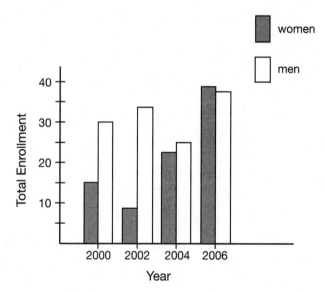

28. A line p passes through the point $(-8,4)$ and has a slope of $\frac{4}{5}$. Which of the following represents the equation for the line p?
a. $4x - y = -52$
b. $4x - y = -60$
c. $4x - 5y = -60$
d. $4x - 5y = -52$

29.

x	0	2	4	6
y	1	4	7	10

The table above shows some points in the x-y coordinate plane that the graph of a line $y = mx + b$ passes through. Based on this information, what is the value of the slope m?
a. $\frac{1}{2}$
b. $\frac{2}{3}$
c. $\frac{3}{2}$
d. 2

30. What are the two linear factors of the polynomial $2x^2 - x$?
a. x and $2x - 1$
b. $2x$ and $x - 1$
c. $2x$ and x
d. $2x$ and $x - 2$

31. A line P graphed in the x-y coordinate plane crosses the x-axis at a point $(-5,0)$. If another line Q has an equation of $y = 3x - 2$, then which of the following statements is true?
a. The x-intercept of line P is closer to the origin than the x-intercept of line Q.
b. The x-coordinate of the x-intercept of line P is smaller than the x-intercept of the x-intercept of line Q.
c. The x-intercepts of both lines lie to the right of the y-axis.
d. The x-intercept of line Q cannot be determined from the given information.

32. A remote-controlled vehicle travels at a constant speed around a testing track for a period of 12 hours. In those 12 hours, the vehicle covers 156 kilometers. In terms of kilometers per hour, at what rate was the vehicle traveling? Write your answer in the box below.

[   ] km/hr

33. The chart represents the number of households in selected cities that have subscribed to a new company's Internet service.

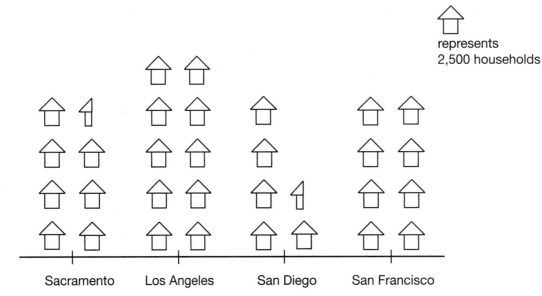

represents
2,500 households

Sacramento   Los Angeles   San Diego   San Francisco

Based on this data, how many households have subscribed to the service in San Diego?

a. 13,750

b. 15,000

c. 18,750

d. 20,000

34. A teacher would like to pick 2 students from her class of 30 (16 girls and 14 boys) to be class leaders. If she picks these students one at a time, without replacement, what is the probability that both class leaders are boys? Round your answer to the nearest whole percent.

a. 14%

b. 21%

c. 47%

d. 91%

35. If $\frac{3}{4}x = 12$, then $x =$

a. 9

b. $11\frac{1}{4}$

c. $12\frac{3}{4}$

d. 16

36. Which of the following lines is parallel to the line $y = \frac{2}{9}x - \frac{1}{5}$?

a. $y = -\frac{9}{2}x + 1$

b. $y = \frac{3}{4}x + 5$

c. $y = \frac{2}{9}x - 8$

d. $y = \frac{3}{4}x - \frac{1}{5}$

37. The figure below is a rectangle with a half-circle attached.

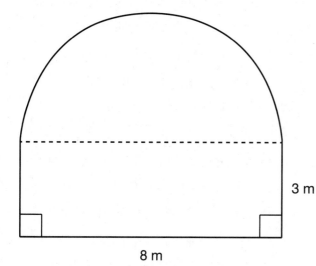

3 m

8 m

Given the indicated dimensions, what is the area of the region in terms of π?
a. 14 + 4π meters
b. 14 + 16π meters
c. 24 + 8π meters
d. 24 + 16π meters

38. What is the value of the expression $-3x + 10y$ when $x = -4$ and $y = -2$?
a. −34
b. 32
c. −8
d. 1

39. $-x^2(x + 1) - (x^3 + 4x^2) =$
a. $-6x^3 - x^2$
b. $-2x^3 - 5x^2$
c. $-2x^3 + 3x^2$
d. $-2x^3 + 4x^2 + 1$

40. Which of the following is the equation of the line that passes through the points (−8,1) and (4,9) in the x-y coordinate plane?
a. $y = \frac{2}{3}x + \frac{19}{3}$
b. $y = \frac{2}{3}x + 9$
c. $y = \frac{3}{2}x + \frac{21}{2}$
d. $y = \frac{3}{2}x + 13$

41. The figure below represents a composite part to be manufactured by fusing together two solid cubes.

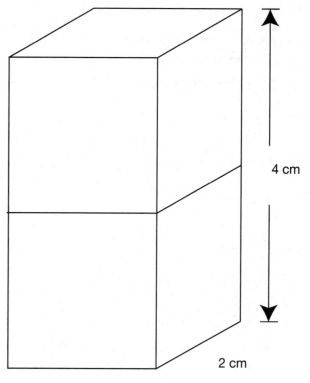

4 cm

2 cm

2 cm

If the cubes used are identical, what is the volume of the resulting part?
a. 4 cm³
b. 8 cm³
c. 16 cm³
d. 40 cm³

42. An IT consultant charges a company $75 an hour to analyze its current systems. Additionally, he charges a 3% project fee and a 1% telecommunications fee on the cost of the billed hours. If a project requires 20 hours for the consultant to complete, what will be the final amount charged to the company?

a. $1,515

b. $1,545

c. $1,560

d. $2,100

43. What expression is equivalent to the sum of $\frac{1}{2}x$ and $\frac{3}{4}x - 5$?

Select from the numbers and expressions listed below, and write the correct values into the boxes to find an equivalent expression.

$\frac{5}{4}x$

$\frac{2}{3}x$

$\frac{3}{4}$

$\frac{5}{2}$

$\frac{1}{2}x$

$\boxed{} - \boxed{}$

44. The ratio of full-time employees to part-time employees in a midsize law firm is 4:3. If there is a total of 20 full-time employees, how many part-time employees work at the firm?

a. 15

b. 19

c. 23

d. 27

45. What is the value of $\frac{x-5}{x^2+1}$ when $x = -3$?

a. $-\frac{3}{2}$

b. $-\frac{4}{5}$

c. $\frac{8}{5}$

d. 1

Answers and Explanations

1. **Choice b is correct.** If the first integer is x, then the second integer is $x + 1$ and their product is $x(x + 1) = x^2 + x = 42$.

   Choice **a** is incorrect. The second integer would be $x + 1$, but the product of both integers should be included in the equation.

   Choice **c** is incorrect. The second integer will be $x + 1$ and neither integer will have a 2 as part of its representation.

   Choice **d** is incorrect. While there are two integers, neither integer will be represented by $2x$.

2. **Choice c is correct.** The middle hash mark between one-half and one represents three-fourths. Point C is between this mark and the one-half mark, indicating it satisfies the given inequality.

   Choice **a** is incorrect. This point is much smaller than one-half. In fact, it is smaller than one-fourth.

   Choice **b** is incorrect. This point is between one-fourth and one-half.

   Choice **d** is incorrect. This point is larger than three-fourths.

3. **Choice c is correct.** Multiplying by 84 is the first step, and this is represented by 84S. The 1,065 is added to this term, leading to the model $P = 84S + 1,065$.

   Choice **a** is incorrect. This model represents multiplying the square footage by 1,149.

   Choice **b** is incorrect. This model represents multiplying by 84 as the last step and would produce different results.

   Choice **d** is incorrect. This model represents just adding 84 and then 1,065 to the square footage.

4.

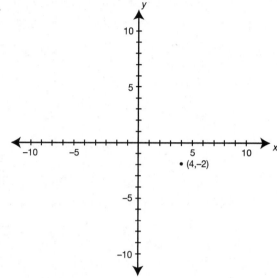

5. Choice b is correct. By the laws of exponents, $\frac{2^5}{2^2} = 2^{5-2} = 2^3$.

Choice **a** is incorrect. When subtracted according to the laws of exponents, there will be a final exponent larger than 1.

Choice **c** is incorrect. The laws of exponents require subtraction here instead of addition.

Choice **d** is incorrect. The laws of exponents require subtraction here instead of multiplication.

6. Choice c is correct. For each possible value of m, there is only one possible value of n.

Choice **a** is incorrect. After and including the indicated point, there are two possible values of n for each value of m.

Choice **b** is incorrect. After the indicated point, there are two possible values of n for each value of m.

Choice **d** is incorrect. At the indicated point, there are two possible values of n for that value of m.

7. Choice c is correct. $\frac{1}{4}(\frac{5}{2} - \frac{1}{6}) = \frac{1}{4}(\frac{15}{6} - \frac{1}{6}) = \frac{1}{4}(\frac{14}{6}) = \frac{7}{12}$.

Choice **a** is incorrect. Denominators are never subtracted when subtracting two fractions.

Choice **b** is incorrect. When rewriting the first fraction with the common denominator of 6, the numerator must also be multiplied by 2.

Choice **d** is incorrect. Parentheses indicate multiplication, not addition. Further, addition of fractions doesn't involve adding the denominators.

8. Choice a is correct. Dividing both sides by three shows that $x - 5 = 1$.

Choice **b** is incorrect. Multiplying the expressions on the left side yields $3x - 15 = 3$, **not** $3x - 15 = 9$.

Choice **c** is incorrect. Dividing both sides by three shows that $x - 5 = 1$. This can be further reduced to $x = 6$, **not** $x = 5$.

Choice **d** is incorrect. Multiplying the expressions on the left side yields $3x - 15 = 3$. This can be further reduced to $3x = 18$, **not** $3x = 8$.

9. Choice a is correct. $f(-8) = -2(-8)^2 + 1 = -2(64) + 1 = -128 + 1 = -127$.

Choice **b** is incorrect. The exponent on the a indicates a should be squared, not multiplied by 2. Further, the result of this will be positive instead of negative.

Choice **c** is incorrect. The exponent on the a indicates a should be squared, not multiplied by 2.

Choice **d** is incorrect. The value of $(-8)^2$ is positive, not negative.

10. Choice c is correct. After subtracting $3x$ from both sides, the resulting inequality is $x - 9 < 1$. Adding 9 to both sides results in the final solution of $x < 10$.

Choice **a** is incorrect. Since the sign of $3x$ is positive, it should be subtracted from both sides. Similarly, in the next step, the 9 should be added to both sides since it is subtracted from $4x$.

Choice **b** is incorrect. After subtracting the $3x$ from both sides, the 9 should be added to both sides since it is subtracted from $4x$.

Choice **d** is incorrect. Since the sign of $3x$ is positive, it should be subtracted from both sides.

11. Choice b is correct. Using FOIL, $(x - 5)(2x + 1)$ $= 2x^2 + x - 10x - 5 = 2x^2 - 9x - 5$.

Choice **a** is incorrect. Using FOIL involves the multiplication of the inner terms instead of the addition of them.

Choice **c** is incorrect. This is the product of only the first two and the last two terms, but FOIL requires the product of the inner and outer terms be included.

Choice **d** is incorrect. While the first term is $2x^2$, the FOIL technique will add many more terms to the final product.

12. The correct answer is 9. Adding 10 to both sides yields the equation $x^2 - 14x + 45 = 0$. The left-hand side of the equation factors into $(x - 5)(x - 9)$, resulting in solutions of 5 and 9. Nine is, of course, the larger of the two solutions to the equation.

13. Choice c is correct. The graph crosses the x-axis at exactly two points, and the fact that all of the turning points are shown indicates it will not cross it again.

Choice **a** is incorrect. A graph with no x-intercepts does not cross the x-axis at any point.

Choice **b** is incorrect. A graph with only one x-intercept would cross the x-axis exactly once. This graph crosses the x-axis more than that.

Choice **d** is incorrect. A graph with infinitely many x-intercepts would have to curve back towards the x-axis and cross it in a regular pattern. That behavior is not indicated by this graph since all the turning points are shown.

14. The correct answer is $798.75. The student will spend $375 \times 2 = \$750$ on the two computers and $750 \times 0.065 = \$48.75$ on the tax: $\$750 + \$48.75 = \$798.75$

15. Choice b is correct. Dividing the number of people by the area yields $236.29 \approx 236.3$

Choice **a** is incorrect. The term *square miles* does not imply that the 86.8 must be squared. It is instead a unit of measure for area.

Choice **c** is incorrect. Since the final result will be people per square miles, taking the square root before dividing is not a needed step.

Choice **d** is incorrect. Although the area is measured in square miles, the values of the population and the area do not need to be squared.

16. Choice b is correct. $\frac{2}{x(x-1)} + \frac{1}{x-1} =$ $\frac{2}{x(x-1)} + \frac{x}{x(x-1)} = \frac{2+x}{x(x-1)}$.

Choice **a** is incorrect. The fractions must have a common denominator before they can be added and once they do, only the numerators are combined.

Choice **c** is incorrect. While the common denominator is $x(x-1)$, $\frac{1}{x-1} \neq \frac{x}{x(x-1)}$.

Choice **d** is incorrect. The x terms in the numerator and denominator are not factors and therefore cannot be cancelled.

17. Choice d is correct. The perimeter is the sum of all side lengths: $2 + 4 + 3 = 9$.

Choice **a** is incorrect. The area of the triangle is 3 square meters, not the perimeter.

Choices **b** and **c** are incorrect. The lengths of all sides must be added to find the perimeter, not just two of them.

18. Choice a is correct. $0.2 \times 24.36 - 0.15 \times 24.36 = 1.22$.

Choice **b** is incorrect. This represents a tip of 15%, not the difference between the two tips.

Choice **c** is incorrect. This represents a tip of 20%, not the difference between the two tips.

Choice **d** is incorrect. The *difference* refers to subtraction, not addition.

19. The scores are added to the dot plot by placing repeated dots over the value on the scale. The circled dots represent the four added students.

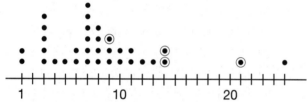

Number of Species Observed

20. Choice a is correct. Following the order of operations, the binomial must first be squared, the 3 distributed, and then like terms combined: $2x + 3(x - 2)^2 = 2x + 3(x^2 - 4x + 4) = 2x + 3x^2 - 12x + 12 = 3x^2 - 10x + 12$.

Choice **b** is incorrect. FOIL must be used to expand the squared term: $(x - 2)^2 \neq x^2 + 4$.

Choice **c** is incorrect. When simplifying, the 3 must multiply each term within the parentheses.

Choice **d** is incorrect. When simplifying, the 3 must multiply the constant term 4.

21. Choice d is correct. The bar representing distances from 1 up to 10 miles has a height of 3, meaning 3 students reported traveling less than 10 miles to campus.

Choice **a** is incorrect. The total number of students surveyed can be found by adding the frequencies. There were $3 + 6 + 4 + 2 + 1 = 16$ students surveyed.

Choice **b** is incorrect. While there was only one student who travels between 37 and 46 miles to campus, there is no way to tell the exact number of miles he travels using this graph.

Choice **c** is incorrect. The 10 and 19 on the horizontal axis represent distance, not frequency.

22. Choice a is correct. The slope of the line represents the unit rate. Using the start point $(0, 50)$ and the end point $(8, 250)$, the slope is $\frac{250 - 50}{8 - 0} = \frac{200}{8} = 25$.

Choice **b** is incorrect. The point 50 on the vertical axis represents the number of packages loaded at the beginning of the day.

Choice **c** is incorrect. There were 125 packages loaded a little after 3 hours, so it cannot be the hourly rate.

Choice **d** is incorrect. This cannot represent the hourly rate because there were 250 packages loaded after 8 hours.

23. Choice c is correct. Using the Pythagorean theorem, $7^2 + 4^2 = c^2$ where c is the length of the hypotenuse. Solving for c, $c^2 = 65$ and $c = \sqrt{65} \approx 8.1$.

Choice **a** is incorrect. The Pythagorean theorem requires that all of the terms be squared, not just the length of the hypotenuse.

Choice **b** is incorrect. When using the Pythagorean theorem $a^2 + b^2 = c^2$, a and b represent the lengths of the legs.

Choice **d** is incorrect. While the Pythagorean theorem does contain a sum, the terms are also squared.

24. Choice b is correct. The highest point in the graph is the maximum, which is 3. This occurs at $x = -1$. This is the vertex of the parabola. Choice **a** is incorrect. The highest point in the graph is the maximum, which is 3. This occurs at $x = -1$. This is the vertex of the parabola. Choice **c** is incorrect. The highest point in the graph is the maximum, not the minimum. Choice **d** is incorrect. The highest point in the graph is the maximum, which is 3. This occurs at $x = -1$. This is the vertex of the parabola.

25. Choice c is correct. If x is the number of miles between the two cities, then $\frac{2.5 \text{ in.}}{10 \text{ mi}} = \frac{7.1 \text{ in.}}{x \text{ mi}}$. Cross multiply and solve the resulting equation:

$2.5x = 71$

$x = \frac{71}{2.5} = 28.4$

Choice **a** is incorrect. This is a proportional relationship, so subtraction does not apply in general.
Choice **b** is incorrect. The final result must be in miles, but multiplying two values that are measured in inches will yield a result in square inches.
Choice **d** is incorrect. This would be the number of miles if each inch represented 10 miles.

26. The correct answer is $192,960.94. If x represents the revenue six months ago, then the equation $1.28x = 246,990$ must be true. Dividing both sides by 1.28 yields $x = 192,960.94$.

27. The correct answer is 2002. The largest difference is indicated by the bars representing the enrollment in one year having the largest discrepancy in height. In 2002, the program had an enrollment of approximately 34 male students and 8 female students. This is the largest height discrepancy shown on the graph.

28. Choice d is correct. Using the point-slope formula, the equation of the line must be

$y - 4 = \frac{4}{5}(x - (-8))$

$y - 4 = \frac{4}{5}(x + 8)$

$y - 4 = \frac{4}{5}x + \frac{32}{5}$

$y = \frac{4}{5}x + \frac{52}{5}$

To rewrite this in $Ax + By = C$ form, bring the x term to the left-hand side and multiply both sides of the equation by -5.
Choice **a** is incorrect. When rewriting the equation in $Ax + By = C$ form, the -5 must be distributed to all of the terms.
Choice **b** is incorrect. In the point-slope formula, the slope must be distributed to both the x term and the constant term. Further, when rewriting the equation in $Ax + By = C$ form, the -5 must be distributed to all of the terms.
Choice **c** is incorrect. In the point-slope formula, the slope must be distributed to both the x term and the constant term.

29. Choice c is correct. Using the first two points, $m = \frac{4 - 1}{2 - 0} = \frac{3}{2}$.
Choice **a** is incorrect. The slope formula is not $\frac{x_1 - y_1}{x_2 - y_2}$. In other words, the formula involves subtracting values from different points.
Choice **b** is incorrect. The change in y is represented in the numerator of the slope formula, not the denominator.
Choice **d** is incorrect. The slope formula is not $\frac{x_2 - y_2}{x_1 - y_1}$. In other words, the formula involves subtracting values from different points.

30. Choice a is correct. Both terms only share x as a factor. When this term is factored out, the resulting expression is $x(2x - 1)$.

Choice **b** is incorrect. The second term does not have a factor of 2, so $2x$ cannot be factored out of the polynomial.

Choice **c** is incorrect. These two expressions are the factors of the first term. Both are not factors of the second term.

Choice **d** is incorrect. The second term does not have a factor of 2, so $2x$ cannot be factored out of the polynomial. Further, $x - 2$ is not a factor of the polynomial.

31. Choice b is correct. The x-coordinate of the x-intercept of line P is -5, while the x-coordinate of the x-intercept of line Q is $\frac{2}{3}$.

Choice **a** is incorrect. The x-intercept of line P is 5 units away from the origin, while the x-intercept of line Q is less than 1 unit away.

Choice **c** is incorrect. The x-coordinate of the x-intercept of line P is negative.

Choice **d** is incorrect. The x-intercept of line Q can be found by letting $y = 0$ and solving for x.

32. The correct answer is 13.

$$\frac{156 \text{ km}}{12 \text{ hr}} = \frac{\frac{156}{12} \text{ km}}{\frac{12}{12} \text{ hr}} = \frac{13 \text{ km}}{1 \text{ hr}}$$

33. Choice a is correct. There are 5.5 house symbols used in the chart for San Diego, indicating $5.5 \times 2{,}500 = 13{,}750$ subscribing households in that city.

Choice **b** is incorrect. There are 5.5 house symbols, not 6 (which would result in 15,000 subscribing households).

Choice **c** is incorrect. This is the number of subscribing households in Sacramento.

Choice **d** is incorrect. This is the number of subscribing households in San Francisco.

34. Choice b is correct. Using the multiplication rule for probability, the probability is $\frac{14}{20} \times \frac{13}{29} \approx 0.21$ or 21%.

Choice **a** is incorrect. Since the students are being selected from the entire class, the denominator should be 30 and not 14.

Choice **c** is incorrect. This represents the probability that one girl is randomly selected. The question is asking for a compound probability of both selected leaders being boys.

Choice **d** is incorrect. The probability of an "and" event should use the multiplication rule, not the addition rule.

35. Choice d is correct. To isolate the x, multiply both sides of the equation by the reciprocal of $\frac{3}{4}$. Thus $x = \frac{4}{3}(12) = 16$.

Choice **a** is incorrect. To cancel out the $\frac{3}{4}$, both sides should be multiplied by the reciprocal instead of the original fraction.

Choice **b** is incorrect. Subtracting the fraction from both sides will not isolate the x since the x is multiplied by the fraction.

Choice **c** is incorrect. Adding the fraction to both sides will not isolate the x since the x is multiplied by the fraction.

36. Choice c is correct. This line has the same slope and therefore, by definition, is a line that is parallel to the original.

Choice **a** is incorrect. This line is perpendicular to the given line.

Choice **b** is incorrect. Although the y-intercept is the negative reciprocal of the y-intercept of the original line, this has no effect on whether the line is parallel or not.

Choice **d** is incorrect. Although the y-intercept is the same as the y-intercept of the original line, this has no effect on whether the line is parallel or not.

37. Choice c is correct. The area of the rectangular region is $8 \times 3 = 24$ square meters, while the area of half circle is $\frac{1}{2}\pi r^2 = \frac{1}{2}\pi(\frac{8}{2})^2 = \frac{1}{2}\pi(16) = 8\pi$.

Choice **a** is incorrect. This is the perimeter of the region.

Choice **b** is incorrect. This would be the perimeter of the region if the radius was 8 meters (this is the diameter) and if it was a full circle instead of a half circle.

Choice **d** is incorrect. The area of the half circle is half of the usual area formula πr^2. This is the area if the full circle was used.

38. Choice c is correct. $-3(-4) + 10(-2) = 12 - 20 = -8$.

Choice **a** is incorrect. This results from mixing up the substitution of x and y. The term multiplied by -3 should be -4.

Choice **b** is incorrect. The product of -3 and -4 is positive since both signs are negative.

Choice **d** is incorrect. When substituting values into the expression, the notation $-3x$ and $10y$ indicates multiplication and not addition.

39. Choice b is correct. $-x^2(x + 1) - (x^3 + 4x^2) = -x^3 - x^2 - x^3 - 4x^2 = -2x^3 - 5x^2$.

Choice **a** is incorrect. The terms within the second set of parentheses are not like terms and therefore cannot be combined.

Choice **c** is incorrect. The negative must be distributed to every term in the second set of parentheses.

Choice **d** is incorrect. The terms in front of both sets of parentheses must be distributed to every term within the parentheses.

40. Choice a is correct. The slope of the line is $m = \frac{9-1}{4-(-8)} = \frac{8}{12} = \frac{2}{3}$. Using this in the point slope formula along with the first point, the equation can be found with the following steps.

$$y - 1 = \frac{2}{3}(x - (-8))$$
$$y - 1 = \frac{2}{3}(x + 8)$$
$$y - 1 = \frac{2}{3}x + \frac{16}{3}$$
$$y = \frac{2}{3}x + \frac{19}{3}$$

Choice **b** is incorrect. In the point slope formula, the slope should multiply the entire term $(x - x_1)$.

Choice **c** is incorrect. The slope of the line should be the change in y divided by the change in x. Additionally, only one point should be used in the formula instead of an x value from one point and a y value from another.

Choice **d** is incorrect. The slope of the line should be $\frac{2}{3}$, the change in y divided by the change in x.

41. Choice c is correct. The volume of one of the cubes is $2 \times 2 \times 2 = 8 \text{ cm}^3$. Since the part consists of two cubes, the final volume is double this, or 16 cm^3.

Choice **a** is incorrect. This is the area of one face of one of the cubes.

Choice **b** is incorrect. This is the volume of only one of the cubes used to make the part.

Choice **d** is incorrect. This is the surface area of the final part.

42. Choice c is correct. $75 \times 20 = 1,500$, $0.01 \times 1,500 = 15$, and $0.03 \times 1,500 = 45$ for a total of $1,500 + 15 + 45 = 1,560$.

Choice **a** is incorrect. This includes only the telecommunications fee, but there is also a 3% project fee.

Choice **b** is incorrect. This includes only the project fee, but there is also a 1% telecommunications fee.

Choice **d** is incorrect. Three percent of a total is found by multiplying by 0.03, not 0.3. Similarly, one percent is found by multiplying by 0.01 instead of 0.1.

43. The correct answer is $\frac{5}{4}x - 5$.
$$\tfrac{1}{2}x + \tfrac{3}{4}x - 5 = \tfrac{2}{4}x + \tfrac{3}{4}x - 5 = \tfrac{5}{4}x - 5.$$

44. Choice a is correct. To maintain the ratio, the fraction of full-time employees to part-time employees must be equivalent to $\frac{4}{3}$. The number of full-time employees can be found by multiplying 4 by 5; therefore, the number of part-time employees can be found by multiplying 3 by 5 to get 15.

Choice **b** is incorrect. Although the difference between 20 and 4 is 16, it can't be used to find the final answer. Ratios work with a common multiplier, not a common sum.

Choice **c** is incorrect. This will not maintain the ratio, since it did not use a common multiplier.

Choice **d** is incorrect. This is approximately correct if the number of part-time employees was 20 instead of full-time employees.

45. Choice b is correct. $\frac{(-3) - 5}{(-3)^2 + 1} = \frac{-8}{10} = -\frac{4}{5}$.

Choice **a** is incorrect. The numerator of the fraction shows subtraction of 5 from x, not multiplication.

Choice **c** is incorrect. The value of $(-3)^2$ is 9, not 6.

Choice **d** is incorrect. The value of $(-3)^2$ is 9, not -9.

7 ▶ GED® REASONING THROUGH LANGUAGE ARTS TEST 2

This practice test is modeled on the format, content, and timing of the official GED® Reasoning through Language Arts test.

Part I

Like the official exam, this section presents a series of questions that assess your ability to read, write, edit, and understand standard written English. You'll be asked to answer questions based on informational and literary reading passages. Refer to the passages as often as necessary when answering the questions.

Work carefully, but do not spend too much time on any one question. Be sure you answer every question.

Set a timer for 95 minutes (1 hour and 35 minutes), and try to take this test uninterrupted, under quiet conditions.

Part II

The official GED® Reasoning through Language Arts test also includes an Extended Response question—an essay question. Set a timer for 45 minutes and try to read the given passage and brainstorm, write, and proofread your essay uninterrupted, under quiet conditions

Complete answer explanations for every test question and sample essays at different scoring levels follow the exam. Good luck!

PART I

48 total questions
95 minutes to complete

Please use the following to answer questions 1–8.

This excerpt is from the Declaration of Independence.

1   When in the Course of human events, it becomes necessary for one people to dissolve the political bands which have connected them with another, and to assume among the powers of the earth, the separate and equal station to which the Laws of Nature and of Nature's God entitle them, a decent respect to the opinions of mankind requires that they should declare the causes which impel them to the separation.

2   We hold these truths to be self-evident, that all men are created equal, that they are endowed by their Creator with certain unalienable Rights, that among these are Life, Liberty and the pursuit of Happiness.—That to secure these rights, Governments are instituted among Men, deriving their just powers from the consent of the governed,—That whenever any Form of Government becomes destructive of these ends, it is the Right of the People to alter or to abolish it, and to institute new Government, laying its foundation on such principles and organizing its powers in such form, as to them shall seem most likely to effect their Safety and Happiness. Prudence, indeed, will dictate that Governments long established should not be changed for light and transient causes; and accordingly all experience hath shewn, that mankind are more disposed to suffer, while evils are sufferable, than to right themselves by abolishing the forms to which they are accustomed. But when a long train of abuses and usurpations, pursuing invariably the same Object evinces a design to reduce them under absolute Despotism, it is their right, it is their duty, to throw off such Government, and to provide new Guards for their future security.—Such has been the patient sufferance of these Colonies; and such is now the necessity which constrains them to alter their former Systems of Government. The history of the present King of Great Britain is a history of repeated injuries and usurpations, all having in direct object the establishment of an absolute Tyranny over these States. To prove this, let Facts be submitted to a candid world.

3   He has refused his Assent to Laws, the most wholesome and necessary for the public good. He has forbidden his Governors to pass Laws of immediate and pressing importance, unless suspended in their operation till his Assent should be obtained; and when so suspended, he has utterly neglected to attend to them. He has refused to pass other Laws for the accommodation of large districts of people, unless those people would relinquish the right of Representation in the Legislature, a right inestimable to them and formidable to tyrants only. He has called together legislative bodies at places unusual, uncomfortable, and distant from the depository of their public Records, for the sole purpose of fatiguing them into compliance with his measures. He has dissolved Representative Houses repeatedly, for opposing with manly firmness his invasions on the rights of the people.

1. Write your answers in the boxes below.

Based on the excerpt, "he has dissolved Representative Houses repeatedly" is an example of an injustice committed by the ⬚ King ⬚ of ⬚ Great Britain ⬚.

2. Paragraph 3 can be summed up as
  a. a list of laws for life in the colonies written by the King of Great Britain
  b. a list of laws created for the newly independent United States of America
  c. a list praising the many good acts carried out by the King of Great Britain
  d. a list of injustices committed by the King of Great Britain against the colonies

3. Which of the following quotations expresses the Declaration's main idea that the American colonies want independence from Great Britain?
  a. "We hold these truths to be self-evident, that all men are created equal"
  b. "it becomes necessary for one people to dissolve the political bands which have connected them with another"
  c. "He has refused to pass other Laws for the accommodation of large districts of people"
  d. "they are endowed by their Creator with certain unalienable Rights"

4. Which of the following phrases builds on the argument that governments should get their powers from the consent of the governed?
  a. "he has refused his Assent to Laws, the most wholesome and necessary for the public good"
  b. "whenever any Form of Government becomes destructive of these ends, it is the Right of the People to alter or to abolish it"
  c. "he has dissolved Representative Houses repeatedly"
  d. "he has called together legislative bodies at places unusual, uncomfortable, and distant from the depository of their public Records"

5. What evidence supports the claim that the King of Great Britain has wronged the colonists?
  a. a list of court rulings against the King in favor of the colonists
  b. a list of all his wrongdoings provided by other world leaders
  c. a list of the King's wrongdoings
  d. a list of names of colonists whom have been personally wronged

6. How would you evaluate the list of grievances given to support the claim that the King of England wronged the colonists?
  a. relevant and sufficient
  b. relevant and insufficient
  c. irrelevant and sufficient
  d. irrelevant and insufficient

7. Which of the following claims is supported by evidence?
  a. All men are equal.
  b. The King of Great Britain is a tyrannical leader.
  c. All men have certain unalienable rights.
  d. Governments should be controlled by the governed.

8. The phrase "to secure these rights, Governments are instituted among Men, deriving their just powers from the consent of the governed" is an example of which of the following?
   a. an explanation
   b. factual evidence
   c. valid reasoning
   d. false reasoning

Please use the following to answer questions 9–12.

This excerpt is from *This Side of Paradise*, by F. Scott Fitzgerald.

1   Amory Blaine inherited from his mother every trait, except the stray inexpressible few, that made him worthwhile. His father, an ineffectual, inarticulate man with a taste for Byron and a habit of drowsing over the *Encyclopædia Britannica*, grew wealthy at thirty through the death of two elder brothers, successful Chicago brokers, and in the first flush of feeling that the world was his, went to Bar Harbor and met Beatrice O'Hara. In consequence, Stephen Blaine handed down to posterity his height of just under six feet and his tendency to waver at crucial moments, these two abstractions appearing in his son Amory. For many years he hovered in the background of his family's life, an unassertive figure with a face half-obliterated by lifeless, silky hair, continually occupied in "taking care" of his wife, continually harassed by the idea that he didn't and couldn't understand her.

2   But Beatrice Blaine! There was a woman! Early pictures taken on her father's estate at Lake Geneva, Wisconsin, or in Rome at the Sacred Heart Convent—an educational extravagance that in her youth was only for the daughters of the exceptionally wealthy—showed the exquisite delicacy of her features, the consummate art and simplicity of her clothes. A brilliant education she had—her youth passed in renaissance glory, she was versed in the latest gossip of the Older Roman Families; known by name as a fabulously wealthy American girl to Cardinal Vitori and Queen Margherita and more subtle celebrities that one must have had some culture even to have heard of. She learned in England to prefer whiskey and soda to wine, and her small talk was broadened in two senses during a winter in Vienna. All in all Beatrice O'Hara absorbed the sort of education that will be quite impossible ever again; a tutelage measured by the number of things and people one could be contemptuous of and charming about; a culture rich in all arts and traditions, barren of all ideas, in the last of those days when the great gardener clipped the inferior roses to produce one perfect bud.

3   In her less important moments she returned to America, met Stephen Blaine and married him— this almost entirely because she was a little bit weary, a little bit sad. Her only child was carried through a tiresome season and brought into the world on a spring day in ninety-six.

4   When Amory was five he was already a delightful companion for her. He was an auburn-haired boy, with great, handsome eyes which he would grow up to in time, a facile imaginative mind

and a taste for fancy dress. From his fourth to his tenth year he *did* the country with his mother in her father's private car, from Coronado, where his mother became so bored that she had a nervous breakdown in a fashionable hotel, down to Mexico City, where she took a mild, almost epidemic consumption. This trouble pleased her, and later she made use of it as an intrinsic part of her atmosphere—especially after several astounding bracers.

5   So, while more or less fortunate little rich boys were defying governesses on the beach at Newport, or being spanked or tutored or read to from "Do and Dare," or "Frank on the Mississippi," Amory was biting acquiescent bell-boys in the Waldorf, outgrowing a natural repugnance to chamber music and symphonies, and deriving a highly specialized education from his mother.

9. The first paragraph is
a. an argument
b. dialogue
c. a description of settings
d. a description of characters

10. In the second paragraph of the excerpt from *This Side of Paradise*, which of the following words would change the tone of the last sentence if it replaced **rich**?
a. abounding
b. heavy
c. lacking
d. plentiful

11. In paragraph 3, what does the word **tiresome** mean?
a. joyous
b. wearisome
c. angry
d. abusive

12. What is the main idea of the last paragraph?
a. Amory loves symphonies.
b. Amory has a taste for adventure.
c. Amory is like other rich boys.
d. Amory is not like other rich boys his age.

Please use the following passage to answer questions 13–14.

This excerpt is from a speech by George W. Bush delivered on March 19, 2008.

1   Operation Iraqi Freedom was a remarkable display of military effectiveness. Forces from the UK, Australia, Poland, and other allies joined our troops in the initial operations. As they advanced, our troops fought their way through sandstorms so intense that they blackened the daytime sky. Our troops engaged in pitched battles with Fedayeen Saddam, death squads acting on the orders of Saddam Hussein that obeyed neither the conventions of war nor the dictates of conscience. These death squads hid in schools, and they hid in hospitals, hoping to draw fire against Iraqi civilians. They used women and children as human shields. They stopped at nothing in their efforts to prevent us from prevailing, but they couldn't stop the coalition advance.

2   Aided by the most effective and precise air campaign in history, coalition forces raced across 350 miles of enemy territory, destroying Republican Guard divisions, pushing through the Karbala Gap, capturing Saddam International Airport, and liberating Baghdad in less than one month. . . .

3   Because we acted, Saddam Hussein no longer fills fields with the remains of innocent men, women, and children. . . . Because we acted, Saddam's regime is no longer invading its neighbors or attacking them with chemical weapons and ballistic missiles.

13. Based on this speech excerpt about Operation Iraqi Freedom, take the following list of events and write them in the correct order of occurrence on the lines below.

coalition forces cross 350 miles of enemy territory
Operation Iraqi Freedom is launched
Baghdad is liberated

1. _____

2. _____

3. _____

14. In the excerpt from Bush's speech, what does the Middle Eastern setting, comprising "sandstorms so intense that they blackened the daytime sky," add to the first paragraph, which mentions troops fighting death squads?
a. a heightened sense of beauty
b. a heightened sense of contentment
c. a heightened sense of danger
d. a decreased sense of danger

Please use the following to answer questions 15–20.

The 1976 Democratic National Convention Keynote Address, delivered by Barbara Jordan

1   Throughout—throughout our history, when people have looked for new ways to solve their problems and to uphold the principles of this nation, many times they have turned to political parties. They have often turned to the Democratic Party. What is it? What is it about the Democratic Party that makes it the instrument the people use when they search for ways to shape their future? Well, I believe the answer to that question lies in our concept of governing. Our concept of governing is derived from our view of people. It is a concept deeply rooted in a set of beliefs firmly etched in the national conscience of all of us.

2   Now, what are these beliefs? First, we believe in equality for all and privileges for none. This is a belief—this is a belief that each American, regardless of background, has equal standing in the public forum—all of us. Because—because we believe this idea so firmly, we are an inclusive rather than an exclusive party. Let everybody come.

3   I think it no accident that most of those immigrating to America in the 19th century identified with the Democratic Party. We are a heterogeneous party made up of Americans of diverse backgrounds. We believe that the people are the source of all governmental power, that the authority of the people is to be extended, not restricted.

4   This—this can be accomplished only by providing each citizen with every opportunity to participate in the management of the government. They must have that, we believe. We believe that the government which represents the authority of all the people, not just one interest group, but all the people, has an obligation to actively—actively—seek to remove those obstacles which would block individual achievement—obstacles emanating from race, sex, economic condition. The government must remove them, seek to remove them.

5   We are a party—we are a party of innovation. We do not reject our traditions, but we are willing to adapt to changing circumstances, when change we must. We are willing to suffer the discomfort of change in order to achieve a better future. We have a positive vision of the future founded on the belief that the gap between the promise and reality of America can one day be finally closed. We believe that.

6   This, my friends is the bedrock of our concept of governing. This is a part of the reason why Americans have turned to the Democratic Party. These are the foundations upon which a national community can be built. Let all understand that these guiding principles cannot be discarded for short-term political gains. They represent what this country is all about. They are indigenous to the American idea. And these are principles which are not negotiable.

15. What is the main idea of the second paragraph?

   a. Every citizen is welcomed by the Democratic Party.

   b. Immigrants have often chosen to support the Democratic Party.

   c. Barbara Jordan approves of the Democratic Party.

   d. The Democratic Party accepts only the best of the best.

16. Which of the following statements supports Barbara Jordan's belief that the government must represent all people?

   a. "Because we believe this idea so firmly, we are an inclusive rather than an exclusive party."

   b. "This can be accomplished only by providing each citizen with every opportunity to participate in the management of the government."

   c. "We do not reject our traditions, but we are willing to adapt to changing circumstances, when change we must."

   d. "These are the foundations upon which a national community can be built."

17. Based on the text, which of the following scenarios would Barbara Jordan most likely support?

   a. A Democratic Party presidential candidate holding a private dinner for a select group of people.

   b. Members of a political party focusing on recruiting only those who can donate large amounts of money.

   c. A Democratic candidate running for the state senate.

   d. A local Democratic Party group holding an open forum for members of the community.

18. Which of the following statements best summarizes the main idea of the address?

   a. Many people have chosen to support the Democratic Party over the years.

   b. The values of the Democratic Party represent American ideals.

   c. The Democratic Party has evolved when necessary.

   d. all of the above

19. In which of the following phrases does Barbara Jordan criticize the Democratic Party?

   a. When she calls it "the instrument the people use when they search for ways to shape their future."

   b. When she says that those in the party "believe in equality for all and privileges for none."

   c. When she says that it is a "party of innovation."

   d. none of the above

20. From which statement can you infer that Barbara Jordan believes the government should enact laws against race and gender discrimination?

   a. "What is it about the Democratic Party that makes it the instrument the people use when they search for ways to shape their future?"

   b. "We believe that the people are the source of all governmental power; that the authority of the people is to be extended, not restricted."

   c. "We have a positive vision of the future founded on the belief that the gap between the promise and reality of America can one day be finally closed."

   d. "We believe that the government which represents the authority of all the people... has an obligation to actively—*actively*—seek to remove those obstacles which would block individual achievement."

Please use the following to answer questions 21–25.

To: All Staff
From: Allison Lewis, Manager
Date: July 15, 2014
Subject: Piles of Books

It has come to our attention that there have been piles of books that (1) on the floor in the fiction, cooking, and teen sections of the bookstore by the end of every day. It has gotten so bad that some customers are complaining that they are in the way of a large portion of shelved books. (2), we are introducing a new policy that mandates employees check their assigned sections for piles every hour and that employees then shelf any books found out of place.

(3) make sure to follow this procedure regularly. Even piles of a few books can cause unnecessary obstacles for customers.

Thank you for (4) cooperation!

(5)

Allison Lewis

21. Choose the correct form of **accumulate** for (1).
   a. accumulate
   b. accumulates
   c. accumulated
   d. will accumulate

22. Which word fits correctly in (2)?
   a. Therefore
   b. However
   c. Meanwhile
   d. Instead

23. Which word fits correctly in (3)?
   a. please
   b. pleases
   c. Please
   d. Pleases

24. Which word fits correctly in (4)?
   a. my
   b. your
   c. their
   d. her

25. Which word fits correctly in (5)?
   a. Best.
   b. Best!
   c. Best'
   d. Best,

Please use the following to answer questions 26–29.

This excerpt is from *The Fall of the House of Usher*, by Edgar Allan Poe.

During the whole of a dull, dark, and soundless day in the autumn of the year, when the clouds hung oppressively low in the heavens, I had been passing alone, on horseback, through a singularly dreary tract of country; and at length found myself, as the shades of the evening drew on, within view of the melancholy House of Usher. I know not how it was; but, with the first glimpse of the building, a sense of insufferable gloom pervaded my spirit. I say insufferable; for the feeling was unrelieved by any of that half-pleasurable, because poetic, sentiment, with which the mind usually receives even the sternest natural images of the desolate or terrible. I looked upon the scene before me—upon the mere house, and the simple landscape features of the domain—upon the bleak walls—upon the vacant eye-like windows—upon a few rank sedges—and upon a few white trunks of decayed trees—with an utter depression of soul which I can compare to no earthly sensation more properly than to the after-dream of the reveler upon opium—the bitter lapse into everyday life—the hideous dropping off of the veil. There was an iciness, a sinking, a sickening of the heart—an unredeemed dreariness of thought which no goading of the imagination could torture into aught of the sublime. What was it—I paused to think—what was it that so unnerved me in the contemplation of the House of Usher? It was a mystery all insoluble; nor could I grapple with the shadowy fancies that crowded upon me as I pondered. I was forced to fall back upon the unsatisfactory conclusion that while, beyond doubt, there are combinations of very simple natural objects which have the power of thus affecting us, still the analysis of this power lies among considerations beyond our depth. It was possible, I reflected, that a mere different arrangement of the particulars of the scene, of the details of the picture, would be sufficient to modify, or perhaps to annihilate its capacity for sorrowful impression; and, acting upon this idea, I reined my horse to the precipitous brink of a black and lurid tarn that lay in unruffled luster by the dwelling, and gazed down—but with a shudder even more thrilling than before—upon the remodeled and inverted images of the gray sedge, and the ghastly tree stems, and the vacant and eye-like windows.

26. The words **sorrowful, sickening, melancholy,** and **dreary** serve to give the excerpt a
a. joyous tone.
b. foreboding tone.
c. courageous tone.
d. silly tone.

27. Based on this excerpt, take the following list of events and write them in the correct order of occurrence on the lines below
rides through the countryside
feels a sense of gloom
reins his horse near the house
comes to the House of Usher
1. _____
2. _____
3. _____
4. _____

28. The phrase "vacant eye-like windows" is an example of
   a. alliteration.
   b. hyperbole
   c. onomatopoeia.
   d. personification.

29. Replacing "insufferable gloom" with which of the following words changes the tone of the phrase "a sense of insufferable gloom pervaded my spirit"?
   a. melancholy
   b. joy
   c. sadness
   d. despair

Please use the following to answer questions 30–34.

From the personal memoirs of Ulysses S. Grant, LXX

1   Things began to quiet down, and as the certainty that there would be no more armed resistance became clearer, the troops in North Carolina and Virginia were ordered to march immediately to the capital, and go into camp there until mustered out. Suitable garrisons were left at the prominent places throughout the South to insure obedience to the laws that might be enacted for the government of the several States, and to insure security to the lives and property of all classes. I do not know how far this was necessary, but I deemed it necessary, at that time, that such a course should be pursued. I think now that these garrisons were continued after they ceased to be absolutely required; but it is not to be expected that such a rebellion as was fought between the sections from 1861 to 1865 could terminate without leaving many serious apprehensions in the mind of the people as to what should be done.

2   Sherman marched his troops from Goldsboro, up to Manchester, on the south side of the James River, opposite Richmond, and there put them in camp, while he went back to Savannah to see what the situation was there.

3   It was during this trip that the last outrage was committed upon him. Halleck had been sent to Richmond to command Virginia, and had issued orders prohibiting even Sherman's own troops from obeying his, Sherman's, orders. Sherman met the papers on his return, containing this order of Halleck, and very justly felt indignant at the outrage. On his arrival at Fortress Monroe returning from Savannah, Sherman received an invitation from Halleck to come to Richmond and be his guest. This he indignantly refused, and informed Halleck, furthermore, that he had seen his order. He also stated that he was coming up to take command of his troops, and as he marched through it would probably be as well for Halleck not to show himself, because he (Sherman) would not be responsible for what some rash person might do through indignation for the treatment he had received. Very soon after that, Sherman received orders from me to proceed to Washington City, and to go into camp on the south side of the city pending the mustering-out of the troops.

continues

4   The march of Sherman's army from Atlanta to the sea and north to Goldsboro, while it was not accompanied with the danger that was anticipated, yet was magnificent in its results, and equally magnificent in the way it was conducted. It had an important bearing, in various ways, upon the great object we had in view, that of closing the war. All the States east of the Mississippi River up to the State of Georgia, had felt the hardships of the war. Georgia, and South Carolina, and almost all of North Carolina, up to this time, had been exempt from invasion by the Northern armies, except upon their immediate sea coasts. Their newspapers had given such an account of Confederate success, that the people who remained at home had been convinced that the Yankees had been whipped from first to last, and driven from pillar to post, and that now they could hardly be holding out for any other purpose than to find a way out of the war with honor to themselves.

5   Even during this march of Sherman's the newspapers in his front were proclaiming daily that his army was nothing better than a mob of men who were frightened out of their wits and hastening, panic-stricken, to try to get under the cover of our navy for protection against the Southern people. As the army was seen marching on triumphantly, however, the minds of the people became disabused and they saw the true state of affairs. In turn they became disheartened, and would have been glad to submit without compromise.

30. Why were garrisons left in the South?
  a. Violence was still prevalent.
  b. The Civil War is brewing.
  c. Grant thought it was necessary at the time.
  d. Sherman made the order.

31. What historical event can you infer was drawing to a close at the time this was written?

32. How would the tone of the passage change if the word **outrage** was replaced with **injustice** in the sentence, "It was during this trip that the last outrage was committed upon him"?
  a. It would support Grant's disapproval of Sherman's March.
  b. It would strengthen Grant's support of Sherman's March as necessary.
  c. It would increase Grant's list of criticisms of Sherman.
  d. It would confirm Grant's claim that the Confederates believed they had succeeded.

33. Which of the following quotations reveals Grant's disagreement with the Confederate viewpoint after the Civil War?
  a. "[B]ut it is not to be expected that such a rebellion as was fought between the sections from 1861 to 1865 could terminate without leaving many serious apprehensions in the mind of the people as to what should be done."
  b. "It was during this trip that the last outrage was committed upon him."
  c. "Their newspapers had given such an account of Confederate success, that the people who remained at home had been convinced that the Yankees had been whipped from first to last, and driven from pillar to post…"
  d. "In turn they became disheartened, and would have been glad to submit without comprise."

34. Put the events in chronological order.

    A—Sherman's men were ordered not to listen to him

    B—the Confederates "saw the true state of affairs"

    C—the Civil War

    D—Sherman's March

a. C, A, D, B

b. C, A, B, D

c. A, C, D, B

d. A, C, B, D

35. What does the word **triumphantly** mean in the following sentence: "As the army was seen marching on triumphantly, however, the minds of the people became disabused and they saw the true state of affairs"?

a. sheepishly

b. victoriously

c. angrily

d. defeatedly

Please use the following to answer questions 36–39.

"Watching Volcanoes," by Millie Ceron

1 Scientists who watch volcanoes bear a great responsibility. It is up to them to alert the public when they think that a volcano is about to erupt. But it is not always easy to tell when an eruption is imminent. I know, because my whole career as a scientist has been spent studying volcanoes. I've learned that predicting eruptions is a very inexact science. There often are certain warning signs, but they can be very difficult to interpret. What should you do when you see them? You certainly don't want to cause a panic or tell people to flee unless it is really necessary, yet you also don't want to underestimate the danger. Scientists like me usually try to steer a path between these two extremes. But we also try to err on the side of caution: It's always better to be safe than sorry!

2 What are the signs that an eruption may soon occur? The main ones are earthquakes beneath the mountain, bulges in the sides of the mountain, and the escape of volcanic gases.

3 **Watching for Earthquakes.** Earthquakes often occur for some time before an eruption of *magma* (molten rock) and volcanic gases force their way up through underground channels. Sometimes the force causes a continuous shaking called *tremor*. To record earthquakes, a device called a *seismometer* is used. Four to eight seismometers are typically installed close to or on the mountain. Only by being very close to the volcano can seismometers pick up the tiny earthquakes that may be the first sign that a volcano may erupt.

4 When an eruption is just about to take place, earthquakes often occur in "swarms." Scientists monitor these swarms around the clock. The reason is that variations in the type and strength of the quakes are often the best indication that an eruption is just about to happen.

continues

5   **Watching for Bulges in the Sides of the Mountain.** During the months or weeks prior to an eruption, magma rises inside a volcano. The pressure created by this magma often causes the sides of the mountain to "tilt." Sometimes it even causes visible bulges in the mountainside. To monitor these bulges, scientists use a sensitive instrument called a *tiltmeter*. Today they also use satellite-based technology to take precise measurements. By these methods scientists discovered that in the months before Mount Saint Helens erupted in 1982, one side of the mountain swelled by more than 100 meters.

6   **Watching for Volcanic Gases.** The gases dissolved in magma provide the main force in a volcanic eruption. Consequently, it is important to find out whether any gases are present and if so, what kinds of gases. However, collecting these gases is not easy. They are often found escaping from vents high up on the mountain or in the crater. Scientists may visit the vents themselves and collect the gases in bottles for analysis in the laboratory. But such visits are dangerous: the climb can be difficult, the gases themselves can be hazardous to breathe, and there is always the danger of an eruption. Scientists may also place automated gas monitors near the vents, but these devices are often destroyed by the acidic gases. Another way to collect the gases is by flying through the gas clouds above the volcano in specially equipped airplanes. But it is difficult to obtain good samples by this method, and bad weather can keep planes on the ground just when monitoring is most urgent. However, when scientists succeed in collecting volcanic gases, they can tell a lot about how a volcano works and what effects it may have on Earth's climate and environment.

"The 1992 Eruptions at Mt. Spurr, Alaska," by Ling Chen

1   Mt. Spurr is a small volcano located 80 miles west of Anchorage, Alaska. In August 1991, eight seismographs placed on the mountain began recording many very small earthquakes. Airborne gas sampling was used to check for the presence of volcanic gases.

2   In early June 1992, earthquake activity increased. Then on June 27 a "swarm" of earthquakes suggested magma moving at shallow depth. As the earthquakes grew stronger, scientists broadcast a warning that an eruption might be about to occur. Later that day, pilots reported ash plumes erupting from the mountain.

3   After the June 27 eruption, earthquake activity declined rapidly to its lowest level in months. Scientists concluded that the danger of further eruptions was low. During July, bad weather often grounded pilots, preventing airborne observation of the volcano and collection of volcanic gas samples. Weeks passed during which little occurred at the mountain.

4   On August 18, however, a pilot suddenly reported a huge ash plume above the crater. Scientists immediately broadcast a warning that an eruption was occurring.

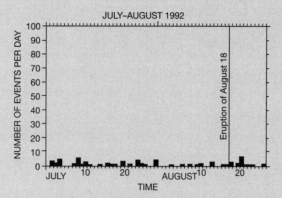

JULY–AUGUST 1992

This graph shows earthquake activity recorded at Mt. Spurr before the eruption of August 18. The eruption ended after a few hours, and earthquake activity remained low, so the likelihood of further eruptions again seemed to be low.

5   That fall, however, earthquake activity increased once again beneath Mt. Spurr. "Swarms" of strong earthquakes were recorded in both early October and early November. Each time, scientists issued warnings that "a large eruption is likely within the next 24 to 48 hours." However, no eruption took place. When another "swarm" of earthquakes occurred in December, scientists decided not to issue an eruption warning.

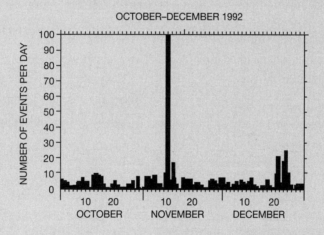

OCTOBER–DECEMBER 1992

This graph shows earthquake activity recorded at Mt. Spurr from October through December 1992.

36. What is the main purpose of paragraph 3 in "Watching for Volcanoes"?
   a. to describe how scientists monitor earthquakes to predict volcanic eruptions
   b. to define scientific terms, such as magma, tremor, and swarms
   c. to explain how scientists use seismometers to record earthquakes
   d. to show how earthquakes cause volcanic gases to escape

37. Which of the following best summarizes "Watching Volcanoes"?
   a. Scientists monitor bulges in the sides of mountains with tiltmeters because bulges may indicate a volcanic eruption will soon occur.
   b. Scientists should not visit vents on mountaintops to collect and analyze gases because it is extremely dangerous.
   c. Scientists were concerned enough about a small volcano near Anchorage, Alaska, to issue a warning it might erupt in June, 1992.
   d. Scientists who watch volcanoes monitor signs of eruption by various means to ensure the public is aware of possible dangers.

38. How are "Watching Volcanoes" and "The 1992 Eruptions at Mt. Spurr, Alaska" different?
   a. "Watching Volcanoes" focuses on a particular eruption, and "The 1992 Eruptions at Mt. Spurr, Alaska" is about volcanoes in general.
   b. "Watching Volcanoes" is a personal account, and "The 1992 Eruptions at Mt. Spurr, Alaska" is an objective report.
   c. "Watching Volcanoes" discusses seismometers, and "The 1992 Eruptions at Mt. Spurr, Alaska" does not.
   d. "Watching Volcanoes" is a diary entry, and "The 1992 Eruptions at Mt. Spurr, Alaska" is a newspaper article.

39. Considering that there were never more than 10 events in a single day from July to August 1992, why might the first graph allot space for as many as 100 events?
   a. to illustrate how Mt. Spurr was not capable of erupting
   b. to forecast a major rise of events in September
   c. to contrast the dramatic number of events in November on the second graph
   d. because this is the standard graph that all volcano-watching scientists use

Please use the following to answer questions 40–43.

This excerpt is from *Pride and Prejudice*, by Jane Austen.

1   It is a truth universally acknowledged that a single man in possession of a good fortune must be in want of a wife.

2   However little known the feelings or views of such a man may be on his first entering a neighbourhood, this truth is so well fixed in the minds of the surrounding families, that he is considered as the rightful property of someone or other of their daughters.

3   "My dear Mr. Bennet," said his lady to him one day, "have you heard that Netherfield Park is let at last?"

4   Mr. Bennet replied that he had not.

5   "But it is," returned she; "for Mrs. Long has just been here, and she told me all about it."

6   Mr. Bennet made no answer.

7   "Do not you want to know who has taken it?" cried his wife, impatiently.

8   "You want to tell me, and I have no objection to hearing it."

9   This was invitation enough.

10   "Why, my dear, you must know, Mrs. Long says that Netherfield is taken by a young man of large fortune from the north of England; that he came down on Monday in a chaise and four to see the place, and was so much delighted with it that he agreed with Mr. Morris immediately; that he is to take possession before Michaelmas, and some of his servants are to be in the house by the end of next week."

11   'What is his name?'

12   "Bingley."

13   "Is he married or single?"

14   "Oh, single, my dear, to be sure! A single man of large fortune; four or five thousand a year. What a fine thing for our girls!"

15   "How so? How can it affect them?"

16   "My dear Mr. Bennet,' replied his wife, 'how can you be so tiresome? You must know that I am thinking of his marrying one of them."

17   "Is that his design in settling here?"

18   "Design? Nonsense, how can you talk so! But it is very likely that hemay fall in love with one of them, and therefore you must visit him as soon as he comes."

19   "I see no occasion for that. You and the girls may go, or you may send them by themselves, which perhaps will be still better, for, as you are as handsome as any of them, Mr. Bingley might like you the best of the party."

20   "My dear, you flatter me. I certainly *have* had my share of beauty, but I do not pretend to be anything extraordinary now. When a woman has five grown-up daughters, she ought to give over thinking of her own beauty."

21   "In such cases, a woman has not often much beauty to think of."

continues

22 "But, my dear, you must indeed go and see Mr. Bingley when he comes into the neighbourhood."

23 "It is more than I engage for, I assure you."

24 "But consider your daughters. Only think what an establishment it would be for one of them. Sir William and Lady Lucas are determined to go, merely on that account; for in general, you know, they visit no newcomers. Indeed you must go, for it will be impossible for *us* to visit him, if you do not."

25 "You are over scrupulous, surely. I daresay Mr. Bingley will be very glad to see you; and I will send a few lines by you to assure him of my hearty consent to his marrying whichever he chooses of the girls; though I must throw in a good word for my little Lizzy."

26 "I desire you will do no such thing. Lizzy is not a bit better than the others: and I am sure she is not half so handsome as Jane, nor half so good-humoured as Lydia. But you are always giving *her* the preference."

27 "They have none of them much to recommend them,' replied he: 'they are all silly and ignorant like other girls; but Lizzy has something more of quickness than her sisters."

28 "Mr. Bennet, how can you abuse your own children in such a way? You take delight in vexing me. You have no compassion on my poor nerves."

29 "You mistake me, my dear. I have a high respect for your nerves. They are my old friends. I have heard you mention them with consideration these twenty years at least."

30 "Ah, you do not know what I suffer."

31 "But I hope you will get over it, and live to see many young men of four thousand a year come into the neighbourhood."

32 "It will be no use to us, if twenty such should come, since you will not visit them."

33 "Depend upon it, my dear, that when there are twenty, I will visit them all."

34 Mr. Bennet was so odd a mixture of quick parts, sarcastic humour, reserve, and caprice, that the experience of three-and-twenty years had been insufficient to make his wife understand his character. *Her* mind was less difficult to develop. She was a woman of mean understanding, little information, and uncertain temper. When she was discontented, she fancied herself nervous. The business of her life was to get her daughters married: its solace was visiting and news.

40. What is the number of the paragraph that supports the idea that a wealthy man is always looking for a wife?

Paragraph [   ]

41. What is the theme of the excerpt?
   a. travel
   b. divorce
   c. holidays
   d. marriage

42. In paragraph 14, what does "four or five thousand a year" refer to?
   a. the number of Mr. Bingley's annual trips to the Bennets' town
   b. Mr. Bingley's annual income
   c. Mr. Bennet's annual income
   d. Mrs. Long's annual income

43. What conclusion can you draw about Mrs. Bennet's wishes?
   a. She wants to marry Mr. Bingley for his money.
   b. She wants one of her daughters to marry Mr. Bingley.
   c. She doesn't want any of her daughters to marry Mr. Bingley.
   d. She wishes she had married someone with more money.

Please use the following to answer questions 44–48.

To: All Staff
From: Allison Lewis, Manager
Date: June 5, 2012
Subject: Bookstore Procedures

I am writing to clear up some issues dealing with our bookstores procedures. I have been getting a lot of questions about what procedures bookstore staff members are meant to follow on every shift. Recently, I have taken it upon myself to write a list of the procedures for reference.

1. at the beginning of a shift, all staff must sign in through our computer system.
2. Staffs members assigned two the floor shift should check for misplaced books regularly and reshelf those books.
3. Staff members assigned to the stock shift should keep the warehouse clean and organized.
4. No staff member is allowed to give a discount to any customer without manager approval.
5. Staff members do not receive free and complimentary drinks at the in-store café.
6. Customers are not allowed to preorder books that are not yet on our preorder list.
7. Before leaving a shift, all staff members must perform one last check for cleanliness and organization of the store and must sign out though our computer system.
8. If a staff member forget to sign in or sign out, he or she must consult the manager before estimating his or her sign in and sign out times.

Thank you for your cooperation!

Best,
Allison Lewis

44. In the first sentence of the company memo, what should be added to make it correct?
a. an apostrophe at the end of *procedures*
b. an apostrophe at the end of *bookstores*
c. an apostrophe between *bookstore* and *s*
d. nothing

45. Re-read the first list item:

1. at the beginning of a shift, all staff must sign in through our computer system.

Now, rewrite the sentence to correct any errors by writing it in the box below:

1.

46. In the second list item of the company memo, what should be changed to make it correct?
a. change *two* to *to*
b. change *for* to *four*
c. change *and* to *or*
d. no change

47. In the fifth list item, which of the following changes would improve the sentence?
a. delete *and complimentary*
b. delete *in-store café*
c. insert *on the house* before *free*
d. no change

48. In the eighth list item of the company memo, what should be changed in order to make it correct?
a. change *forget* to *forgets*
b. change *he or she* to *they*
c. change *consult* to *consults*
d. no change

Part II

1 question
45 minutes to complete

This practice allows you to compose your response to the given task and then compare it with examples of responses at the different score levels. You will also get a scoring guide that includes a detailed explanation of how official GED® test graders will score your response. You may use this scoring guide to score your own response.

Before you begin, it is important to note that on the official test this task must be completed in no more than 45 minutes. But don't rush to complete your response; take time to carefully read the passage(s) and the question prompt. Then think about how you would like to respond.

As you write your essay, be sure to:

- Decide which position presented in the passages is better supported by evidence.
- Explain why your chosen position has better support.
- Recognize that the position with better support may not be the position you agree with.
- Present multiple pieces of evidence from the passage to defend your assertions.
- Thoroughly construct your main points, organizing them logically, with strong supporting details.
- Connect your sentences, paragraphs, and ideas with transitional words and phrases.
- Express your ideas clearly and choose your words carefully.
- Use varied sentence structures to increase the clarity of your response.
- Reread and revise your response.

Good luck!

Please use the following passages to answer the essay question.

An Analysis of Stem Cell Research

1   Stem cell research is research using embryonic and "somatic" or "adult" stem cells for the purpose of advancing medicine. This research has been in existence since the beginning of the 20th century, and over the years many breakthroughs have come from it. In 1998, scientists discovered methods to derive stem cells from human embryos. In 2006, researchers made another breakthrough, which involved reprogramming some adult cells in certain conditions to assume a stem cell-like state. Stem cells themselves are useful in medical research because they are at the early state of reproduction, where the cell can either remain a stem cell or become a cell that would be involved in the formation of bones, brain cells, skin, the nervous system, organs, muscles and every other part of the body.

Benefits of Stem Cell Research

2   Theoretically, research points to stem cell research being of great value in medical advancement. At this time, it is not yet clear how much can be done with stem cell research, and the possible benefits are incalculable. It could lead to cures for diabetes or heart disease. It is also seen as a potential resource to help cure cancer, Parkinson's Disease, or even to regenerate a severed spinal cord and allow someone to walk who has been confined to a wheel chair. Although this sounds miraculous, it will not happen without extensive work and time.

3   Currently, adult stem cell therapies are used in the form of bone marrow transplants for treating leukemia. In 2006, researchers created artificial liver cells from umbilical cord blood stem cells. And in 2008, a study was published of the first successful cartilage regeneration in a human knee using adult stem cells. The variety of ways in which stem cell research could aid in curing many diseases has just begun to be explored.

4   While there are questions regarding human embryo stem cells for research, there are a variety of ways to acquire stem cells. As noted in a 2008 Stanford publication, regarding human embryo stem cell research specifically, a majority of the researchers are not actually touching newly derived stem cells, but are instead using the lineage and data of stem cells that have already been researched by other scientists. They have made these cell lines available for others to work with and learn from. Along with advances regarding adult stem cell research, this could be a fruitful direction for medical inquiry to go.

continues

Arguments Against Stem Cell Research

5 Stem cell research is a risky endeavor that does not have clear cut benefits and a lot of moral questions involved. While it seems clear that certain diseases are being treated by stem cell therapies, there are too many questions regarding further study and use.

6 With human embryo stem cells, a major concern is where they are coming from. One suggestion is for these stem cells to be taken from embryos that have been created for reproduction via *in vitro* fertilization. These embryos could be donated for scientific research after it is confirmed that they are not going to be used for reproduction. While this seems like a simple solution, there's also the question of the actual usefulness of those stem cells. With all stem cell therapies, in 2010, *Consumer Reports* noted the concern regarding transplanted cells forming tumors and becoming cancerous if the cell's division continued uncontrollably. There are also concerns of immune rejection by the patient being treated. While immunosuppressant drugs are used in organ transplant surgery, would this work on a body with new cells injected into it? There's also the additional question of whether the correct cell types can be induced in the stem cells, since the stem cells themselves are undifferentiated and can become many different kinds of cells.

7 While certain therapies have been successfully created, this research is still very untested. More conversations and clear education of the public is needed regarding this controversial form of medical therapy and the research behind it.

QUESTION:
While the first passage outlines the benefits of and identifies arguments for stem cell research, the second passage identifies arguments against stem cell research.

In your response, analyze both passages to determine which position is best supported. Use relevant and specific evidence from both sources to support your response.

Answers and Explanations

Part I

1. **The correct answer is the King of Great Britain.** The second to the last sentence in the second paragraph states, "The history of the present King of Great Britain is a history of repeated injuries and usurpations, all having in direct object the establishment of an absolute Tyranny over these States." The America colonists rebelled against the King of Great Britain's control of the colonies.

2. **Choice d is correct.** This paragraph incorporates a list of injustices that had been committed against the colonies by the King of Great Britain. The previous paragraphs describe suffering that the King caused the colonies, and paragraph 3 provides examples of those injuries.

   Choice **a** is incorrect. This paragraph incorporates a list of injustices that had been committed against the colonies by the King of Great Britain. It is not a list of laws written by the King, but a list of acts he committed.

   Choice **b** is incorrect. This paragraph incorporates a list of injustices that had been committed against the colonies by the King of Great Britain. It is not a list of laws for the United States of America because the colonies were not yet independent when the Declaration was written.

   Choice **c** is incorrect. This paragraph incorporates a list of injustices that had been committed against the colonies by the King of Great Britain. It is not a list of his good acts due to the fact that they are all negative things, and because the previous paragraphs mention that the King has committed repeated injuries against the colonies.

3. **Choice b is correct.** This quotation explicitly states that one group of people wishes to dissolve political ties with another group of people, meaning the colonies dissolving political ties with Great Britain.

   Choice **a** is incorrect. This quotation supports the idea of equality for all men, but does not express the desire to be free from Great Britain.

   Choice **c** is incorrect. This quotation expresses one of the grievances that the colonists have against the King of Great Britain. It is one of the reasons why the colonies want to split from Great Britain, but it does not express that desire itself.

   Choice **d** is incorrect. This quotation supports the idea of certain rights for all men, but does not express the desire to be free from Great Britain.

4. **Choice b is correct.** This phrase goes into more depth about what it means to have a government that gains its power from the consent of the governed and that is essentially controlled by the governed. This helps build the argument for popular sovereignty that this excerpt expresses.

   Choice **a** is incorrect. This phrase expresses a grievance that the colonists have against the King of Great Britain. It does not specifically help to build an argument for popular sovereignty.

   Choice **c** is incorrect. This phrase expresses a grievance that the colonists have against the King of Great Britain. It does not specifically help to build an argument for popular sovereignty.

   Choice **d** is incorrect. This phrase expresses a grievance that the colonists have against the King of Great Britain. It does not specifically help to build an argument for popular sovereignty.

5. Choice c is correct. The final paragraph of the excerpt is a list of the King's wrongdoings against the colonies.

Choice **a** is incorrect. The excerpt does not list court cases against the King.

Choice **b** is incorrect. The list of wrongdoings in the excerpt is by American colonists, not by other world leaders.

Choice **d** is incorrect. This excerpt does not name any specific individuals; it attempts to speak for the colonists as a whole.

6. Choice a is correct. The information given in the list of grievances is made up of examples of wrongdoings that the King has done against the colonists. This is definitely relevant to a claim that the King has carried out wrongs against the colonists. Furthermore, the list goes on for a long paragraph, making it more than sufficient to support the claim.

Choice **b** is incorrect. While the choice of relevancy is correct, the list goes on for a long paragraph, making it more than sufficient to support the claim. Therefore, the choice of insufficiency is incorrect.

Choice **c** is incorrect. While the choice of sufficiency is correct, the information given in the list of grievances is made up of examples of wrongdoings that are relevant to the claim. Therefore, the choice of irrelevancy is incorrect.

Choice **d** is incorrect. The information given in the list of grievances is made up of examples of wrongdoings that the King has done against the colonists. This is definitely relevant to a claim that the King has carried out wrongs against the colonists. Furthermore, the list goes on for a long paragraph, making it more than sufficient to support the claim.

7. Choice b is correct. The whole last paragraph of the excerpt is a list of tyrannical action the King of Great Britain committed against the colonists.

Choice **a** is incorrect. The excerpt claims that "all men are created equal," but it does not provide evidence as to why this is true. No evidence is given to support this claim.

Choice **c** is incorrect. The excerpt claims that all men "are endowed by their Creator with certain unalienable Rights," but it does not provide evidence to support this claim.

Choice **d** is incorrect. The excerpt discusses the idea of popular sovereignty, but it provides no evidence to support this claim.

8. Choice d is correct. Factually, there is no validity to the claim that the only way to secure certain rights is through a government controlled by the governed. Logically, there is really no reason why this would be the only way to secure those rights. Therefore, this is an example of false reasoning.

Choice **a** is incorrect. This statement is not really an explanation of anything but rather an opinion that in order to secure certain rights, governments should derive their power from the governed.

Choice **b** is incorrect. This statement does not give any evidence based in actual fact. Instead, it expresses an opinion that in order to secure certain rights, governments should derive their power from the governed.

Choice **c** is incorrect. Factually, there is no validity to the claim that the only way to secure certain rights is through a government controlled by the governed. Logically, there is really no reason why this would be the only way to secure those rights. Therefore, this is an example of false reasoning, not valid reasoning.

9. **Choice d is correct.** The first paragraph largely consists of descriptions of many of the author's characters. He describes their appearances and personalities and generally uses this first paragraph to introduce his readers to the characters of his story.

Choice **a** is incorrect. In the first paragraph, the author is not arguing a point. Instead, he is simply making observations, albeit biased and opinionated observations, about his characters in order to describe them.

Choice **b** is incorrect. In the first paragraph, there is no dialogue. None of the characters are talking amongst themselves. Instead, the paragraph involves description of many of the characters.

Choice **c** is incorrect. While there is description in the first paragraph, it is description of characters, not settings or even a main setting for the story. Instead, the author uses the first paragraph to set up the personalities and appearances of his characters.

10. **Choice c is correct.** *Lacking* is the opposite of *rich* in this context. Therefore, if it were to replace *rich* in the sentence, the whole tone and meaning of the sentence would be changed to the opposite of what the author intends to convey.

Choice **a** is incorrect. *Abounding* is a synonym of the word *rich* as it's used in this context. Therefore, it would not change the tone or meaning of the sentence if it replaced *rich*.

Choice **b** is incorrect. *Heavy* is a synonym of the word *rich* as it's used in this context. Therefore, it would not change the tone or meaning of the sentence if it replaced *rich*.

Choice **d** is incorrect. *Plentiful* is a synonym of the word *rich* as it's used in this context. Therefore, it would not change the tone or meaning of the sentence if it replaced *rich*.

11. **Choice b is correct.** *Tiresome* means fatiguing, wearisome, or tedious.

12. **Choice d is correct.** The paragraph describes how Armory is not like other rich boys his age. Choice **a** is incorrect. Amory doesn't love symphonies, but as the last paragraph states, he is "outgrowing a natural repugnance to chamber music and symphonies."

Choice **b** is incorrect. This paragraph makes no mention of whether Amory has a taste for adventure.

Choice **c** is incorrect. The opposite is true. The last paragraph describes how Armory is different than other rich boys.

13. **The correct order is:**
    1. **Operation Iraqi Freedom is launched**
    2. **coalition forces cross 350 miles of enemy territory**
    3. **Baghdad is liberated.**

This order is correct due to the implied order of events that Bush mentions in the excerpt. Operation Iraqi Freedom had to have been launched before coalition forces could cross 350 miles of enemy territory. The ultimate outcome of the operation was the liberation of Baghdad; therefore, that is the last event in the progression.

14. Choice c is correct. The setting is described as harsh and unforgiving. This technique is used to heighten the sense of danger to the troops fighting death squads, in order to persuade the audience of its truth.

Choice **a** is incorrect. The choice of describing an extreme climate with intense sandstorms in this paragraph is not meant to express beauty. The setting is described as harsh and unforgiving, not beautiful. This technique is used to heighten the sense of danger to the troops fighting death squads, in order to persuade the audience of its truth.

Choice **b** is incorrect. The choice of describing an extreme climate with intense sandstorms in this paragraph is not meant to express contentment. The setting is described as harsh and unforgiving, not a place to feel content. This technique is used to heighten the sense of danger to the troops fighting death squads, in order to persuade the audience of its truth.

Choice **d** is incorrect. The setting is described as harsh and unforgiving. This technique is used to heighten the sense of danger to the troops fighting death squads, in order to persuade the audience of its truth.

15. Choice a is correct. In the paragraph, Jordan states that the party is "an inclusive rather than an exclusive party" and that "everybody" should come.

Choice **b** is incorrect. This is what the third paragraph is about, not the second paragraph.

Choice **c** is incorrect. Although it can be inferred that Jordan approves of the party, this is not the main point of the second paragraph.

Choice **d** is incorrect. This is the opposite of the meaning of the second paragraph.

16. Choice b is correct. Here, Jordan says that everyone should be able to participate in government. This is what the prompt is asking for.

Choice **a** is incorrect. In this sentence, Jordan is stating that the Democratic Party accepts all people. It slightly fits the prompt, but there is a better answer.

Choice **c** is incorrect. Jordan is speaking about how the party evolves, not about how the government represents all people.

Choice **d** is incorrect. This is a summary of all the values that Jordan brings up and is too broad to be just about the representation of everyone.

17. Choice d is correct. Jordan says the party is for all people and that everyone should be represented in government. An open forum is an inclusive event that allows people to speak their mind.

Choice **a** is incorrect. Jordan explicitly states that the Democratic Party is inclusive. This would be an exclusive event, contrary to what she states.

Choice **b** is incorrect. This is an example of exclusivity, which is not in line with the values she expresses.

Choice **c** is incorrect. Although this would be a logical choice, this is a broader answer, and there is a better choice. Jordan does not talk about senate races in the passage.

18. Choice b is correct. Throughout her address, Jordan compares American values to the party's values and claims that they are in line with each other. This is the best summary.

Choice **a** is incorrect. This is a detail Jordan includes, but it does not represent the main idea of her address.

Choice **c** is incorrect. This is another detail rather than a summary.

Choice **d** is incorrect. This cannot be correct because choices **a** and **c** are wrong.

19. Choice d is correct. Jordan praises the Democratic Party throughout her speech. Choice **a** is incorrect. This phrase praises the party.

Choice **b** is incorrect. Jordan is commending the party.

Choice **c** is incorrect. Jordan is ascribing a positive quality, innovation, to her party's character.

20. Choice d is correct. Jordan does not come right out and say that the government should pass laws to combat racism and gender discrimination, which would block individual achievement, but she stresses the word "actively" in connection with the government's "obligation" to "remove those obstacles." Passing laws is "active" on the part of the government, and it is logical to infer that Jordan would support laws to curb discrimination.

Choice **a** is incorrect. Jordan is asking why people are drawn to her party, not calling on government to enact anti-discrimination laws.

Choice **b** is incorrect. Jordan is discussing political power in a democracy, not anti-discrimination law.

Choice **c** is incorrect. Jordan is talking about the beliefs of the Democratic Party, not about the U.S. government.

21. Choice a is correct. In order to make the verb agree with the plural subject, *piles of books*, the verb needs to be in present tense and not end in *s*.

Choice **b** is incorrect. In order to make the verb agree with the plural subject, *piles of books*, the verb needs to be in present tense and not end in *s* (*accumulate*), not the present tense ending in *s* (*accumulates*).

Choice **c** is incorrect. In order to make the verb agree with the plural subject, *piles of books*, the verb needs to be in present tense (*accumulate*), not in the past tense (*accumulated*).

Choice **d** is incorrect. In order to make the verb agree with the plural subject, *piles of books*, the verb needs to be in present tense (*accumulate*), not in the future tense (*will accumulate*).

22. Choice a is correct. *Therefore* is the correct transition word to use when describing a cause-and-effect relationship. And as the first word in the sentence, the word is correctly capitalized.

Choice **b** is incorrect. *However* is a transition word used to show contrast. Since the accumulating piles of books cause the effect of instituting a new policy, *Therefore* is the correct transition word to use when describing a cause-and-effect relationship.

Choice **c** is incorrect. *Meanwhile* denotes time. Since the accumulating piles of books cause the effect of instituting a new policy, *Therefore* is the correct transition word to use when describing a cause-and-effect relationship.

Choice **d** is incorrect. *Instead* is a transition word used to show contrast. Since the accumulating piles of books cause the effect of instituting a new policy, *Therefore* is the correct transition word to use when describing a cause-and-effect relationship.

23. Choice c is correct. Because this word starts a sentence, the first letter needs to be capitalized. Choice **a** is incorrect. Because this word starts a sentence, the first letter needs to be capitalized. Choice **b** is incorrect. Because this word starts a sentence, the first letter needs to be capitalized. Also, *please* is being used as a command, and the addition of an *s* at the end does not make sense in this context.
Choice **d** is incorrect. *Please* is being used as a command, and the addition of an *s* at the end does not make sense in this context.

24. Choice b is correct. Of the possessive pronouns listed, *your* in the second person is correct to address the reader.

25. Choice d is correct. The closing of a letter or memo ends with a comma, followed on the next line by the letter writer's name.
Choice **a** is incorrect. The closing of a letter or memo ends with a comma, followed on the next line by the letter writer's name.
Choice **b** is incorrect. The closing of a letter or memo ends with a comma, followed on the next line by the letter writer's name.
Choice **c** is incorrect. The closing of a letter or memo ends with a comma, followed on the next line by the letter writer's name.

26. Choice b is correct. The author chose these words to create a dark and foreboding tone.

27. The correct order is:
  1. rides through the countryside
  2. comes to the House of Usher
  3. feels a sense of gloom
  4. reins his horse near the house

This is based on the order of events recounted by the narrator in the excerpt.

28. Choice d is correct. Personification is giving human characteristics to inanimate objects. The phrase "vacant eye-like windows" gives the human quality of vacant eyes to windows.
Choice **a** is incorrect. Alliteration is a repetition of consonant sounds at the beginning of several words in a row. An example would be "brightly beautiful butterflies."
Choice **b** is incorrect. Hyperbole is extreme exaggeration, for example: "He walks louder than an elephant."
Choice **c** is incorrect. Onomatopoeia refers to words that mimic the sounds they describe, for example: "The fire hissed, crackled, and popped."

29. Choice b is correct. The word *joy* changes the tone and meaning of the phrase from an expression of unhappiness and gloom to a positive and happy expression.
Choice **a** is incorrect. *Melancholy* preserves the unhappy and negative tone of the original phrase.
Choice **c** is incorrect. *Sadness* preserves the unhappy and negative tone of the original phrase.
Choice **d** is incorrect. *Despair* preserves the unhappy and negative tone of the original phrase.

30. Choice c is correct. Grant admits that he did "not know how far this was necessary," but "deemed it necessary, at that time." He feels later that his decision was justified.
Choice **a** is incorrect. The passage opens with the statement "things began to quiet down," the opposite of widespread violence.
Choice **b** is incorrect. The first words in the first sentence report that the war is winding down.
Choice **d** is incorrect. Grant deemed the garrisons necessary and felt justified later, calling the garrisons "absolutely required."

31. **The correct answer is the Civil War.** It can be inferred from the passage that the Civil War had just concluded. The passage clearly describes the "rebellion as was fought between the sections from 1861 to 1865." There are many other context clues. In addition, the excerpt is from Grant's memoir after 1865 and Sherman's March through the South.

32. **Choice b is correct.** Grant refers to Sherman's March as "magnificent" and as signifying "the closing of the war."
Choice **a** is incorrect. Grant obviously approves of the march.
Choice **c** is incorrect. Grant is sympathizing with Sherman, not criticizing him.
Choice **d** is incorrect. The word change is unrelated to Grant's feelings about how "their newspapers had given such an account of Confederate success."

33. **Choice c is correct.** Grant is describing how the Confederate view is false.
Choice **a** is incorrect. Grant is expressing sympathy with the general consensus of feeling after the war.
Choice **b** is incorrect. This sentence comments on Sherman's March, not Grant's disagreement with the Confederate viewpoint.
Choice **d** is incorrect. This sentence describes how Grant assumed the Confederates felt upon seeing Sherman, not Grant's disagreement with the Confederate viewpoint.

34. **Choice a is correct.** The correct order is C—the Civil War, A—Sherman's men were ordered not to listen to him, D—Sherman's March, then B—the Confederates "saw the true state of affairs."

35. **Choice b is correct.** Grant is describing how seeing the victorious soldiers' march reminded the South of what really happened.
Choice **a** is incorrect. The opposite is true for the victorious army. For example, Grant emphasizes how the march was a positive thing because it set the Confederates straight on who won.
Choice **c** is incorrect. There is no evidence in the excerpt to support his conclusion.
Choice **d** is incorrect. The opposite is true for the victorious army.

36. **Choice a is correct.** Paragraph 3 is mainly about how scientists monitor earthquakes to predict volcanic eruptions.
Choice **b** is incorrect. Although these terms are defined in this paragraph, they are supporting details.
Choice **c** is incorrect. The paragraph does not explain how seismometers work.
Choice **d** is incorrect. Although the paragraph mentions that volcanic gases force their way up through underground channels, this is a small detail and not the paragraph's main idea.

37. **Choice d is correct.** This best summarizes the main ideas of "Watching Volcanoes" by referencing the scientists who watch volcanoes, the ways they monitor volcanoes, and why their work is important.
Choice **a** is incorrect. This is a good summary of the section titled "Watching for Bulges in the Sides of the Mountain," but it does not summarize the entire passage.
Choice **b** is incorrect. The article mentions that vents are dangerous, not that scientists should not visit them for study. This is a small detail and not a summary of the complete article.
Choice **c** is incorrect. This answer refers to the second article, "The 1992 Eruptions at Mt. Spurr, Alaska," not "Watching Volcanoes."

38. Choice b is correct. "Watching Volcanoes" is a first-person account of watching volcanoes from the perspective of a volcano-watching scientist. "The 1992 Eruptions at Mt. Spurr, Alaska" is an objective report without any indication that the journalist is involved in volcano science.

Choice **a** is incorrect. The opposite is true. "Watching Volcanoes" discusses volcanoes in general, and "The 1992 Eruptions at Mt. Spurr, Alaska" focuses on the volcano at Mt. Spurr, Alaska.

Choice **c** is incorrect. Both passages discuss seismometers, the instruments that scientists use to measure earthquake magnitude.

Choice **d** is incorrect. Although "Watching Volcanoes" is written from the first-person point of view like a diary, it does not describe what the writer did on a particular day as a diary does. Although it is possible that "The 1992 Eruptions at Mt. Spurr, Alaska" was published in a newspaper, there is no way of knowing this based on the passage.

39. Choice c is correct. Having vertical axes to 100 incidents on both graphs dramatizes the explosion of 90 more incidents than on any day in the first graph occurring in November 1992 in the second graph.

Choice **a** is incorrect. Based on the dramatic rise in events in November 1992 shown in the second graph, the volcano was close to erupting, and the threat was serious enough that scientists warned, "a large eruption is likely within the next 24 to 48 hours."

Choice **b** is incorrect. September is not charted on either graph.

Choice **d** is incorrect. There is no evidence to support this claim.

40. The correct answer is paragraph 1. Paragraph 1 explicitly states that "a single man in possession of a good fortune must be in want of a wife."

41. Choice d is correct. The topic of marriage is the focus of the introductory paragraphs as well as the majority of the dialogue.

Choice **a** is incorrect. Travel is not the main topic of the excerpt.

Choice **b** is incorrect. Divorce is not a topic in the excerpt.

Choice **c** is incorrect. The Michaelmas holiday is a minor topic in the excerpt, not the main topic.

42. Choice b is correct. Mrs. Bennet is discussing Bingly's fortune—in other words, his income.

Choice **a** is incorrect. Mrs. Bennet is discussing Bingly's fortune—in other words, his income.

Choice **c** is incorrect. Mrs. Bennet is talking to Mr. Bennet in this dialogue, and she would not need to be telling her husband about his own money in the third person. Furthermore, they are just beginning to discuss Mr. Bingley when this number amount is mentioned.

Choice **d** is incorrect. Mrs. Bennet is discussing Bingly's fortune—in other words, his income.

43. Choice b is correct. This whole excerpt is about the supposition that wealthy men need to find wives and the topic of marriage in general. Mrs. Bennet spends most of the dialogue discussing the merits of Mr. Bingley and how he would be a good match for one of her daughters.
Choice **a** is incorrect. Mrs. Bennet is a married woman, and every time she mentions marriage it is in reference to her daughters.
Choice **c** is incorrect. This whole excerpt is about the supposition that wealthy men need to find wives and the topic of marriage in general.
Choice **d** is incorrect. The only time that Mrs. Bennet mentions money is in reference to the wealth of Mr. Bingley and how that makes him a good match for one of her daughters. She never implies that she wishes she had married someone wealthier.

44. Choice c is correct. The noun possessing *procedures* is singular.
Choice **a** is incorrect. *Procedures* is not being used as a possessive noun in this context. Therefore, an apostrophe is not needed.
Choice **b** is incorrect. There is one bookstore, so the possessive noun is singular, not plural.
Choice **d** is incorrect. The singular noun *bookstore* possesses *procedures*, so an apostrophe should be inserted between *bookstore* and *s*.

45. The correct answer is: At the beginning of a shift, all staff must sign in through our computer system. The first word in a sentence must always be capitalized.

46. Choice a is correct. This is a common homonym error. *Two* is a number designation, and in this context, the preposition *to* is necessary instead. This is to reference what the staff members are assigned to, not a number designation.
Choice **b** is incorrect. This change would cause a homonym error. The preposition *for* is needed to denote an action that the staff members should take. The homonym *four* denoting number does not make sense in this context.
Choice **c** is incorrect. The procedure listed here has two parts. The staff members need to look for misplaced books *and* reshelf them. The procedure does not imply that staff members can choose to do one thing or the other.
Choice **d** is incorrect. *Two* is a number designation, and in this context, the preposition *to* is necessary instead. This is to reference what the staff members are assigned to, not a number designation.

47. Choice a is correct. *Free* and *complimentary* mean essentially the same thing. *And complimentary* adds an unnecessary wordiness to the sentence and should be deleted.
Choice **b** is incorrect. *In-store café* is the object of the preposition *at* and is needed in order to make the prepositional phrase complete.
Choice **c** is incorrect. *Free, complimentary,* and *on the house* all mean the same thing. Therefore, the use of all three together causes unnecessary wordiness.
Choice **d** is incorrect. *Free* and *complimentary* mean essentially the same thing. *And complimentary* adds an unnecessary wordiness to the sentence and should be deleted.

48. Choice a is correct. In order for the subject *staff member* to agree with the verb, *forget* must end in an *s*. This is a common subject-verb agreement rule.

Choice **b** is incorrect. Since *he or she* is referencing a *staff member*, all the subjects in the sentence need to be singular. The change to *they* would change this number agreement, making the pronoun plural that is referencing a singular noun, which is incorrect.

Choice **c** is incorrect. In order for the subject *he or she* to agree with the verb, *consult* should not end in an *s*. This is a common subject-verb agreement rule.

Choice **d** is incorrect. In order for the subject *staff member* to agree with the verb, *forget* must end in an *s*. This is a common subject-verb agreement rule.

Part II

Your Extended Response will be scored based on three traits, or elements:

Trait 1: Analysis of arguments and use of evidence

Trait 2: Development of ideas and structure

Trait 3: Clarity and command of standard English conventions

Your essay will be scored on a 6-point scale—each trait is worth up to 2 points. The final score is counted twice, so the maximum number of points you can earn is 12.

Trait 1 tests your ability to write an essay that takes a stance based on the information in the reading passages. To earn the highest score possible, you must carefully read the information and express a clear opinion on what you have read. You will be scored on how well you use the information from the passages to support your argument.

Your response will also be scored on how well you analyze the author's arguments in the passages. To earn the highest score possible, you should discuss whether or not you think the author is making a good argument, and why or why not.

For your reference, here is a table that readers will use when scoring your essay with a 2, 1, or 0.

TRAIT 1: CREATION OF ARGUMENTS AND USE OF EVIDENCE	
2	• Makes text-based argument(s) and establishes an intent connected to the prompt • Presents specific and related evidence from source text(s) to support argument (may include a few unrelated pieces of evidence or unsupported claims) • Analyzes the topic and/or the strength of the argument within the source text(s) (e.g., distinguishes between supported and unsupported claims, makes valid inferences about underlying assumptions, identifies false reasoning, evaluates the credibility of sources)
1	• Makes an argument with some connection to the prompt • Presents some evidence from source text(s) to support argument (may include a mix of related and unrelated evidence that may or may not cite the text) • Partly analyzes the topic and/or the strength of the argument within the source text(s); may be limited, oversimplified, or inaccurate
0	• May attempt to make an argument OR lacks an intent or connection to the prompt OR attempts neither • Presents little or no evidence from source text(s) (sections of text may be copied from source directly) • Minimally analyzes the topic and/or the strength of the argument within the source text(s); may present no analysis, or little or no understanding of the given argument
Non-scorable	• Response consists only of text copied from the prompt or source text(s) • Response shows that test-taker has not read the prompt or is entirely off-topic • Response is incomprehensible • Response is not in English • No response has been attempted (has been left blank)

Trait 2 tests whether you respond to the writing prompt with a well-structured essay. Support of your thesis must come from evidence in the passages, as well as personal opinions and experiences that build on your central idea. Your ideas must be fully explained and include specific details. Your essay should use words and phrases that allow your details and ideas to flow naturally. Here is a table that outlines what is involved in earning a score of 2, 1, or 0.

TRAIT 2: DEVELOPMENT OF IDEAS AND ORGANIZATIONAL STRUCTURE	
2	• Contains ideas that are generally logical and well-developed; most ideas are expanded upon • Contains a logical sequence of ideas with clear connections between specific details and main ideas • Develops an organizational structure that conveys the message and goal of the response; appropriately uses transitional devices • Develops and maintains an appropriate style and tone that signal awareness of the audience and purpose of the task • Uses appropriate words to express ideas clearly
1	• Contains ideas that are partially developed and/or may demonstrate vague or simplistic logic; only some ideas are expanded upon • Contains some evidence of a sequence of ideas, but specific details may be unconnected to main ideas • Develops an organizational structure that may partially group ideas or is partially effective at conveying the message of the response; inconsistently uses transitional devices • May inconsistently maintain an appropriate style and tone to signal an awareness of the audience and purpose of the task • May contain misused words and/or words that do not express ideas clearly
0	• Contains ideas that are ineffectively or illogically developed, with little or no elaboration of main ideas • Contains an unclear or no sequence of ideas; specific details may be absent or unrelated to main ideas • Develops an ineffective or no organizational structure; inappropriately uses transitional devices, or does not use them at all • Uses an inappropriate style and tone that signal limited or no awareness of audience and purpose • May contain many misused words, overuse of slang, and/or express ideas in an unclear or repetitious manner
Non-scorable	• Response consists only of text copied from the prompt or source text(s) • Response shows that test-taker has not read the prompt or is entirely off-topic • Response is incomprehensible • Response is not in English • No response has been attempted (has been left blank)

Trait 3 tests how you create the sentences that make up your essay. To earn a high score, you will need to write sentences with variety—some short, some long, some simple, some complex. You will also need to prove that you have a good handle on standard English, including correct word choice, grammar, and sentence structure.

Here is a table that outlines what is involved in attaining a score of 2, 1, or 0.

TRAIT 3: CLARITY AND COMMAND OF STANDARD ENGLISH CONVENTIONS	
2	• Demonstrates generally correct sentence structure and an overall fluency that enhances clarity with regard to the following skills: 1) Diverse sentence structure within a paragraph or paragraphs 2) Correct use of subordination, coordination, and parallelism 3) Avoidance of awkward sentence structures and wordiness 4) Use of transitional words, conjunctive adverbs, and other words that enhance clarity and logic 5) Avoidance of run-on sentences, sentence fragments, and fused sentences • Demonstrates proficient use of conventions with regard to the following skills: 1) Subject-verb agreement 2) Placement of modifiers and correct word order 3) Pronoun usage, including pronoun antecedent agreement, unclear pronoun references, and pronoun case 4) Frequently confused words and homonyms, including contractions 5) Use of apostrophes with possessive nouns 6) Use of punctuation (e.g., commas in a series or in appositives and other non-essential elements, end marks, and punctuation for clause separation) 7) Capitalization (e.g., beginnings of sentences, proper nouns, and titles) • May contain some errors in mechanics and conventions that do not impede comprehension; overall usage is at a level suitable for on-demand draft writing
1	• Demonstrates inconsistent sentence structure; may contain some choppy, repetitive, awkward, or run-on sentences that may limit clarity; demonstrates inconsistent use of skills 1–5 as listed under Trait 3, Score Point 2 • Demonstrates inconsistent use of basic conventions with regard to skills 1–7 as listed under Trait 3, Score Point 2 • May contain many errors in mechanics and conventions that occasionally impede comprehension; overall usage is at the minimum level acceptable for on-demand draft writing
0	• Demonstrates improper sentence structure to the extent that meaning may be unclear; demonstrates minimal use of skills 1–5 as listed under Trait 3, Score Point 2 • Demonstrates minimal use of basic conventions with regard to skills 1–7 as listed under Trait 3, Score Point 2 • Contains numerous significant errors in mechanics and conventions that impede comprehension; overall usage is at an unacceptable level for on-demand draft writing OR • Response is insufficient to show level of proficiency involving conventions and usage
Non-scorable	• Response consists only of text copied from the prompt or source text(s) • Response shows that test-taker has not read the prompt or is entirely off-topic • Response is incomprehensible • Response is not in English • No response has been attempted (has been left blank)

Sample Score 6 Essay

Stem cell research is a complicated topic to evaluate. While it is noted as having a lot of potential with regard to medical advancements, there are several elements of it that can cause moral quandaries, such as the use of human embryos in the research. At the same time, it is providing valuable therapies for diseases such as leukemia and could treat diseases like diabetes and heart disease. With that in mind and on reviewing the two passages, I find that I must argue in favor of stem cell research.

Since the passage against stem cell research makes several valid points, especially questioning the source of the stem cells used in the research, this is sure to inspire many readers to question the morality of the supporting argument. This concern does not actually have any evidence behind it, saying that only human embryo stem cells are being used, so it is difficult to know where this concern came from. In addition, the particular evidence noting that stem cell research itself is potentially harmful has no scientific basis and was simply based on concerns from the populace, as noted by Consumer Reports, than actual research. At the end of the third paragraph, this passage even questions whether scientists could differentiate the cells properly to make them become what is needed for that specific stem cell therapy. Would the stem cells become an actual brain cell or would it just become a bunch of organ cells and cause a tumorous growth? This is stated without any evidence to backup up the concern at all. While it is clear that the reason stem cell research is interesting in any form is that the cells themselves can be formed into any other cell needed, this worry about differentiation seems to be idle speculation rather than something that would legitimately make this research impossible.

In contrast, the passage supporting stem cell research is full of dates and specific examples. While the against passage only notes an article from Consumer Reports, *this passage notes research done in the 1900s, all the way through 2008. It points out some of the current research and medical benefits of stem cell research being used right now, including bone marrow transfu-sions to treat leukemia and the generation of artificial liver cells just in 2006. It also notes that the major concern regarding the source of the stem cells should be less of a concern due to a report from Stanford, a major research institute, about how researchers acquire the data of human embryo stem cells. It appears that not every single researcher is getting a new set of embryo stem cells to work off of. Instead, the information about one set is shared among all of the researchers. Also, the passage pointed to a 2008 article about medical advancements using adult stem cells. If stem cell research should be argued against, there needs to be more thorough and specific evidence provided to support that argument.*

It is clear that the arguments against stem cell research are antiquated and have been addressed by the medical community. Perhaps there is research regarding why stem cell research should not be pursued, but it is unspecified in these passages. Overall, while the supporting passage addresses many of the same concerns as the "against" passage, it is better organized and supported throughout with actual referenced research.

About this essay:

This essay has earned the maximum number of points in each trait for a total of 6 points.

Trait 1: Creation of Arguments and Use of Evidence

This response evaluates the arguments in the source text, develops an effective position supported by the text, and fulfills the criteria to earn 2 points for Trait 1.

This response establishes its stance at the conclusion of the first paragraph (*I find that I must argue in favor of stem cell research*) and provides a summary of support for that stance in the second and third paragraphs.

In the second paragraph, the writer also weighs the validity of the evidence in the "against" argument, for example: "*the particular evidence noting that stem cell research itself is potentially harmful has no scientific basis and was simply based on concerns from the populace, as noted by Consumer Reports, than actual research."*

Trait 2: Development of Ideas and Organizational Structure

This response is well developed and fulfills the criteria to earn 2 points for Trait 2. It is well organized, opens with a definitive stance, offers a discussion of the pros and cons of stem cell research and the evidence provided, and then provides a summary in support of the chosen stance. The writer provides multiple, specific examples and then elaborates on them, using an appropriately formal tone throughout.

Trait 3: Clarity and Command of Standard English Conventions

This response also fulfills the criteria for draft writing and earns 2 points for Trait 3. Besides employing sophisticated sentence structure (*Since the passage against stem cell research makes several valid points, especially questioning the source of the stem cells used in the research, this is sure to inspire many readers to question the morality of the supporting argument. This concern does not actually have any evidence behind it, saying that only human embryo stem cells are being used, so it is difficult to know where this concern came from . . .*), this response uses clear transitions in its "compare and contrast" construction. (*In contrast, the passage supporting stem cell research is full of dates and specific examples . . .*)

In addition, the writer adheres to proper grammar and usage.

Sample Score 4 Essay

It seems clear that we must not allow stem cell research. It may have been around since the early 1900s, but that does not outweigh the moral questions it raises.

I am against stem cell research for mainly the same reasons stated in the passage. Since stem cell research has been around, there is no clear answer

regarding where the human embryo stem cells come from. This was not answered in the supporting passage.

What's more, I also think the possibility that the cells could form tumors and become cancerous, as noted in the against passage, is pretty worrying. At the very least, more education and research into the risks of stem cells is very necessary.

Finally, while it may be true that the arguments for stem cell research list many favorable benefits, and those aspects of stem cell research seem intriguing, the arguments against the research are better than the ones for it. At the very least there needs to be more education on the dangers.

About this essay:

This essay earned 1 point each for Trait 1 and Trait 2, and 2 points for Trait 3.

Trait 1: Creation of Arguments and Use of Evidence

This response makes a simple argument, supports it with some evidence from the source text, and offers a partial analysis of the opposing argument, earning it 1 point for Trait 1.

The writer generates an argument against stem cell research and makes a clear statement of her position in the first paragraph (*It seems clear that we must not allow stem cell research*), in the second paragraph (*I am against stem cell research for mainly the same reasons*), and final paragraph (*the arguments against the research are better than the ones for it*).

The writer does cite some evidence from the source text to support her position (*Since stem cell research has been around, there is no clear answer regarding where the human embryo stem cells come from*). The writer offers a partial analysis of the issue (*At the very least, more education and research into the risks of stem cells is very necessary*) and (*It's true; there are arguments for stem cell research that list a lot of favorable benefits*); however, this analysis is simplistic and limited.

In addition, in the second paragraph the writer offers a partial evaluation of the validity of the "for" arguments (*there is no clear answer regarding where the human embryo stem cells come from. This was not answered in the supporting passage*).

Trait 2: Development of Ideas and Organizational Structure

Although this response has a general organization and focus, the supporting ideas are developed unevenly; thus, it earns only one point in this trait.

This response establishes a discernable organizational structure by introducing stance and a comparison of the source text's two positions (*It seems clear that we must not allow stem cell research. It may have been around since the early 1900s, but that does not outweigh the moral questions it raises*).

The second and third paragraphs focus on the troubling aspects of stem cell research, and the writer offers a clear progression of ideas. Her main points are clear but not sufficiently elaborated upon. Her argument is based solely on what is offered in the passage (*I am against stem cell research for mainly the same reasons stated in the passage*).

The concluding paragraph offers a very basic comparison of the "for" and "against" arguments, but not much development is offered (*Though the good aspects of stem cell research seem intriguing, the arguments against the research are better than the ones for it*).

Trait 3: Clarity and Command of Standard English Conventions

This response earns the full two points for Trait 3. It employs sophisticated sentence structure (*Finally, while it may be true that the arguments for stem cell research list many favorable benefits, and those aspects of stem cell research seem intriguing, the arguments against the research are better than the ones for it*) and clear transitions (*What's more . . . Finally . . .*).

In addition, the writer adheres to proper grammar and usage.

Sample Score 0 Essay

Stem cell research is way too confusing and disturbing for a lot of people. While these scientists think that listing all of the accomplishemtns will mean that stem cell research should continue it's not clear at all whether that's true. If perhaps you had loukemia, then it would be ok for it to continue.

Also we don't know where the human embryo stem cells come from also some of them could become cancerous and that isn't a good idea either I thought Loukemia was some kind of cancer, that makes it even more confusing. Also the differentiation of cells. If you can't get the right kind of cells for your therapy, then those cells are useless and are a waste.

I think it's a better idea to not have stem cell research until we know more about what it could do. There are too many factors that seem harmful or dangerous in some way.

About this essay:

This essay earned 0 points in Trait 1, Trait 2, and Trait 3.

Trait 1: Creation of Arguments and Use of Evidence

In general, this response provides a minimal summary of the source text and lacks insight and topic analysis, earning this response 0 points for Trait 1.

The writer fails to summarize source texts in a coherent and organized structure. Though this response addresses the source material, the writer fails to cite evidence to support any arguments and does not take a firm stance until the final paragraph (*I think it's a better idea to not have stem cell research until we know more about what it could do*). She also seems to flip-flop on her stance (*While these scientists think that listing all of the accomplishemtns will mean that stem cell research should continue it's not clear at all whether that's true. If perhaps you had loukemia, then it would be ok for it to continue*).

Trait 2: Development of Ideas and Organizational Structure

Overall, the response is poorly developed, disorganized, and lacks any clear progression of ideas, earning it 0 points for Trait 2.

The writer uses informal and colloquial language (*Stem cell research is way too confusing and disturbing for a lot of people*) and fails to demonstrate awareness of audience and purpose. The response lacks organizational structure and a clear progression of ideas.

Trait 3: Clarity and Command of Standard English Conventions

Many sentences lack sense and fluency and are incorrect and awkward. The writer misuses and confuses words, punctuation, and usage as well as the conventions of English in general, making the response almost incomprehensible and earning it 0 points for Trait 3.

This short response shows flawed sentence structure, including run-on sentences (*Also we don't know where the human embryo stem cells come from also some of them could become cancerous and that isn't a good idea either I thought Loukemia was some kind of cancer, that makes it even more confusing. . . .*) and fragments (*Also the differentiation of cells*).

8 ▶ GED® SCIENCE TEST 2

This practice test is modeled on the format, content, and timing of the official GED® Science test and, like the official exam, presents a series of questions that focus on the fundamentals of scientific reasoning.

Work carefully, but do not spend too much time on any one question. Be sure you answer every question.

Set a timer for 90 minutes (1 hour and 30 minutes), and try to take this test uninterrupted, under quiet conditions.

Complete answer explanations for every test question follow the exam. Good luck!

35 total questions
90 minutes to complete

1. Kenya is a country located on the eastern edge of the African continent.

The graph below shows the number of hours during which the sun is visible in Kenya each month.

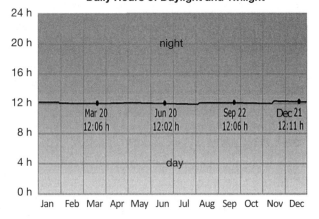

Daily Hours of Daylight and Twilight

Which statement correctly explains the lack of variation in daylight hours over the course of the year?
a. The length of the day is not dependent on daylight saving time.
b. Kenya receives direct sun all year long because it is on the equator.
c. Countries in the northern and southern hemispheres have opposite seasons.
d. The Earth's rotation places Kenya an equal distance from the sun during spring and fall.

2. The equation for photosynthesis is shown below.

$$6CO_2 + 6H_2O + Energy \rightarrow C_6H_{12}O_6 + 6O_2$$

Which of these correctly identifies the reactants in the equation?
a. glucose, oxygen
b. carbon dioxide, water
c. oxygen, carbon dioxide
d. oxygen, water, glucose

3. Circle the graph below that correctly depicts constant positive velocity.

(A)

(B)

(C)

(D)

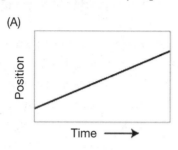
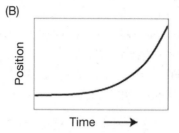
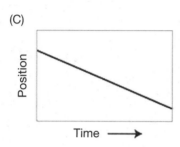
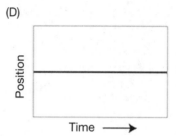

4. The diagram below shows the difference between an eye with normal vision and one with nearsighted vision.

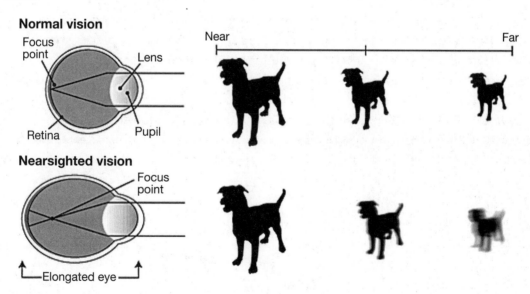

Which part of the eye is best described as a layer at the back of the eye containing light-sensitive cells that trigger nerve impulses to the brain?

a. lens

b. pupil

c. retina

d. focus point

5. Water moves easily across cell membranes through special protein-lined channels. If the total concentration of all dissolved solutes is not equal on both sides, there will be a net movement of water molecules into or out of the cell. The diagram below shows red blood cells in solutions with three different salt concentrations.

Red Blood Cells in Solutions of Different NaCl Concentrations

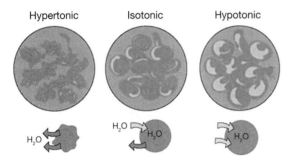

According to this diagram, when will homeostasis occur in red blood cells?

a. when the osmotic pressure of water is equal

b. when the concentration of salt is higher outside the cell

c. when the amount of water inside the cell is higher than outside the cell

d. when the osmotic flow of water out of the cell is greater than the salt solution inside the cell

Please use the following to answer questions 6–8.

Tetanus is a non-contagious infection caused by *Clostridium tetani*—rod-shaped, anaerobic bacteria. *C. tetani* affects skeletal muscles by releasing an endotoxin manufactured in the outer portion of the cell wall. The toxin infects the central nervous system and causes prolonged muscle spasms. Infection occurs through contamination of wounds and can be prevented by proper immunization. Most developed countries provide tetanus vaccinations as a standard of health care.

Tetanus is often associated with rust. Rusting occurs when oxygen, water, and iron interact in a process called oxidation. Over time, the iron mass will convert to iron oxide, or rust. A rusted surface provides a thriving environment for organisms with low oxygen needs.

Tetanus occurs worldwide but is most common in hot, damp climates with manure-treated soils. *C. tetani* endospores are widely distributed in the intestines of many animals such as cattle, chickens, and sheep.

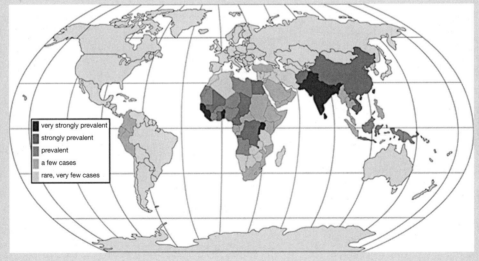

6. Explain how a non-contagious disease, such as tetanus, comes to be so widespread in certain parts of the world. Include multiple pieces of evidence from the text to support your answer.

Write your answer on the lines below. This task may take approximately 10 minutes to complete.

_____

_____

_____

_____

_____

_____

_____

_____

_____

_____

_____

_____

_____

_____

_____

_____

_____

7. Anaerobic bacteria such as *Clostridium tetani* use the process of fermentation to obtain nutrition. The bacteria use organic compounds, typically found in the intestinal tract of animals, to ferment sugars for energy, and produce various acids and alcohol byproducts.

Identify the correct products in the fermentation equation below. Fill in each box with the correct term from the list below.

oxygen

water

ethanol

energy

glucose → [   ] + carbon
dioxide (+ [   ] released)

8. The diagram below shows some basic components of bacterial cells.

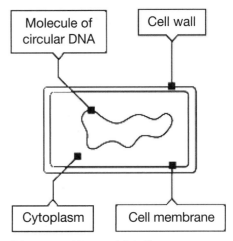

Diagram of bacterial cell

Based on the information in the passage and in the diagram, determine which cellular component is responsible for both the shape of *Clostridium tetani* and endotoxin production.

a. DNA

b. cell wall

c. cytoplasm

d. cell membrane

Please use the following to answer questions 9–11.

Bufo marinus, commonly referred to as the cane toad, can measure 6–9 inches long and weigh up to 4 pounds. The cane toad is nocturnal, breeds year round, and releases a toxin from the shoulders that is fatal to vertebrates. It eats crawling insects, small birds, mammals, and other amphibians, including smaller cane toads. It is native to tropical America but is permanently established in Australia. In the 1930s, sugarcane farmers imported the toads to Australia in attempts to control cane beetles.

Adult cane beetles measure about 13 millimeters long and are black, hard-shelled, dome-shaped flying insects with strong legs. They eat the leaves of sugar cane while their larvae hatch underground and destroy the roots. The flying beetles and burrowing larvae are difficult to eradicate. There is no evidence that the introduced cane toads have had any impact on cane-beetle populations. Cane toads have, however, had a significant impact on Australian ecology, including the depletion of native species that die when eating cane toads, the poisoning of pets and humans, and the decline of native animals preyed upon by the toads. While many populations of native species declined in the decades following the introduction of cane toads, some are now beginning to recover. One species of crow has even learned how to eat cane toads from the underbelly in order to avoid the venom.

9. Which of the following pieces of evidence supports the theory that the behaviors of other organisms are limiting resources for young cane toads?

   a. Adult cane toads often prey on juvenile cane toads.

   b. Cane-beetle larvae are buried underground and are inaccessible to cane toads.

   c. Adult cane beetles have heavy exoskeletons and the ability to fly.

   d. Cane-toad tadpoles can exist only in aquatic environments.

10. Based on the information in the passage, which of these terms best describes the effect seen in crows that eat cane toads?

   a. speciation

   b. adaptation

   c. development

   d. homeostasis

11. Discuss the impact that cane toads have had on the Australian ecosystem.

Include multiple pieces of evidence from the text to support your answer.

Write your answer on the lines below. This task may take approximately 10 minutes to complete.

Please use the following to answer questions 12–14.

In a marine ecosystem, there is a unique relationship between corals and the photosynthetic protists that live on the coral reefs. The single-celled protists, called zooxanthellae, live in the tissue of corals and go about the business of transforming large amounts of carbon dioxide into usable energy. The photosynthetic products are used by the corals for metabolic functions or as building blocks in the making of proteins, fats, and carbohydrates.

Although much of a coral's energy needs is supplied by these zooxanthellae, most corals also capture food particles with their stinging tentacles. Prey ranges in size from small fish to microscopic zooplankton. These food sources supply corals and zooxanthellae with nitrogen.

12. Based on the passage, corals and zooxanthellae demonstrate which type of symbiotic relationship?
   a. mutualism
   b. parasitism
   c. amensalism
   d. commensalism

13. Examine the trophic levels of a marine food web in the diagram below. The trophic pyramid groups organisms by the role that they play in the food web.

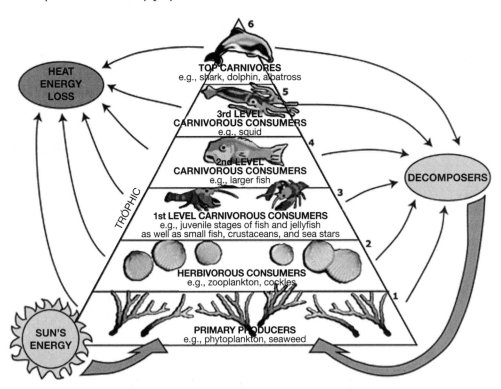

Write the appropriate answers in the boxes below.

Zooxanthellae are described in the passage as ⬚.

Based on the trophic levels identified in this pyramid, zooxanthellae would be classified as

⬚.

14. The diagram below shows a marine food web.

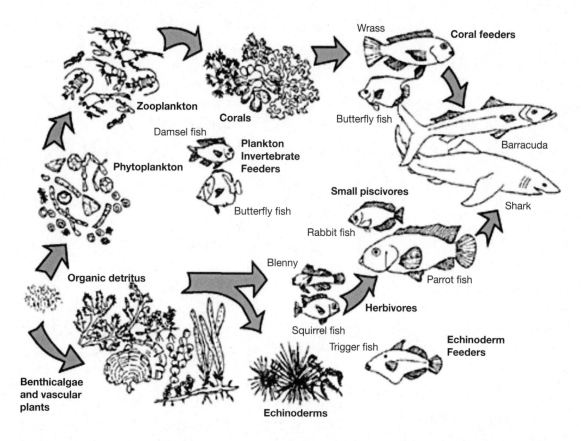

Using the information provided in the passage, identify the organism in the marine food web that supplies coral with energy. Circle the picture of the organism you want to select.

15. As seen in the following diagram, living things are highly organized, with specialized structures performing specific functions at every level of organization.

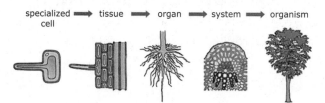

Select the correct sequence of cellular organization. Begin with the most specialized component.

a. red blood cell → blood → heart → cardiovascular system

b. cardiovascular system → heart → blood → red blood cell

c. red blood cell → blood → cardiovascular system → heart

d. heart → cardiovascular system → blood → red blood cell

16. The letters below show the genotypes of two parents.

$$Yy \times Yy$$

The Punnett square below shows the possible combinations of parent alleles. Write the remaining correct combination of the parent alleles in the gray box.

	Y	**y**
Y	YY	Yy
y	Yy	

17. Work is a force acting on an object to move it across a distance. Inclined planes make work easier by providing a smooth surface for objects to slide or roll across.

Pushing a stroller up a ramp is easier than pushing it up a flight of stairs. When going down a ramp, the gravitational pull on the stroller may be all that the stroller needs to begin rolling and gain velocity.

The velocity of a moving object can be determined by the following formula:
$$velocity = \frac{distance}{time}$$

If a stroller travels with a forward velocity of 4 m/s for a time of 2 seconds, then the distance covered is ⬚ meters. (You may use a calculator to complete this question.)

18. Which of the following materials would be a good insulator?
a. tile floor, because it transfers heat away from skin
b. steel spoon, because it conducts heat from boiling liquids
c. wool blanket, because it slows the transfer of heat from skin
d. copper pipe, because it accelerates the transfer of heated materials

19. Every chemical reaction needs a certain amount of energy to get started, as illustrated in the graph below.

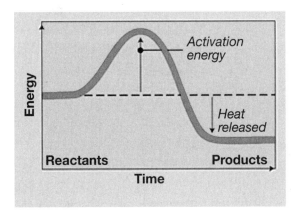

What type of reaction is shown?
a. endothermic, because energy is required after activation to continue the reaction
b. exothermic, because additional energy is needed in order to complete the reaction
c. exothermic, because the energy level of the products is lower than the energy level of the starting materials
d. endothermic, because the energy level of the final materials is higher than that of the starting materials

20. The amount of kinetic energy a moving object has depends on its velocity and mass. Kinetic energy can be calculated by using the following formula:

$$\text{Kinetic Energy} = \frac{\text{mass} \times \text{velocity}^2}{2}$$

Which of the following would have the most kinetic energy?
a. a truck driving 10 m/s
b. a bicycle traveling 10 m/s
c. a car stopped at a red light
d. a school bus parked on a hill

21. Carlos wants to make his home more energy efficient, and he wants an affordable and environmentally responsible solution. Carlos lives in the western United States. His house is located on a small lot in an urban neighborhood that is sparsely landscaped.

Which of these options would meet all of Carlos's needs and criteria?
a. Place solar panels on the roof.
b. Install a wind turbine in the front yard.
c. Replace an oil-fired furnace with a wood-burning stove.
d. Contact electricity companies to compare prices and negotiate rates.

22. The chart below presents information on ultraviolet radiation. It is divided into wavelength ranges identified as UVA, UVB, and UVC.

RADIATION	UVA	UVB	UVC
Main human effect	Aging	Burning	
Wavelength	400 nm to 315 nm	315 nm to 280 nm	280 nm to 100 nm
% reaching Earth 12 noon	95%	5%	0%
% reaching Earth before 10 A.M. and after 12 P.M.	99%	1%	0%
% reaching the Earth (average)	97%	3%	0%
NOTES:		creates Vitamin D	

People are most likely to be at risk of sunburn at
a. 10:00 A.M., because the UVA rays are the greatest.
b. 12:00 P.M., because more UVB rays reach the Earth.
c. 2:00 P.M., because UVC rays are least harmful.
d. 4:00 P.M., because the UVA rays have less strength.

23. Almost all of the weight of a carbon atom comes from which of these particles?

   a. protons only

   b. neutrons and electrons

   c. protons and neutrons

   d. protons, electrons, and neutrons

24. Examine the diagram of an atom below.

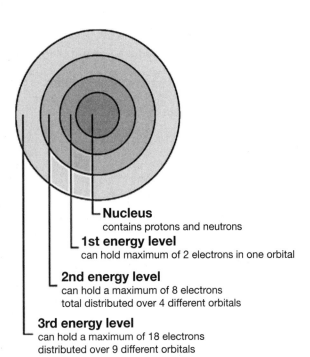

Nucleus
contains protons and neutrons

1st energy level
can hold maximum of 2 electrons in one orbital

2nd energy level
can hold a maximum of 8 electrons
total distributed over 4 different orbitals

3rd energy level
can hold a maximum of 18 electrons
distributed over 9 different orbitals

Which of these would be found in the 1st energy level?

   a. 8 neutrons

   b. 18 electrons

   c. protons and neutrons

   d. no more than 2 electrons

25. A cleaning service wants to offer a natural alternative to the industrial products it normally uses. Instead of bleach, the company uses a mixture of vinegar and baking soda. When the liquid vinegar and powdered baking soda combine, a bubbly gas is produced. What chemical property is observed?

   a. flammability

   b. color change

   c. volume

   d. reactivity

26. The following chart lists the mechanical properties of different metals and alloys.

TOUGHNESS	BRITTLENESS	DUCTILITY	MALLEABILITY	CORROSION RESISTANCE
Copper	White Cast Iron	Gold	Gold	Gold
Nickel	Gray Cast Iron	Silver	Silver	Platinum
Iron	Hardened Steel	Platinum	Aluminum	Silver
Magnesium	Bismuth	Iron	Copper	Mercury
Zinc	Manganese	Nickel	Tin	Copper
Aluminum	Bronzes	Copper	Lead	Lead
Lead	Aluminum	Aluminum	Zinc	Tin
Tin	Brass	Tungsten	Iron	Nickel
Cobalt	Structural Steels	Zinc		Iron
Bismuth	Zinc	Tin		Zinc
	Monel	Lead		Magnesium
	Tin			Aluminum
	Copper			
	Iron			

A jewelry designer wants to work with new types of materials. She needs a metal that is easy to shape, not easily broken, and resistant to tarnishing. Based on the chart, which material would be the best choice?

a. gold

b. nickel

c. bismuth

d. manganese

27. Hydrogen peroxide (H_2O_2) is stored in dark, opaque containers to slow the natural breakdown of the compound.

Write the missing number of water molecules in the box below.

The reaction is summarized by this formula:

$$2H_2O_2 \rightarrow \boxed{} H_2O + O_2$$

28. In a chemical formula, subscripts show the ratio of one kind of atom to another. For example, NH_3 shows that there are 3 hydrogen atoms for every 1 nitrogen atom.

Examine the following ratios:

- twice as many sodium atoms as carbon atoms
- three times as many oxygen atoms as carbon atoms

Which chemical formula correctly shows the ratios described?

a. Na_2CO_3

b. $NaCO_3$

c. Na_3CO_2

d. Na_6CO_{12}

29. The chart below displays solubility rules.

Soluble Compounds	Combinations That Are Not Soluble
Almost all salts of Na^+, K^+, and NH_4^+	
All salts of Cl^-, Br^-, I^-	Ag^+, Hg_2^{+2}, Pb^{+2}
Salts of F^-	Mg^{+2}, Ca^{+2}, Sr^{+2}, Ba^{+2}, Pb^{+2}
Salts of: nitrates, NO_3^- chlorates, ClO_3^- perchlorates, ClO_4^- acetates, $C_2H_3O_2^-$	
All salts of sulfates, SO_4^{-2}	Ba^{+2}, Sr^{+2}, Pb^{+2}

Based on the chart, which compound would be insoluble?

a. $Mg(OH)_2$, because it contains magnesium

b. NaOH, because it is a hydroxide compound

c. KNO_3, because it is a potassium compound

d. LiCl, because it contains a group 1A element

Please use the following to answer questions 30–32.

Billions of barrels of oil are believed to be locked in soft, finely stratified sedimentary shale formations throughout the United States. Natural gas and oil companies are hard at work freeing these resources. Hydraulic fracturing, more commonly referred to as *fracking*, is a drilling process in which millions of gallons of fresh water, sand, and chemicals are injected under high pressure into a well. This cracks the existing rock and releases the natural gas and oil.

The fluids used in hydraulic fracturing, and the wastewater that comes back up the well, need to be disposed of. The safest, most cost-efficient method of disposal involves injecting the fluids into disposal wells thousands of feet underground. The wells are encased in layers of concrete and usually store the waste from several different wells. Each holds about 4.5 million gallons of chemical-laced water.

Sometimes injections of waste into these wells cause earthquakes. These earthquakes occur as crevices that previously contained oil are filled with water. The resulting pressure change needed to push the water underground can trigger a slip in a nearby fault line.

30. Based on the information in the passage, where are the natural-gas deposits that are targeted by hydraulic fracturing?

a. underneath sand

b. in shale formations

c. inside concrete wells

d. below the water table

31. On the map below, the circles indicate locations of earthquakes caused by or related to energy technologies. The larger the circle, the larger the earthquake.

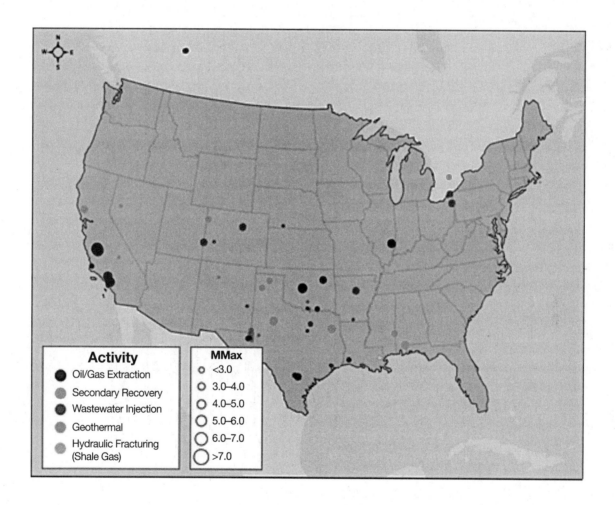

Activity		MMax
● Oil/Gas Extraction		○ <3.0
● Secondary Recovery		○ 3.0–4.0
● Wastewater Injection		○ 4.0–5.0
● Geothermal		○ 5.0–6.0
● Hydraulic Fracturing (Shale Gas)		○ 6.0–7.0
		○ >7.0

Circle the activity in the key that results in earthquakes with the greatest magnitude.

32. According to the information in the passage, which of the following statements best describes concerns about the possible sustainability of hydraulic fracturing?

a. Ongoing fracking could pollute the air.

b. The potential for earthquakes is increasing.

c. Fresh water supplies in shale outcroppings are scarce.

d. Gas and oil surpluses cause less reliance on wind and solar resources.

Please use the following to answer questions 33–35.

Ocean acidification occurs when seawater absorbs carbon dioxide from the atmosphere. This causes the water to become more acidic. Dissolved carbon dioxide increases the hydrogen ion concentration in the ocean, which decreases the ocean's pH level. Calcifying organisms such as corals, oysters, and sea urchins find it more difficult to build shells and skeletons in acidic water.

Carbon dioxide in the atmosphere comes from many sources. When humans burn oil or gas to generate power, carbon dioxide is released. Carbon dioxide is also a greenhouse gas, which means it leads to warmer temperatures on Earth's surface by trapping heat in the air.

34. Based on the passage, which effect from carbon dioxide could have a direct negative impact on marine food webs?
a. reduced calcification of coral
b. increased air pollution from cars
c. rising sea levels from melting glaciers
d. warmer temperatures on Earth's surface

35. Which type of coastal erosion would be most impacted by ocean acidification?
a. abrasion
b. attrition
c. corrosion
d. hydraulic action

33.

Atmospheric CO$_2$ at Mauna Loa Observatory

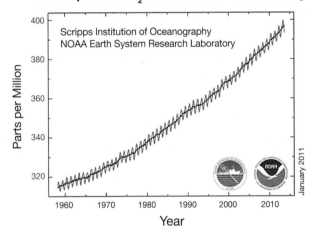

Based on the graph above and the information in the passage, what year presented the lowest risk of ocean acidification?
a. 1960
b. 1970
c. 1990
d. 2010

Answers and Explanations

1. **Choice b is correct.** Kenya is located on the equator. The tilt of the Earth's axis does not substantially change the length of daily exposure of equatorial countries to the sun. Thus, the length of the day does not vary substantially over the course of the year.

   Choice **a** is incorrect. Daylight saving time is the practice of advancing clocks during the lighter months so that evenings have more daylight and mornings have less. In equatorial countries, such as Kenya, there is little variation between daylight and morning hours, and there is no observation of daylight saving time.

   Choice **c** is incorrect. The difference of seasons in opposing hemispheres is due to the tilt of the Earth's axis and the proximity of the hemisphere to the sun. In winter, the northern hemisphere is tilted away from the sun. During winter months, the hemispheres will also experience shorter daylight hours. Kenya, an equatorial country, experiences little variance in daylight hours.

   Choice **d** is incorrect. It is true that equatorial countries such as Kenya will not change position with relation to the sun in fall and spring as the Earth rotates. However, this does not correctly explain the lack of variation in daylight hours over the course of an entire year.

2. **Choice b is correct.** Carbon dioxide combines with water in the presence of energy. These reactants produce glucose in addition to oxygen as a waste material.

   Choice **a** is incorrect. Glucose and oxygen are products of the photosynthesis reaction.

   Choice **c** is incorrect. While carbon dioxide is a reactant of photosynthesis, oxygen is one of the products, along with glucose.

   Choice **d** is incorrect. Water is incorrectly grouped with oxygen and glucose, which are both products of photosynthesis.

3. **Choice a is correct.** Velocity is speed with direction, and it is calculated by dividing the distance traveled by the time it took to cover that distance. On this graph, time is increasing to the right, and position is increasing constantly with time. At any point on graph A, the position divided by time will produce the same number, indicating constant positive velocity.

   Choice **b** is incorrect. The line on graph B is curving upward. This larger slope is indicative of a larger velocity. This shows a positive increase in velocity because the line is getting steeper, indicating acceleration.

   Choice **c** is incorrect. Graph C is representative of an object that is moving with a negative velocity (as denoted by the negative slope). There is a constant, negative velocity (as denoted by the constant, negative slope).

   Choice **d** is incorrect. If an object is not moving, a horizontal line is shown on a position-time graph. Time is increasing to the right, but the position does not change, so there is no movement. A straight-line graph, such as graph D, indicates an object at rest.

4. **Choice c is correct.** The retina is defined as a layer of light-sensitive tissue lining the inner surface of the eye at the back of the eyeball. The cells that are sensitive to light trigger nerve impulses that travel along the optic nerve to the brain, where a visual image is formed.
Choice **a** is incorrect. The lens is a transparent, biconvex body located in the front of the eye that focuses light rays entering through the pupil to form an image on the retina.
Choice **b** is incorrect. The pupil is a black circular opening located near the front of the eye, through which light passes to the retina.
Choice **d** is incorrect. The focus point, also called an image point, is the point where light rays originating from a point on the object converge. Although the focus is conceptually a point, physically the focus has a spatial extent, called the *blur circle*. The focus point differs based on the shape of the eye and elongation of the retina.

5. **Choice a is correct.** When the osmotic pressure outside the red blood cells is the same as the pressure inside the cells, the solution is isotonic with respect to the cytoplasm. This is the usual condition of red blood cells in plasma in a state of homeostasis.
Choice **b** is incorrect. When the concentration of NaCl is higher outside the cell, it is hypertonic. This results in an osmotic flow from the cell to the more concentrated solution outside the cell, instead of an equilibrium needed to maintain homeostasis.
Choice **c** is incorrect. When the solution outside of the red blood cells has a lower osmotic pressure than the cytoplasm inside the red blood cells, the solution is hypotonic with respect to the cells. The cells take in water in an attempt to equalize the osmotic pressure, causing them to swell and potentially burst.
Choice **d** is incorrect. The osmotic pressure of the solution outside the blood cells is higher than the osmotic pressure inside the cells. The water inside the blood cells exits the cells in an attempt to equalize the osmotic pressure, causing the cells to shrink.

6. The highest number of points you can earn on this short-response essay is 3.

A **3-point response** contains:
- a clear and well-developed explanation of how tetanus endospores are transmitted and prevented
- a well-developed explanation correlating the prevalence of tetanus in nations least likely to vaccinate with the high rate of occurrence, noting the favorable climate for tetanus endospores
- complete support from the passage

Sample 3-point response:

It is probable that the countries with the highest incidence of tetanus infection are those least likely to vaccinate while also harboring the most favorable soil and climate conditions for C. tetani endospores. Though C. tetani thrives on the low-oxygen surfaces of rusted metals, it is most common in the hot, damp climates of equatorial countries. Developed, vaccinating nations, such as the United States, Canada, and Australia, have low or no reported cases of tetanus. However, tetanus is strongly prevalent in third-world countries such as India and those found in Africa. Less developed, third-world nations are less likely to immunize people, thus the rates of tetanus infections are strongly prevalent, even though it is not contagious. Toxins from C. tetani enter unvaccinated bodies through open wounds, attack the central nervous system, and cause prolonged muscle spasms.

A **2-point response** contains:

- an adequate or partially articulated explanation of how tetanus endospores are transmitted and prevented
- a partial explanation correlating the prevalence of tetanus in nations least likely to vaccinate with the high rate of occurrence
- partial support from the passage

Sample 2-point response:

People can get tetanus if they are wounded by some kind of rusty metal object. They can also get tetanus from manure-treated soil. Tetanus is caused by a bacteria called C. tetani and it can be prevented with a vaccine. Some countries in Africa may not vaccinate against tetanus.

A **1-point response** contains:

- a minimal or implied explanation of how tetanus endospores are transmitted and prevented
- no explanation correlating the prevalence of tetanus in nations least likely to vaccinate with the high rate of occurrence, noting the favorable climate for tetanus endospores
- minimal or implied support from the passage

Sample 1-point response:

More people in Africa get tetanus than in the rest of the world. It is hot in Africa and there are a lot of animals that have tetanus. People can get tetanus from soil or wounds.

A **0-point response** contains:

- no explanation of how tetanus endospores are transmitted and prevented
- no explanation correlating the prevalence of tetanus in nations least likely to vaccinate with the high rate of occurrence, noting the favorable climate for tetanus endospores
- no support from the passage

7. glucose $\longrightarrow$ **ETHANOL** + carbon dioxide (+ **ENERGY** released)

The first product is **ethanol**. In this item, the phrase "alcohol byproducts" clues the choice for the first product. Oxygen is clearly incorrect, as both the item and the passage indicate that the bacteria are anaerobic, thus cannot use oxygen to respire. Water is a factor in the anaerobic fermentation process in that anaerobes are commonly found and used in waste water treatments, but it is not a component in the simplified fermentation equation.

The second product is **energy**. In this item, the statement "the bacteria use organic compounds, typically found in the intestinal tract of animals, to ferment sugars for energy" indicates that the purpose of fermentation is to create energy to be released.

8. Choice b is correct. The cell wall provides rigidity to maintain cell shape. Additionally, endotoxins are produced in the outer portion of the cell wall.

Choice **a** is incorrect. DNA contains the genetic code for enzymes involved in respiration, along with other important information for the life of the cell. Endotoxins are produced in the outer cell wall.

Choice **c** is incorrect. Enzymes are made and chemical reactions involved in respiration are carried out within the cytoplasm of bacteria. However, endotoxins are produced in the outer cell wall, which is also the component that gives shape and rigidity to the cell.

Choice **d** is incorrect. The cell membrane is a non-rigid porous structure that allows gases and water to pass in and out of the cell while controlling the passage of other chemicals. Endotoxins are produced in the outer cell wall.

9. Choice a is correct. Adult cane toads could be a limiting factor for the juvenile cane toad population because large cane toads prey on other amphibians, even smaller cane toads.

Choice **b** is incorrect. Because cane beetle larvae are buried underground, they are not accessible to the predation of cane toads. Furthermore, cane toads are such diverse predators that the unavailability of one prey species would have little to no effect on their overall population.

Choice **c** is incorrect. Adult cane beetles have heavy exoskeletons and strong legs fitted with spikes. They are difficult to prey upon. They have the ability to fly, while cane toads do not, so they are not a prey resource for the toads.

Choice **d** is incorrect. Cane toad tadpoles do not limit the success of young, or juvenile, cane toads because they are confined to aquatic habitats, while juvenile cane toads can live terrestrially.

10. Choice b is correct. Adaptation is the evolutionary process whereby an organism becomes better able to live in its habitat or habitats. Over time, the crows learned a way to prey upon cane toads without exposing themselves to the toxins released from the cane toad's shoulders.

Choice **a** is incorrect. Speciation is the evolutionary process by which new biological species arise.

Choice **c** is incorrect. Development is a general term referring to physical growth and change in an individual organism.

Choice **d** is incorrect. Homeostasis is a property of a system that regulates its internal environment and tends to maintain a stable, relatively constant condition of properties such as temperature or pH.

11. The highest number of points you can earn on this short-response essay is 3.

A **3-point response** contains:

■ a clear and well-developed explanation of cane toads as an invasive species in Australia

■ complete support from the passage

Sample 3-point response:
Cane toads are non-native to Australia. They were imported nearly 100 years ago in an attempt to control the cane beetle, a pest that destroys sugarcane. Cane toads had no significant impact on the flying and burrowing beetle. However, they had a devastating impact on Australian ecology that includes the depletion of native species. Many species have been in decline for decades and are only recently beginning to recover.

A **2-point response** contains:
- an adequate or partially articulated explanation of cane toads as an invasive species in Australia
- partial support from the passage

Sample 2-point response:
Cane toads are not from Australia. They were brought from the Americas to eat cane beetles and are toxic to Australian animals. The only species they don't impact negatively is the cane beetle.

A **1-point response** contains:
- a minimal or implied explanation of cane toads as an invasive species in Australia
- minimal or implied support from the passage

Sample 1-point response:
Some animals are killed by cane toads when they try to eat the toxic toads. Pets and humans have been poisoned. Only a few animals have learned how to eat the toads without dying themselves.

A **0-point response** contains:
- no explanation of cane toads as an invasive species in Australia.
- no support from the passage

12. **Choice a is correct.** The unique mutualism between corals and their photosynthetic zooxanthellae is the driving force behind the settlement, growth, and productivity of coral reefs. This mutualistic relationship is beneficial to the zooxanthellae by providing a host and expelled carbon dioxide for photosynthesis. The corals benefit when they use the products of the zooxanthellae's photosynthesis for metabolic functions or as building blocks in the making of proteins, fats, and carbohydrates.
Choice b is incorrect. A parasitic relationship is one in which one member of the association benefits while the other is harmed. Parasitic symbioses take many forms, from endoparasites that live within the host's body to ectoparasites that live on its surface. In addition, parasites may be necrotrophic (they kill their host) or biotrophic (they rely on their host surviving).
Choice c is incorrect. Amensalism is the type of relationship in which one species is inhibited or completely obliterated and the other is unaffected. An example is a sapling growing under the shadow of a mature tree. The mature tree can begin to rob the sapling of necessary sunlight, and if the mature tree is very large, it can take up rainwater and deplete soil nutrients.
Choice d is incorrect. Commensalism describes a relationship between two living organisms where one benefits and the other is not significantly harmed or helped. Commensal relationships may involve one organism using another for transportation or for housing, or it may also involve one organism using something another organism created after death.

13. Box 1: Zooxanthellae are described in the passage as **mutualistic photosynthesizers**. Producers are described as autotrophic, which means they are able to make their own food. Just like producers on land, producers in the marine environment convert energy from the sun into food energy through photosynthesis. Phytoplankton are the most abundant and widespread producers in the marine environment. **Box 2:** Based on the trophic levels identified in this pyramid, zooxanthellae would be classified as **primary producers**. Organisms in food webs are commonly divided into trophic levels. These levels can be illustrated in a trophic pyramid, where organisms are grouped by the roles they play in the food web. For example, the first level forms the base of the pyramid and is made up of producers. The second level is made up of herbivorous consumers, and so on. On average, only 10% of the energy from an organism is transferred to its consumer. The rest is lost as waste, movement energy, heat energy, and so on. As a result, each trophic level supports a smaller number of organisms—in other words, it has less biomass. This means that a top-level consumer, such as a shark, is supported by millions of primary producers from the base of the food web or trophic pyramid.

14. The correct answer is zooplankton. The passage states that "although much of a coral's energy needs are supplied by these zooxanthellae, most corals also capture food particles with their stinging tentacles. Prey ranges in size from small fish to microscopic zooplankton." The marine food web clearly depicts an arrow originating with zooplankton that points toward coral. This indicates that the flow of energy moves from zooplankton into coral.

15. Choice a is correct. The correct sequence moves from most specialized to higher levels of organization.
Choice **b** is incorrect. The correct sequence moves from most specialized to higher levels of organization; this choice moves in the opposite way.
Choice **c** is incorrect. The cardiovascular system is a higher level of organization than the heart.
Choice **d** is incorrect. The correct sequence moves from most specialized to higher levels of organization. Red blood cell should be the most specialized item at the far left, with cardiovascular system listed on the far right as the highest level of organization.

16. The correct answer is yy. In a Punnett square, the alleles combine, one from the side and one from the top, in each box. The two lower case "y" alleles combine in the bottom right box of the Punnett square, indicating that a recessive phenotype is possible when two heterozygous genotypes combine.

17. The correct answer is 8 meters. The formula for velocity, $v = \frac{distance}{time}$, can be rearranged to solve for distance. In this case, $d = v \times t$, which is 4 m/s multiplied by 2 seconds.

18. Choice c is correct. Materials such as wool are good insulators because they are poor conductors of heat. A wool blanket will slow the transfer of heat from the body so that it feels warmer.

Choice **a** is incorrect. A material that does not conduct heat well is an insulator. A tile floor would act as a conductor because it transfers heat away from the skin easily, causing the surface of the floor to feel cooler.

Choice **b** is incorrect. Metals such as silver and stainless steel are good conductors of heat. A metal spoon transfers the heat from the hot liquid to any surface it contacts, even skin.

Choice **d** is incorrect. A copper pipe is an excellent conductor of heat and electricity, making it a poor insulator.

19. Choice c is correct. The graph shows that additional energy is not needed to complete the reaction; energy is given off as the reaction takes place. As a result, the energy level of the products is lower than the energy level of the starting materials.

Choice **a** is incorrect. The graph illustrates an exothermic reaction because the energy level of the products is lower than the energy level of the starting materials.

Choice **b** is incorrect. While the graph does indicate an exothermic reaction, the rationale is incorrect in that there is no additional energy necessary to complete the reaction. The graph illustrates energy given off, instead of being used, after activation.

Choice **d** is incorrect. The graph does not show an endothermic reaction. This graph shows a product energy level lower than the reactant energy level.

20. Choice a is correct. While a truck and a school bus may have similar mass, the school bus is parked, indicating a velocity of zero. Thus the truck moving at any velocity will have the highest kinetic energy. Similarly, even though the bicycle is in motion, the greater mass of the truck will contribute to its larger kinetic energy.

Choice **b** is incorrect. A bicycle traveling at 10 m/s will have less kinetic energy than a truck traveling at the same velocity because it has less mass than the truck.

Choice **c** is incorrect. A car stopped at a red light has a velocity of zero, so it will have zero kinetic energy.

Choice **d** is incorrect. A school bus that is parked will have a velocity of zero, translating to zero kinetic energy.

21. Choice a is correct. Incorporating solar panels into his home would allow Carlos to use less fossil fuel energy while saving money.

Choice **b** is incorrect. While wind turbines could be an environmentally sound decision, they are not affordable, nor are they likely to be allowed in Carlos's neighborhood.

Choice **c** is incorrect. Replacing an oil-burning furnace with a wood-burning stove would cost a lot of money and provide no long-term savings or environmental benefits.

Choice **d** is incorrect. Changing electricity companies or lowering existing rates will not make Carlos's home more energy efficient.

22. Choice b is correct. UVB rays cause sunburns. The greatest percentage of UVB rays reach the Earth at noon (12 P.M.), making it the most likely time of day for sunburn to occur.
Choice **a** is incorrect. UVA rays do great damage and are associated with the signs of aging. While they are in abundance from 10 A.M.–2 P.M., they are not the cause of sunburns.
Choice **c** is incorrect. UVC rays do not reach the Earth at any time of day and are not the cause of sunburns.
Choice **d** is incorrect. UVA rays are lessened by 4 P.M., but they are not the cause of sunburns.

23. Choice c is correct. Almost all of the weight of an atom comes from the protons and neutrons in its nucleus. Neutrons weigh approximately 1 atomic mass unit, and protons weigh 1 atomic mass unit (1.67×10^{-24} grams).
Choice **a** is incorrect. Protons are positively charged particles that weigh 1 atomic mass unit (1.67×10^{-24} grams) and are located in the nucleus. They account for the atomic number of the element, but the atomic mass, or weight, is a combination of the weights of protons and neutrons.
Choice **b** is incorrect. The majority of the atomic weight of an atom is determined by the neutrons and protons. Electrons are negatively charged particles that weigh zero atomic mass units and are located in the various orbitals of the energy levels outside the nucleus. An electron actually weighs 9.11×10^{-28} grams. This means it would take about 1,830 electrons to equal the mass of one proton.
Choice **d** is incorrect. An electron actually weighs 9.11×10^{-28} grams. This means it would take about 1,830 electrons to equal the mass of one proton, so they are too light to factor into the overall weight of the atom. Almost all of the weight of an atom is made up of the protons and neutrons in its nucleus.

24. Choice d is correct. The first energy level of an atom can hold a maximum of 2 electrons in one orbital. Each energy level is capable of holding a specific number of electrons.
Choice **a** is incorrect. Neutrons are found only in the nucleus of an atom. The second energy level of an atom can hold a maximum of 8 electrons spread over 4 different orbitals.
Choice **b** is incorrect. The maximum number of electrons in the third energy level of an atom is 18, and they are distributed over 9 different orbitals.
Choice **c** is incorrect. Protons and neutrons are found only in the nucleus of an atom.

25. Choice d is correct. Reactivity is the tendency of a substance to undergo a chemical reaction, either by itself or with other materials, and to release energy. Reactivity with other chemicals was evidenced when the baking soda and vinegar combined and reacted to create carbon dioxide gas, as seen by the bubbles.
Choice **a** is incorrect. While flammability is a chemical property, it was not observed during the reaction between the baking soda and vinegar.
Choice **b** is incorrect. Color change can indicate a reaction, but it was not observed in this scenario.
Choice **c** is incorrect. Volume is a physical property of liquids, not a chemical property seen in this situation.

26. Choice a is correct. Gold is the best choice because it tops the list for corrosion resistance and will not tarnish. It is also malleable, so it is easy to shape, but will not break easily because it is not brittle.

Choice **b** is incorrect. Nickel is not highly malleable, which would make it difficult to shape for jewelry design.

Choice **c** is incorrect. Bismuth is highly brittle and is not considered very malleable, making it a poor choice for jewelry.

Choice **d** is incorrect. Manganese is a very brittle metal that does not shape well and does not resist corrosion well.

27. The correct answer is 2.

The breakdown of hydrogen peroxide into water and oxygen is summarized as $2H_2O_2 \rightarrow 2H_2O + O_2$. The 2 balances the equation because there are 2 water molecules to equal 4 hydrogens.

28. Choice a is correct. The correct formula described is Na_2CO_3, which shows sodium with a subscript of 2, indicating twice as many atoms as the one carbon atom. Oxygen has a subscript of 3, meaning 3 times more than the single carbon atom.

Choice **b** is incorrect. The correct formula should have a subscript of 2 next to sodium because it is to have twice as many sodium atoms as the single carbon atom.

Choice **c** is incorrect. The 3 sodium atoms are more than the "twice as many sodium atoms as carbon atoms" described in the question.

Choice **d** is incorrect. This formula shows 6 times more sodium atoms than carbon atoms and 12 times as many oxygen atoms.

29. Choice a is correct. The rules of solubility state that all hydroxide (OH) compounds are insoluble except those of Group I-A (alkali metals) and Ba^{2+}, Ca^{2+}, and Sr^{2+}. $Mg(OH)_2$ is insoluble because Mg is listed in the chart under the heading of "combinations that are not soluble."

Choice **b** is incorrect. NaOH is soluble, completely dissociating in aqueous solution. Sodium (Na) compounds are soluble, according to the chart.

Choice **c** is incorrect. Salts of K^+ and NO_3 are listed as soluble on the chart. KNO_3 would be classified as completely soluble by the general solubility rules 1 and 3.

Choice **d** is incorrect. Salts of Cl^- are listed as soluble on the chart, so LiCl is a soluble compound. The solubility rules state that all compounds of Group IA elements (the alkali metals) are soluble.

30. Choice b is correct. Soft, finely stratified sedimentary shale formations are home to billions of barrels of oil as well as natural gas.

Choice **a** is incorrect. The natural gas and oil deposits are found in shale formations. Sand, chemicals, and water are used in extraction of the gas and oil through fracking.

Choice **c** is incorrect. Concrete wells are used to house the disposed wastewater from the hydraulic fracturing process, after the shale formation is fractured.

Choice **d** is incorrect. While the oil and gas can be located far below the water table, the best answer, as referenced in the passage, is "billions of barrels of oil are believed to be locked in soft, finely stratified sedimentary shale formations all over the United States."

31. **The correct answer is Oil/Gas Extraction.** The circles in the activity legend indicate the location of earthquakes that were caused or "likely related" to energy technologies. The larger the circle, the larger the earthquake. The largest circles on the map are black, which represents "Oil/Gas Extraction."

32. **Choice c is correct.** Water is scarce in the regions targeted by hydraulic fracturing, and the sustainability of fresh water must be addressed. When "millions of gallons of fresh water, sand, and chemicals are injected under high pressure into a well," the reality of the vast amounts of this resource being used comes to light.
Choice **a** is incorrect. Air pollution is a concern, but it does not address the sustainability concerns. The primary sustainable resource used in hydraulic fracturing is water.
Choice **b** is incorrect. The potential for earthquakes is not a sustainability issue. The resource that must be sustained in order for fracking to continue is water.
Choice **d** is incorrect. Solar and wind resources are not the sustainability issue being raised in the process of hydraulic fracturing. Rather, the millions of gallons of fresh water used in the injection of the wells is the issue.

33. **Choice a is correct.** Ocean acidification occurs when seawater absorbs carbon dioxide from the atmosphere. The point on the graph indicating the lowest concentration of atmospheric CO_2 is 1960.
Choice **b** is incorrect. 1970 shows more parts per million of atmospheric CO_2, which contributes to ocean acidification, than 1960.
Choice **c** is incorrect. 1990 shows significantly more atmospheric carbon dioxide than 1960.
Choice **d** is incorrect. More than 380 parts per million of CO_2 were detected in the atmosphere in 2010.

34. **Choice a is correct.** Increased acidification of ocean waters creates a poor environment for calcifying marine animals. Corals are primary consumers in marine food webs. When corals cannot properly function and begin to die, the secondary and tertiary consumers are negatively impacted.
Choice **b** is incorrect. Increased air pollution from cars does pour more CO_2 into the atmosphere, but this does not directly impact marine food webs.
Choice **c** is incorrect. Rising sea levels can be a result of overall global temperatures, which can be an effect of greenhouse gases. However, this does not have a direct effect on marine food webs.
Choice **d** is incorrect. Greenhouse gases increasing Earth's temperatures will indirectly affect many food webs, but it is not the best answer. The direct negative effect will be seen in coral calcification.

35. Choice c is correct. The process of corrosion occurs when materials with a low pH chemically weather cliff rocks with a high pH. The increased acidity of seawater significantly contributes to the way sea cliffs break apart. Choice **a** is incorrect. Abrasion is also called corrasion; this action is how sea cliffs erode. Various sizes of rock are carried by fast-moving waves that break against cliffs, wearing them down like sandpaper. Large pieces of the upper cliff face break or fall off because of gravity. Choice **b** is incorrect. Attrition is a type of mechanical weathering, in which rock particles are worn against other rock particles so they break up and wear each other down into smooth, round pebbles. This is usually caused by a combination of tidal action and coastal winds.
Choice **d** is incorrect. In hydraulic action erosion, air is forced into tiny fissures and cracks in large rocks by the breaking of large waves. This air pressure exerts enough force on these rocks that they eventually weaken enough to collapse.

9 ▶ GED® SOCIAL STUDIES TEST 2

This practice test is modeled on the format, content, and timing of the official GED® Social Studies test and, like the official exam, presents a series of questions that focus on the fundamentals of social studies reasoning.

Part I

You'll be asked to answer questions based on brief texts, maps, graphics, and tables. Refer to the provided information as often as necessary when answering the questions.

Work carefully, but do not spend too much time on any one question. Be sure you answer every question.

Set a timer for 65 minutes (1 hour and 5 minutes), and try to take this test uninterrupted, under quiet conditions.

Part II

The official GED® Social Studies test also includes an Extended Response question—an essay question. Set a timer for 25 minutes and try to read the given passage, brainstorm, write, and proofread your essay uninterrupted, under quiet conditions

Complete answer explanations for every test question and sample essays at different scoring levels follow the exam. Good luck!

PART I

35 total questions
66 minutes to complete

Please use the following to answer questions 1–3.

The chart below shows the different types of democracy.

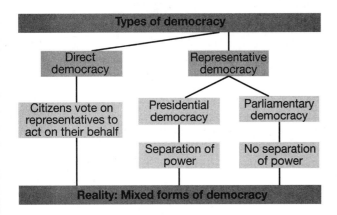

1. Which of the following is generally unique to presidential democracy?
   a. Citizens participate in voting.
   b. The executive power is separate from the legislature.
   c. The executive power is a part of the legislature.
   d. The head of the state is not directly elected by the people.

2. What specific type of democracy is the United States?
   a. Direct democracy
   b. Representative democracy
   c. Parliamentary democracy
   d. Presidential democracy

3. Using the chart, what can you infer about representative democracy?
   a. Each individual's choices are not represented when lawmakers make decisions.
   b. Every citizen's vote on laws is represented when lawmakers make decisions.
   c. The president or prime minister writes the laws.
   d. It is the same as direct democracy.

Please use the following to answer questions 4–5.

The chart below outlines the three branches of United States government.

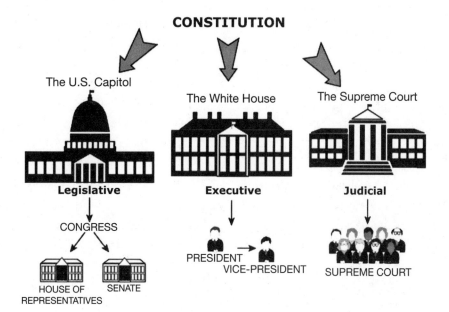

4. What are the branches of government?
   a. House of Representatives and the Senate
   b. House of Representatives, the Senate, and the Supreme Court
   c. President and Vice President
   d. Legislative, executive, and judicial

5. Write the appropriate branch of government in the box below.
   The [   ] branch interprets and applies the law.

Please use the following to answer questions 6–7.

The excerpt below was spoken by Sojourner Truth.

> That man over there says that women need to be helped into carriages, and lifted over ditches, and to have the best place everywhere. Nobody ever helps me into carriages, or over mud-puddles, or gives me any best place! And ain't I a woman? Look at me! Look at my arm! I have ploughed and planted, and gathered into barns, and no man could head me! And ain't I a woman? I could work as much and eat as much as a man—when I could get it—and bear the lash as well! And ain't I a woman? I have borne thirteen children, and seen most all sold off to slavery, and when I cried out with my mother's grief, none but Jesus heard me! And ain't I a woman?

6. Sojourner Truth is making the case for
  a. women's rights.
  b. abolition of slavery.
  c. the opportunity to work.
  d. special treatment for women.

7. The most important source of Sojourner Truth's credibility was
  a. her physical toughness.
  b. her personal beauty and charm.
  c. her moral strength.
  d. her eloquent use of language.

Please use the following to answer questions 8–9.

When the Spanish Conquistadors came to the Americas in the 16th century and destroyed Native American civilizations, one of the greatest civilizations, the Classical Maya, had already disappeared. The archeological evidence shows that a relatively peaceful civilization became more violent with the conquest of Tikal, the greatest Mayan city, in 378 by the mysterious warrior Fire Is Born. Even though Tikal was rebuilt and remained one of the dominant Mayan city-states for hundreds of years, it and the other Mayan cities fell into disrepair and were eventually abandoned.

  Researchers have worked for years to identify the causes for this collapse. According to National Geographic's article "The Maya: Glory and Ruin," by Guy Gugliotta:

  Scholars have looked at various afflictions across the Mayan world, including overpopulation, environmental damage, famine, and drought.

  They have also focused on the one thing that appears to have happened everywhere during the prolonged decline: As resources grew scarce, the kuhul ajaw lost their divine luster, and, with it, the confidence of their subjects, both noble and commoner. Instability and desperation in turn fueled more destructive wars. What had been ritualized contests fought for glory or captives turned into spasms of savagery like the one that obliterated Cancuén. Says Simon Martin of the University of Pennsylvania Museum: "The system broke down and ran out of control."

8. Which of the following was the most important cause of the collapse of the Classical Mayan civilization?
  a. The conquest of Tikal in 378 by Fire Is Born
  b. Loss of confidence of the people in the system
  c. Ritualized warfare for glory and captives
  d. The invasion of the Spanish Conquistadors

9. Write your answer in the box below.
  The Mayan rulers were called the [   ].

Please use the following to answer questions 10–11.

"I Didn't Raise My Boy to Be a Soldier"
(1915)
Lyrics by Al Bryan, music by Al Piantadosi
I didn't raise my boy to be a soldier,
I brought him up to be my pride and joy.
Who dares to place a musket on his shoul-
    der
To shoot some other mother's darling boy?
Let nations arbitrate their future troubles,
It's time to lay the sword and gun away;
There'd be no war today if mothers would
    all say,
"I didn't raise my boy to be a soldier."

"Over There"
(1917)
Music and Lyrics by George Cohan
Johnnie get your gun, get your gun, get
    your gun.
Take it on the run, on the run, on the run.
Hear them calling you and me, every son of
    liberty;
Hurry right away, no delay, go today.
Make your daddy glad to have had such a
    lad
Tell your sweetheart not to pine; to be
    proud her boy's in line.

10. These two popular American songs deal with the position of the United States at the time of World War I. What is the best conclusion based on these two sources?
   a. American parents were proud to have their children join the army.
   b. American soldiers in World War I fought for liberty.
   c. World War I was unnecessary.
   d. World War I was controversial and elicited different points of view.

11. Which propaganda technique is being used in "Over There"?
   a. Testimonial
   b. Name calling
   c. Bandwagon
   d. Fear

Please use the following to answer questions 12–14.

This excerpt is from the Declaration of Independence.

We hold these truths to be self-evident, that all men are created equal, that they are endowed by their Creator with certain unalienable Rights, that among these are Life, Liberty and the pursuit of Happiness.—That to secure these rights, Governments are instituted among Men, deriving their just powers from the consent of the governed,—That whenever any Form of Government becomes destructive of these ends, it is the Right of the People to alter or to abolish it, and to institute new Government, laying its foundation on such principles and organizing its powers in such form, as to them shall seem most likely to effect their Safety and Happiness. Prudence, indeed, will dictate that Governments long established should not be changed for light and transient causes; and accordingly all experience hath shewn, that mankind are more disposed to suffer, while evils are sufferable, than to right themselves by abolishing the forms to which they are accustomed. But when a long train of abuses and usurpations, pursuing invariably the same Object evinces a design to reduce them under absolute Despotism, it is their right, it is their duty, to throw off such Government, and to provide new Guards for their future security.—Such has been the patient sufferance of these Colonies; and such is now the necessity which constrains them to alter their former Systems of Government. The history of the present King of Great Britain is a history of repeated injuries and usurpations, all having in direct object the establishment of an absolute Tyranny over these States. To prove this, let Facts be submitted to a candid world.

This excerpt is from the Second Treatise on Civil Government, by John Locke.

"To understand political power right, and derive it from its original, we must consider, what state all men are naturally in, and that is, a state of perfect freedom to order their actions, and dispose of their possessions and persons, as they think fit, within the bounds of the law of nature, without asking leave or depending upon the will of any other man."

12. Which sentence best represents the main idea expressed in this passage of the Declaration of Independence?
   a. "We hold these truths to be self-evident, that all men are created equal, that they are endowed by their Creator with certain unalienable Rights . . ."
   b. "That whenever any Form of Government becomes destructive of these ends, it is the Right of the People to alter or to abolish it, and to institute new Government . . ."
   c. "The history of the present King of Great Britain is a history of repeated injuries and usurpations, all having in direct object the establishment of an absolute Tyranny over these States."
   d. "To prove this, let Facts be submitted to a candid world."

13. The writers of the Declaration of Independence wanted the decent respect of the opinions of mankind. Their argument primarily rested on what foundation?
   a. an appeal to reason
   b. a plea for emotional connection
   c. a demand for religious faith
   d. a request for partisan feeling

14. In considering the second excerpt and comparing it to the Declaration of Independence, which ideas in the two excerpts are similar?
   a. Locke's ideas regarding a freedom created without asking leave or depending upon the will of any other man are similar to the Declaration's ideas regarding a government that secures men's rights.
   b. Locke's ideas regarding the state of perfect freedom are similar to the Declaration's ideas regarding unalienable rights.
   c. Locke's ideas regarding political power are similar to the Declaration's ideas regarding the pursuit of happiness.
   d. Locke's ideas regarding the consent of the governed are similar to the Declaration's ideas regarding the disposition of possessions and persons.

15. The following is an excerpt from an executive order issued by a president of the United States.

> That on the first day of January, in the year of our Lord one thousand eight hundred and sixty-three, all persons held as slaves within any State or designated part of a State, the people whereof shall then be in rebellion against the United States, shall be then, thenceforward, and forever free; and the Executive Government of the United States, including the military and naval authority thereof, will recognize and maintain the freedom of such persons, and will do no act or acts to repress such persons, or any of them, in any efforts they may make for their actual freedom.

Who was the author of this executive order?
   a. George Washington
   b. Abraham Lincoln
   c. Thomas Jefferson
   d. James Madison

Please use the following to answer questions 16–18.

The following is an excerpt from the United States Supreme Court decision of *Plessy v. Ferguson* (1896).

> Legislation is powerless to eradicate racial instincts or to abolish distinctions based upon physical differences.

The following is an excerpt from the United States Supreme Court decision of *Brown v. Board of Education* (1954).

> To separate [children in grade and high schools] from others of similar age and qualifications solely because of their race generates a feeling of inferiority as to their status in the community that may affect their hearts and minds in a way unlikely to ever be undone . . . Whatever may have been the extent of psychological knowledge at the time of *Plessy v. Ferguson*, this finding is amply supported by modern authority . . .We conclude that in the field of public education the doctrine of "separate but equal" has no place.

The following is an excerpt from the First Amendment.

> Congress shall make no law respecting an establishment of religion, or prohibiting the free exercise thereof; or abridging the freedom of speech, or of the press; or the right of the people peaceably to assemble, and to petition the Government for a redress of grievances.

The following is an excerpt from the Sixth Amendment.

> In all criminal prosecutions, the accused shall enjoy the right to a speedy and public trial, by an impartial jury of the State and district wherein the crime shall have been committed, which district shall have been previously ascertained by law, and to be informed of the nature and cause of the accusation; to be confronted with the witnesses against him; to have compulsory process for obtaining witnesses in his favor, and to have the Assistance of Counsel for his defence.

The following is an excerpt from the Thirteenth Amendment.

> **Section 1.**
> Neither slavery nor involuntary servitude, except as a punishment for crime whereof the party shall have been duly convicted, shall exist within the United States, or any place subject to their jurisdiction.

The following is an excerpt from the Fourteenth Amendment.

> **Section 1.**
> All persons born or naturalized in the United States, and subject to the jurisdiction thereof, are citizens of the United States and of the State wherein they reside. No State shall make or enforce any law which shall abridge the privileges or immunities of citizens of the United States; nor shall any State deprive any person of life, liberty, or property, without due process of law; nor deny to any person within its jurisdiction the equal protection of the laws.

16. Which of the following statements is supported by evidence from the excerpts?
    a. The U.S. Supreme Court occasionally changes its mind.
    b. The *Brown* decision declared segregation was constitutional and overturned the *Plessy* decision.
    c. It is impossible to make laws to eliminate racial instincts.
    d. Interpretive problems can be solved by returning to the actual words of the Constitution.

17. Which of the following was central to the arguments presented to the Supreme Court in *Plessy v. Ferguson*?
    a. the First Amendment
    b. the Sixth Amendment
    c. the Thirteenth Amendment
    d. the Fourteenth Amendment

18. Which of the following was LEAST likely to have influenced the Supreme Court's decision in *Brown v. Board of Education*?
    a. A statement signed by some of the leading experts in the fields of psychology, biology, cultural anthropology, and ethnology that rejected race theories and pseudo-science used to justify the Holocaust.
    b. A study of race relations that detailed the obstacles facing African Americans in 1940s American society.
    c. A study that found contrasts among children who attended segregated schools in Washington, D.C., versus those in integrated schools in New York.
    d. The first African American quarterback played in the National Football League during the modern era.

19.

Which of the following can you infer from this cartoon?
    a. Economic freedoms are the same as political freedoms.
    b. The economy has no effect on political freedoms in the United States.
    c. Political freedoms can be hindered by the economy.
    d. Race remains a key factor in the economic opportunities available to Americans.

Please use the following to answer questions 20–21.

The following is an excerpt from "On Indian Removal," by President Andrew Jackson (1830).

What good man would prefer a country covered with forests, and ranged by a few thousand savages to our extensive Republic, studded with cities, towns, and prosperous farms embellished with all the improvements which art can devise or industry execute, occupied by more than 12,000,000 happy people, and filled with all the blessings of liberty, civilization and religion? . . .

The tribes which occupied the countries not constituting the Eastern States were annihilated or have melted away to make room for the whites. The waves of population and civilization are rolling to the westward, and we now propose to acquire the countries occupied by the red men of the South and West by a fair exchange, and, at the expense of the United States, to send them to land where their existence may be prolonged and perhaps made perpetual.

The following is the painting *American Progress*, by John Gast (1872).

John Gast, American Progress, 1872.
Chromolithograph published by George A. Crofutt.
Source: Prints and Photographs Division, Library of Congress.

20. What element from the excerpt or painting would be considered propaganda?

a. The painting shows a progression of transportation ideas from horseback all the way to steam-engine train, which matches the industrial movement of the time.

b. The United States set aside land for displaced Indian tribes.

c. The population of the United States was expanding westward.

d. The woman in the painting representing American Progress wears white robes like a classical Greek or Roman sculpture.

21. In today's society, how would the concept of American Progress and President Andrew Jackson's removal plan be seen?

a. as an infringement on the rights of individuals

b. as valid and necessary for the reclamation of needed farmland

c. as a removal of foreign peoples from American soil

d. as an infringement on the rights of the states

Please use the following to answer question 22.

The following excerpt is from the Majority Decision of *Marbury v. Madison* (1803).

It is emphatically the province and duty of the Judicial Department [the judicial branch] to say what the law is. Those who apply the rule to particular cases must, of necessity, expound and interpret that rule. If two laws conflict with each other, the Courts must decide on the operation of each.

So, if a law [e.g., a statute or treaty] be in opposition to the Constitution, if both the law and the Constitution apply to a particular case, so that the Court must either decide that case conformably to the law, disregarding the Constitution, or conformably to the Constitution, disregarding the law, the Court must determine which of these conflicting rules governs the case. This is of the very essence of judicial duty. If, then, the Courts are to regard the Constitution, and the Constitution is superior to any ordinary act of the Legislature, the Constitution, and not such ordinary act, must govern the case to which they both apply.

Those, then, who controvert the principle that the Constitution is to be considered in court as a paramount law are reduced to the necessity of maintaining that courts must close their eyes on the Constitution, and see only the law [e.g., the statute or treaty].

This doctrine would subvert the very foundation of all written constitutions.

(Chief Justice John Marshall)

The following excerpt is from a letter to Abigail Adams from Thomas Jefferson (1804).

> The Constitution . . . meant that its coordinate branches should be checks on each other. But the opinion which gives to the judges the right to decide what laws are constitutional and what not, not only for themselves in their own sphere of action but for the Legislature and Executive also in their spheres, would make the Judiciary a despotic branch.

22. What can be concluded from these two excerpts?

a. Thomas Jefferson was supportive of the judiciary branch maintaining the constitution.

b. The judiciary branch prior to 1803 did not decide whether laws being formed by the other two branches were constitutional or not.

c. The coordinate branches check and balance each other through the Constitution.

d. The law should be blind to the Constitution and apply to each case as such.

Please use the following to answer question 23.

The following excerpt is from Adam Smith, *The Wealth of Nations*, Book V, Chapter 2 (1776).

> The subjects of every state ought to contribute towards the support of the government, as nearly as possible, in proportion to their respective abilities; that is, in proportion to the revenue which they respectively enjoy under the protection of the state. The expense of government to the individuals of a great nation is like the expense of management to the joint tenants of a great estate, who are all obliged to contribute in proportion to their respective interests in the estate.

The following excerpt is from *On the Duty of Civil Disobedience*, by Henry David Thoreau (1849).

> When a sixth of the population of a nation which has undertaken to be the refuge of liberty are slaves, and a whole country is unjustly overrun and conquered by a foreign army, and subjected to military law, I think that it is not too soon for honest men to rebel and revolutionize. What makes this duty the more urgent is the fact that the country so overrun is not our own, but ours is the invading army.
>
> . . . If a thousand men were not to pay their tax bills this year, that would not be a violent and bloody measure, as it would be to pay them, and enable the State to commit violence and shed innocent blood. This is, in fact, the definition of a peaceable revolution, if any such is possible.

23. Based on the two excerpts, what would you conclude to be true of the statements below?

  a. Adam Smith and Henry David Thoreau would agree on the distribution of taxation within the government.

  b. Adam Smith and Henry David Thoreau would agree on the definition of a peaceable revolution.

  c. Adam Smith and Henry David Thoreau would disagree on the use of military by the government.

  d. Adam Smith and Henry David Thoreau would disagree on the use of taxation as an avenue for government critique.

24.

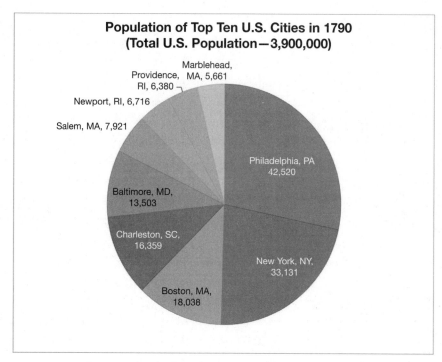

Population of Top Ten U.S. Cities in 1790
(Total U.S. Population—3,900,000)

Marblehead, MA, 5,661
Providence, RI, 6,380
Newport, RI, 6,716
Salem, MA, 7,921
Baltimore, MD, 13,503
Charleston, SC, 16,359
Boston, MA, 18,038
New York, NY, 33,131
Philadelphia, PA 42,520

Using this chart, what can be concluded about the time when this population count was made?

  a. The American Revolution had drastically reduced the number of people living in cities.

  b. The biggest cities had a more diverse population than the smaller cities.

  c. Western expansion was in progress, but modern cities did not have big populations yet.

  d. The majority of the total U.S. population was not located in cities.

25.

Comparison of Chinese and U.S. Energy Statistics

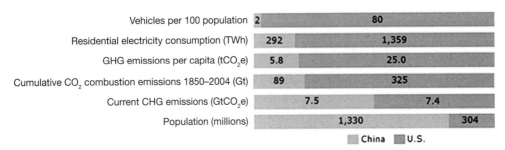

	China	U.S.
Vehicles per 100 population	2	80
Residential electricity consumption (TWh)	292	1,359
GHG emissions per capita (tCO$_2$e)	5.8	25.0
Cumulative CO$_2$ combustion emissions 1850–2004 (Gt)	89	325
Current CHG emissions (GtCO$_2$e)	7.5	7.4
Population (millions)	1,330	304

China ☐ U.S. ☐

According to the graph, the energy statistic that shows the greatest difference between the United States and China is [   ].

Select the correct answer from the choices below to fill in the blank.

Vehicles per 100 population
Residential Electricity Consumption
GHG Emissions per Capita
Population (millions)

26. This map depicts the territories held by various empires in the years before and after European colonization of the Americas.

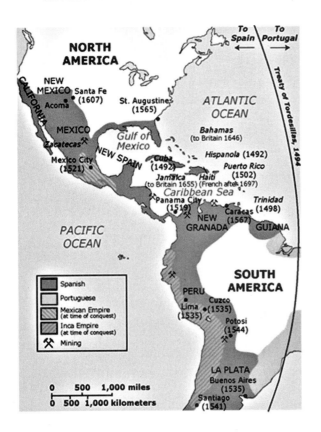

Which nation or people controlled the largest amount of territory in the Americas?
a. the Spanish
b. the Portuguese
c. the Mexican Empire
d. the Inca Empire

27. What is the exclusive control of the supply of a commodity called?
a. market power
b. price discrimination
c. monopoly
d. efficiency

Please use the following to answer questions 28–29.

The following chart depicts the gross domestic product of the United States, China, and Japan between 1960 and 2011.

14.99 Trillion USD (2011)
United States of America
Gross Domestic Product

15T

10T

5T

0

1960   1970   1980   1990   2000   2010

● United States of America
14.99 trillion USD (2011)

● China 7.318 trillion
USD (2011)

● Japan 5.867 trillion
USD (2011)

Please use the following to answer questions 30–31.

Abraham Lincoln and Andrew Johnson: "The Rail Splitter at Work Repairing the Union" (1865).

THE "RAIL SPLITTER" AT WORK REPAIRING THE UNION.

28. Which characteristic best describes the Japanese GDP trend between 1996 and 2010?
  a. stable
  b. turbulent
  c. stagnant
  d. all of the above

29. Which of the following accurately describes the United States GDP between 2008 and 2010?
  a. It increased dramatically.
  b. It decreased slightly before increasing.
  c. It increased slightly before decreasing.
  d. It decreased dramatically.

"Andrew Johnson Kicking out the Freedmen's Bureau," by Thomas Nast in *Harper's Weekly* (1866).

"This Little Boy . . . ," a political cartoon of President Johnson by Thomas Nast in *Harper's Weekly* (1868).

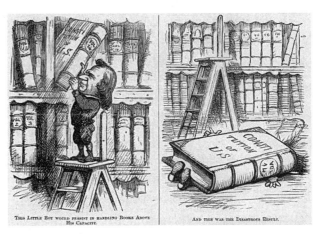

30. Viewing the three political cartoons, what can be surmised about Andrew Johnson's political career over the course of these years?
   a. Andrew Johnson continued the legacy of Abraham Lincoln's Restoration reforms.
   b. Andrew Johnson was well liked by political cartoonists and the populace.
   c. Andrew Johnson did what was necessary to work with the U.S. Constitution.
   d. Andrew Johnson succeeded Abraham Lincoln as president.

31. What aspects of the United States government are illustrated in these political cartoons?
   a. The amendment process and power of veto
   b. The powers of the presidency
   c. The powers of Congress
   d. The Constitution and ratification

32. The following political cartoon appeared in *Harper's Weekly* (1868).

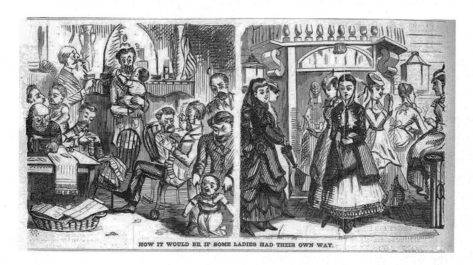

HOW IT WOULD BE, IF SOME LADIES HAD THEIR OWN WAY.

The following is an excerpt from *History of Woman Suffrage*, by Susan B Anthony, Elizabeth Cady Stanton, Matilda Joslyn Gage, and Ida Husted Harper (1886).

"We ask justice, we ask equality, we ask that all civil and political rights that belong to the citizens of the United States be guaranteed to us and our daughters forever."

In what way do these two references to the Women's Suffrage Movement diverge?
a. The political cartoon is focused on women going out to work, while the quote is focused on daughters.
b. The political cartoon is focused on babies, while the quote is focused on citizenship.
c. The political cartoon is focused on women leaving men to take care of the children, while the quote is focused on equality.
d. The political cartoon is focused on men spending time together, while the quote is focused on women spending time together.

Please use the following to answer question 33.

FISCAL YEAR	EXPENDITURES	SURPLUS OR DEFICIT	TOTAL PUBLIC DEBT
UNITED STATES GOVERNMENT FINANCES, 1929–1941 (IN BILLIONS OF DOLLARS)			
1929	$3.127	$0.734	$16.9
1930	3.320	0.738	16.2
1931	3.577	−0.462	16.8
1932	4.659	−2.735	19.5
1933	4.598	−2.602	22.5
1934	6.645	−3.630	27.1
1935	6.497	−2.791	28.7
1936	8.422	−4.425	33.8
1937	7.733	−2.777	36.4
1938	6.765	−1.177	37.2
1939	8.841	−3.862	40.4
1940	9.589	−2.710	43.0
1941	13.980	−4.778	44.0

This excerpt is President Herbert Hoover's annual message to the Congress on the State of the Union, presented in 1930.

"Economic depression cannot be cured by legislative action or executive pronounce-ment. Economic wounds must be healed by the action of the cells of the economic body—the producers and consumers them-selves . . . The best contribution of govern-ment lies in encouragement of this voluntary cooperation in the community. The govern-ment—national, state, and local—can join with the community in such programs and do its part."

33. What do the chart and excerpt indicate about the Great Depression?
   a. Hoover was correct: economic depression cannot be cured by legislative action or executive pronouncement.
   b. Hoover was incorrect: economic depression can be cured by legislative action or executive pronouncement.
   c. The Great Depression did not affect surplus or deficit.
   d. There is not enough data to truly evaluate the government's policies.

Please use the following to answer questions 34–35.

This map illustrates the dates that each state joined the union.

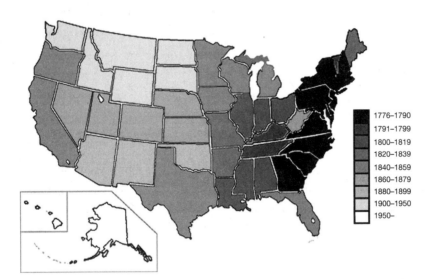

■	1776–1790
■	1791–1799
■	1800–1819
■	1820–1839
■	1840–1859
■	1860–1879
■	1880–1899
■	1900–1950
□	1950–

34. Which conclusion is supported by the map?
   a. The United States expanded from east to west.
   b. The United States expanded from west to east.
   c. The United States expanded from north to south.
   d. There is no general trend in United States expansion.

35. Which of the following statements is best supported by the data presented on the map?

    a. Wisconsin and Minnesota were once considered part of Canada.

    b. California was more difficult to reach than surrounding areas, resulting in a long delay before it became a state.

    c. Texas was considered part of the same territory as New Mexico until the late 19th century.

    d. West Virginia was originally part of Virginia but became a separate state at a later date.

Part II

1 Question
25 minutes to complete

This practice test will familiarize you with the Extended Response question found on the GED® Social Studies test.

Before you begin, it is important to note that on the official test, this task must be completed in no more than 25 minutes. But don't rush to complete your response; take time to carefully read the passage(s) and the prompt. Then think about how you would like to respond to the prompt.

As you write your essay, be sure to:

- Develop an argument about how the ideas expressed in the first passage, an editorial by President Theodore Roosevelt, are related to those expressed in the second passage, a letter to the editor
- Thoroughly construct your main points, organizing them logically, with strong supporting details
- Present multiple pieces of evidence, using ideas from both passages
- Connect your sentences, paragraphs, and ideas with transitional words and phrases
- Express your ideas clearly and choose your words carefully
- Use varied sentence structures to improve the clarity and flow of your response
- Reread and revise your response

Good luck!

Please use the following to answer the essay question.

This excerpt is from an editorial by former president Theodore Roosevelt that was published in the _Kansas City Star_ on May 7, 1918.

The President is merely the most important among a large number of public servants. He should be supported or opposed exactly to the degree which is warranted by his good conduct or bad conduct, his efficiency or inefficiency in rendering loyal, able, and disinterested service to the Nation as a whole. Therefore it is absolutely necessary that there should be full liberty to tell the truth about his acts, and this means that it is exactly necessary to blame him when he does wrong as to praise him when he does right. Any other attitude in an American citizen is both base and servile. To announce that there must be no criticism of the President, or that we are to stand by the President, right or wrong, is not only unpatriotic and servile, but is morally treasonable to the American public. Nothing but the truth should be spoken about him or any one else. But it is even more important to tell the truth, pleasant or unpleasant, about him than about anyone else.

Letter

September 21, 2001

To the Editor:

Yesterday, our president George W. Bush stood in front of Congress and said many things about loyalty to America and the American response to the recent tragic attacks on our country. He stated explicitly "Every nation in every region now has a decision to make: Either you are with us or you are with the terrorists."

I find this wording troublesome for a very specific reason. If this is how the president addresses Congress regarding our possible allies, what will he say about his own citizens and their feelings about the actions of the government to this crisis? While we have not acted yet as a nation regarding the attacks on our country, what if the actions of our government are not what the population agrees with? Will we then be considered "with the terrorists" if we voice our criticism? I worry that freedom of speech, which is one of our basic rights, while not being applied to our allies, could come under fire on our own soil. If we criticize the president, do we then run the risk of being seen as disloyal to our nation and thus have allied ourselves with terrorism?

At the very least, maybe it's important that there is a reminder that freedom of speech is a right placed beyond the reach of government. Criticism of our own government is a form of freedom of speech, and any of our civil liberties must be held sacred especially in times of crisis like this. Until we see what actions the government takes with regard to recent events, I will hold my critique at bay, but I should have the right to critique those actions without being aligned with our enemies. Our government and especially our president should inspire our loyalty through actions, and not through fear or infringing on our individual rights.

—Sandra Greene

Eden Prairie, MN

QUESTION:

In your response, develop an argument about how the letter writer's viewpoint reflects the enduring issue of civil liberties during times of crisis that Theodore Roosevelt expressed in his editorial. Incorporate relevant and specific evidence from the excerpt, the letter, and your own knowledge of the enduring issue and the circumstances surrounding both passages to support your analysis.

Answers and Explanations

Part I

1. **Choice b is correct.** In presidential democracy, the president is separate from the legislature.
Choice **a** is incorrect. In both presidential and parliamentary democracy, the people participate in voting.
Choice **c** is incorrect. In parliamentary democracy, not presidential, the executive power, usually called the prime minister, is a member of parliament or the legislature.
Choice **d** is incorrect. In parliamentary democracy, the parliament or legislature elects the president; this answer is incorrect because that is an attribute of parliamentary not presidential democracy.

2. **Choice d is correct.** In the U.S., citizens elect representatives and vote to elect the president. In addition, the presidential powers are separate from legislative powers. These are all hallmarks of presidential democracy.
Choice **a** is incorrect. This answer neglects the fact that U.S. citizens elect officials to represent them in the legislature.
Choice **b** is incorrect. Although this is technically true, as one can see on the graph, it is not the most specific answer available.
Choice **c** is incorrect. This answer is incorrect because it shows the reader does not understand the difference between parliamentary and presidential democracy, and how the U.S. fits the latter description.

3. **Choice a is correct.** In this type of democracy, people elect representatives who then make decisions on their behalf. People do not each get a vote on legislature.
Choice **b** is incorrect. In this type of democracy, people elect representatives who then make the laws. In direct democracy, each individual's vote is represented.
Choice **c** is incorrect. There is no evidence in this chart to support that conclusion; neither a president nor a prime minister's role is outlined here.
Choice **d** is incorrect. Direct democracy and representative democracy are two separate branches.

4. **Choice d is correct.** This reflects the three branches of the U.S. government.
Choice **a** is incorrect. This choice shows the reader does not comprehend the graphic and lacks basic understanding of the U.S. government.
Choice **b** is incorrect. This choice shows a misinterpretation of the graphic.
Choice **c** is incorrect. This choice shows a misreading of the graphic.

5. **The correct answer is judicial.**
The judicial branch interprets and applies the law. This is the power of the judicial branch as listed in the Constitution. The Supreme Court reviews the laws through the lens of different cases and decides how the law should be understood and used.
The legislative branch is responsible for writing the laws, and the executive branch is responsible for implementing and enforcing the laws written by the legislature.

6. Choice a is correct. By repeating the phrase "Ain't I a woman," Sojourner Truth makes it clear that all women have basic human rights. Choice **b** is incorrect. While she was a former slave and mentions slavery in her speech, it is not the main focus of her speech.

Choice **c** is incorrect. Sojourner states that she worked hard, but that is not the main point of her speech.

Choice **d** is incorrect. By describing her own tough life, she speaks out against special treatment and in favor of equal rights.

7. Choice c is correct. The directness and power of her language emphasizes her moral strength. Her physical strength can be seen as a metaphor for her moral strength.

Choice **a** is incorrect. Her physical toughness alone is only part of her credibility.

Choice **b** is incorrect. Truth makes the point that she is not a dainty creature of privilege, and therefore beauty and charm wouldn't form part of her powers of persuasion.

Choice **d** is incorrect. Her eloquent and direct use of language may be persuasive and helps to clarify her moral character, but it is her character itself that is the ultimate source of her credibility.

8. Choice b is correct. Loss of confidence of the people in the system was the most important cause of the collapse of the Classical Mayan civilization.

Choice **a** is incorrect. The conquest of Tikal in 378 by Fire Is Born was a key step in the collapse of the Mayan system, but it was only one part of a loss of confidence that spanned hundreds of years.

Choice **c** is incorrect. Ritualized warfare was an important part of their stable religious system.

Choice **d** is incorrect. The invasion of the Conquistadors happened hundreds of years later.

9. The correct answer is kuhul ajaw.

The kuhul ajaw was a Mayan ruler. While the passage doesn't state this directly, it makes clear that the kuhul ajaw was the head of the society by what follows the phrase "kuhul ajaw" — "their divine luster . . . the confidence of their subjects."

10. Choice d is correct. The two songs take opposing views as to the value of enlisting and fighting in World War I.

Choice **a** is incorrect. It is supported by "Over There" but not by "I Didn't Raise My Boy to Be a Soldier."

Choice **b** is incorrect. It is supported by "Over There" but not by "I Didn't Raise My Boy to Be a Soldier."

Choice **c** is incorrect. It is proposed by Al Bryan but rejected by George Cohan.

11. Choice c is correct. This technique entices the audience to follow the crowd by appealing to groups held together already by common of nationality, religion, race, etc. Bandwagon propaganda is a common technique used in wartime.

Choice **a** is incorrect. A testimonial typically uses a celebrity in an attempt to have us agree with an idea, such as in a celebrity endorsement. This is not the case in "Over There."

Choice **b** is incorrect. The name-calling propaganda technique connects a person, or idea, to a negative word or symbol in an effort to get the audience to reject the person or the idea. This is not the case in "Over There."

Choice **d** is incorrect. Fear as a propaganda technique focuses on the negative outcomes if the desired course of action is not followed. This is not the case in "Over There."

12. Choice b is correct. This sentence correctly sums up the passage, whose main theme is the right for the United States to break away from an unfair government.

Choice **a** is incorrect. This is a reason that the United States' founding fathers are using to justify the document and its ideals, but it's not the main idea.

Choice **c** is incorrect. Although this is a sentence justifying the theme, it does not represent the main idea.

Choice **d** is incorrect. This sentence is only a transition sentence that introduces the facts.

13. Choice a is correct. The Declaration of Independence reads like a logical treatise. There is nothing in the excerpt that appeals to the reader's emotions, religious beliefs, or partisan feelings.

Choice **b** is incorrect. There is nothing in the excerpt that appeals to the reader's emotions.

Choice **c** is incorrect. There is nothing in the excerpt that appeals to the reader's religious beliefs.

Choice **d** is incorrect. There is nothing in the excerpt that appeals to the reader's partisan feelings.

14. Choice b is correct. John Locke's "state of perfect freedom" and the Declaration of Independence's "unalienable Rights" are similar concepts. John Locke's focus was that all men, through nature, are given this state of freedom, and the Declaration agreed that all men have rights that are not dictated by any other man.

Choice **a** is incorrect. John Locke, while influencing the Declaration of Independence, was more focused on man as an independent person without reliance on others, while the Declaration of Independence stated that government should protect any freedoms men could want. These ideas are not similar.

Choice **c** is incorrect. John Locke's ideas regarding political power are not fully addressed in this excerpt. These ideas may be similar, but are not the best choice.

Choice **d** is incorrect. John Locke did not write about "the consent of the governed," and Declaration of Independence did not mention the disposing of possessions or persons. These ideas have been reversed, so this is not the best choice.

15. Choice b is correct. Lincoln is known for writing the Emancipation Proclamation, of which this is an excerpt, which freed all persons held as slaves.

Choice **a** is incorrect. This excerpt is dated "one thousand eight hundred and sixty-three," long after Washington's death.

Choice **c** is incorrect. This excerpt was written after Jefferson's death.

Choice **d** is incorrect. This choice neglects the evidence of time and content.

16. Choice a is correct. The *Brown* decision overturned the *Plessy* decision, thus demonstrating that the U.S. Supreme Court occasionally changes its mind.

Choice **b** is incorrect. The *Brown* decision overturned the *Plessy* decision; however, in doing so, it declared segregation was unconstitutional.

Choice **c** is incorrect. The *Plessy* decision held that laws could not eliminate racial instincts, but this does not make it a reasonable conclusion; indeed, Brown's authors completely disagreed.

Choice **d** is incorrect. Both decisions were based on the Fourteenth Amendment.

17. Choice d is correct. The Fourteenth Amendment protects the rights of Americans regardless of their race, which was the main issue in the case of *Plessy v. Ferguson*. However, the Supreme Court decided that "separate but equal" facilities offered to people of different races did not violate the Fourteenth Amendment. This viewpoint would stand as law until 1954, when the case *Brown v. Board of Education* essentially reversed this ruling.

Choice **a** is incorrect. The First Amendment deals with free speech and freedom of the press, which is not necessarily relevant in this case.

Choice **b** is incorrect. The Sixth Amendment guarantees the right to a speedy and public trial. This issue was not central to the arguments presented in *Plessy v. Ferguson*.

Choice **c** is incorrect. The Thirteenth Amendment outlawed slavery. Issues of slavery were not central to the arguments presented in *Plessy v. Ferguson*.

18. Choice d is correct. Although this was indeed a sign of the changing times in America, it did not influence the Supreme Court's decision in *Brown v. Board of Education*.

Choice **a** is incorrect. The Supreme Court's decision was, in fact, influenced by "The Race Question," a scholarly statement published by UNESCO in 1950.

Choice **b** is incorrect. The Supreme Court's decision was, in fact, influenced by "An American Dilemma: The Negro Problem and Modern Democracy," a 1,500-page study of race relations published in 1944.

Choice **c** is incorrect. The Supreme Court's decision was, in fact, influenced by a study that found contrasts between children who attended segregated schools in Washington, D.C., and those in integrated schools in New York.

19. Choice c is correct. This answer shows that the reader comprehends that the person in the comic cannot reach "political freedom" because he is being sat on by a piggy bank, a visual symbol of the economy.

Choice **a** is incorrect. There is no evidence or graphic representation in the cartoon that suggests the two are the same.

Choice **b** is incorrect. It neglects the visual representation of money, as symbolized by the piggy bank, as restricting the person from grabbing "political freedom."

Choice **d** is incorrect. The cartoon does not emphasize race as a component that can restrict economic opportunities or political freedoms.

20. Choice d is correct. By dressing this allegorical figure of American Progress in Classical robes as though she were from Greek or Roman times, the painter is suggesting that the United States' displacement of native people is as important to civilization as the creation of democracy and republic in ancient times. This is propaganda.

Choice **a** is incorrect. The painting does show this progression of transportation, which would be seen more as illustrating the industry of the time rather than propaganda.

Choice **b** is incorrect. The United States did actually set aside land for displaced Indian tribes. This was fact rather than propaganda.

Choice **c** is incorrect. The population of the United States was expanding westward. This was fact rather than propaganda.

21. Choice a is correct. American Indians are considered citizens, so in today's society, forcibly removing them would be seen as an infringement on the rights of the individuals.

Choice **b** is incorrect. Although much of where American Indians have lived has become farmland, this would not be seen as a valid reason to move citizens.

Choice **c** is incorrect. Since American Indians are considered citizens, removing them would not be a removal of foreign people.

Choice **d** is incorrect. Although this could be seen as infringing on the rights of the state, this is not the best choice.

22. Choice b is correct. By looking at both excerpts, it's clear that the judiciary branch, prior to *Marbury v. Madison*, was not ruling on whether a law set into place by the legislative and executive branches fell into agreement with the Constitution. Thomas Jefferson's letter shows that he is uncomfortable with the precedent of the judiciary branch having the final say over the creation of laws by the Legislative and Executive, which means that this was not the case previously.

Choice **a** is incorrect. Thomas Jefferson does not support the judiciary branch maintaining the Constitution, as he uses the word "despotic" to describe what he fears it will become.

Choice **c** is incorrect. This is only stated in the letter from Thomas Jefferson and is not referred to in the excerpt from *Marbury v. Madison*.

Choice **d** is incorrect. This is only noted in the excerpt from *Marbury v. Madison* and is argued against within that ruling.

23. Choice d is correct. Since Adam Smith notes that all men ought to contribute via taxation to the government, it seems likely that he would disagree with Henry David Thoreau's notion that not paying taxes is a good way to disagree with government activities.

Choice **a** is incorrect. This is not something that it appears Adam Smith and Henry David Thoreau would agree on. Adam Smith notes that the government should be paid for the protections that each individual enjoys. This would suggest that Smith believes government should use those taxes for citizen protection, which might include military action. Thoreau, however, is against the use of tax money for military action, especially since he was protesting the Mexican-American war during this time.

Choices **b** and **c** are incorrect. These are not things that Adam Smith refers to.

24. Choice d is correct. The total population far exceeds the total population numbers listed for these cities. It can be inferred that most of the population was located not in cities, but in towns and rural areas.
Choice **a** is incorrect. This chart does not address the American Revolution casualties.
Choice **b** is incorrect. There is nothing in this chart to indicate the diversity of the cities at this time.
Choice **c** is incorrect. There is nothing in this chart to indicate the status of Western expansion.

25. The correct answer is Vehicles per 100 Population. The United States has 80 cars per 100 people, while China only has 2; a 78-car difference. This is clearly shown on the graph, which has United States taking up almost all of the bar for that characteristic.

26. Choice a is correct. A significant portion of the map is covered by the color that represents Spain.
Choice **b** is incorrect. In the map, the Portuguese conquests cover a relatively small portion compared to Spain.
Choice **c** is incorrect. The Mexican Empire was conquered; also, it covers a small part of the map.
Choice **d** is incorrect. The Inca Empire was conquered and takes up only a small part of the map.

27. Choice c is correct. This is the correct word for that definition.
Choice **a** is incorrect. This phrase indicates how a company can raise the market price of a good or service over its marginal costs in a profitable way.
Choice **b** is incorrect. This is a phrase used to describe the sales of identical goods and services at different prices from the same company.
Choice **d** is incorrect. This word means how well effort or cost is used.

28. Choice b is correct. The rate rises steadily before suffering turbulent ups and downs from around 1996 to 2010.
Choice **a** is incorrect. This would indicate that the rate rises increasingly without any drops; this is not true according to the graph.
Choice **c** is incorrect. This would indicate that the GDP does not increase at all, which is incorrect as shown on the graph.
Choice **d** is incorrect. The terms contradict each other, so they cannot all be true.

29. Choice b is correct. This answer correctly identifies that the graph drops before rising in the time period mentioned.
Choice **a** is incorrect. The graph obviously shows less dramatic changes during this time.
Choice **c** is incorrect. This choice does not accurately depict the graph.
Choice **d** is incorrect. The graph obviously shows less dramatic changes during this time.

30. Choice d is correct. The only choice that can be correctly surmised is that Andrew Johnson succeeded Abraham Lincoln as president. Between the first image, in which Abraham Lincoln is working on repairing the Union, and the second image, in which Andrew Johnson has the word "veto" above him, he has become president of the United States. A veto is an action exercised only by the president, and Abraham Lincoln would have been president during the reparation of the Union.

Choice **a** is incorrect. These political cartoons seem to show that Johnson did not continue the legacy of Lincoln's Restoration reforms.

Choice **b** is incorrect. These political cartoons do not seem to show Johnson in a favorable way.

Choice **c** is incorrect. One of the political cartoons shows Johnson flattened by the U.S. Constitution.

31. Choice a is correct. Both the Amendment process and the power of the presidential veto are shown in these political cartoons. In the first image, Andrew Johnson and Abraham Lincoln are "repairing the Union" by introducing Amendments to the Constitution. In the second image, Andrew Johnson is shown exercising the right of veto. In the third image, Andrew Johnson is shown being flattened by the Constitution of the United States, which is the document to which Amendments are attached.

Choice **b** is incorrect. While the presidential power of veto is shown in these political cartoons, this is not the best choice.

Choice **c** is incorrect. These political cartoons do not show the powers of Congress.

Choice **d** is incorrect. The Constitution does appear in one of the political cartoons, but nothing about ratification appears.

32. Choice c is correct. The political cartoon shows women leaving the men to take care of the children, and the quote is focused on equality between the genders. The political cartoon reveals some of the fears of the time—that if women were given equal pay, the right to vote, and more, men would be forced into the position of caretakers and housewives. In contrast, the quote simply states a request for equal civil and political rights, without addressing the roles of men and women in the home.

Choice **a** is incorrect. The quote mentions daughters, but it is not focused just on daughters.

Choice **b** is incorrect. While there are babies in the political cartoon, the quote is not about citizenship.

Choice **d** is incorrect. The political cartoon is not about men spending time together, and the quote is not about women spending time together.

33. Choice d is the correct answer. There is not enough data based on this chart to say whether the government policies affected the nation during the Great Depression. This would also require information based on cost of living per person, rates of employment and unemployment, and more to determine this.

Choice **a** is incorrect. There is nothing in the chart to indicate that President Hoover was correct regarding government spending during the Great Depression.

Choice **b** is incorrect. There is nothing in the chart to indicate that President Hoover was incorrect regarding government spending during the Great Depression.

Choice **c** is incorrect. According to information in the table, the Great Depression did affect the surplus and deficit.

34. Choice a is correct. Generally, as shown in the graph, states joined chronologically from east to west.

Choice **b** is incorrect. States on the West Coast joined later than states on the East Coast.

Choice **c** is incorrect. Southern states joined the union earlier or at the same time as northern states.

Choice **d** is incorrect. There is a clear trend indicating that the United States expanded from east to west.

35. Choice d is correct. West Virginia was admitted as a state in 1863, 75 years after most of its surrounding states. This suggests that it broke off from an existing state at a later date. Indeed, West Virginia was originally part of Virginia but separated during the Civil War—in which Virginia aligned with the Confederacy—and entered the Union as a free state.

Choice **a** is incorrect. None of the data shown on the map suggests that Wisconsin and Minnesota were once considered part of Canada.

Choice **b** is incorrect. California was admitted as a state on September 9, 1850, much sooner than most of the states surrounding it.

Choice **c** is incorrect. Texas was admitted as a state on December 29, 1845, while New Mexico was not admitted until 1912.

Part II

Your Extended Response will be scored according to three traits, or elements:

Trait 1: Creation of arguments and use of evidence

Trait 2: Development of ideas and organizational structure

Trait 3: Clarity and command of standard English conventions

Your essay will be scored on a 4-point scale. Trait 1 is worth 0–2 points, and Traits 2 and 3 are worth 0–1 point.

Trait 1 tests your ability to write an essay that takes a stance and makes an argument based on the information in the passages. To earn the highest score possible, you must carefully read the information and express a clear opinion on what you have read. You will be scored on how well you use the information from the passages to support your argument. Your response will also be scored on how well you analyze the information in the passages.

For your reference, here is a table that readers will use when scoring your essay with a 2, 1, or 0.

TRAIT 1: CREATION OF ARGUMENTS AND USE OF EVIDENCE	
2	• Makes a text-based argument that demonstrates a clear understanding of the connections between ideas, figures, and events as presented in the source text(s) and the historical contexts from which they are drawn • Presents specific and related evidence from primary and secondary source text(s) that sufficiently supports an argument • Demonstrates a good connection to both the source text(s) and the prompt
1	• Makes an argument that demonstrates an understanding of the connections between ideas, figures, and events as presented in the source text(s) • Presents some evidence from primary and secondary source texts in support of an argument (may include a mix of related and unrelated textual references) • Demonstrates a connection to both the source text(s) and the prompt
0	• May attempt to make an argument but demonstrates little or no understanding of the ideas, figures, and events presented in the source text(s) or the contexts from which they are drawn • Presents little or no evidence from the primary and secondary source text(s); may or may not demonstrate an attempt to create an argument • Lacks a connection to either the source text(s) or the prompt
Non-scorable	• Response consists only of text copied from the prompt or source text(s) • Response shows that test taker has not read the prompt or is entirely off-topic • Response is incomprehensible • Response is not in English • No response has been attempted (has been left blank)

Trait 2 tests whether you respond to the writing prompt with a well-structured essay. Support of your thesis must come from evidence in the passages, as well as personal opinions and experiences that build on your central idea. Your ideas must be fully explained and include specific details. Your essay should use words and phrases that allow your details and ideas to flow naturally. Here is a table that outlines what is involved in earning a score of 1 or 0.

TRAIT 2: DEVELOPMENT OF IDEAS AND ORGANIZATIONAL STRUCTURE	
1	• Contains a logical sequence of ideas with clear connections between specific details and main ideas • Contains ideas that are developed and generally logical; multiple ideas are expanded upon • Demonstrates an appropriate understanding of the task
0	• Contains an unclear or indiscernible sequence of ideas • Contains ideas that are inadequately developed or illogical; only one idea is expanded upon • Does not demonstrate an understanding of the task
Non-scorable	• Response consists only of text copied from the prompt or source text(s) • Response shows that test taker has not read the prompt or is entirely off-topic • Response is incomprehensible • Response is not in English • No response has been attempted (has been left blank)

Trait 3 tests how you create the sentences that make up your essay. To earn a high score, you will need to write sentences with variety—some short, some long, some simple, some complex. You will also need to prove that you have a good handle on standard English, including correct word choice, grammar, and sentence structure. Here is a table that outlines what is involved in attaining a score of a 1 or 0.

	TRAIT 3: CLARITY AND COMMAND OF STANDARD ENGLISH CONVENTIONS
1	• Demonstrates adequate use of conventions with regard to the following skills: 1) subject-verb agreement 2) placement of modifiers and correct word order 3) pronoun usage, including pronoun antecedent agreement, unclear pronoun references, and pronoun case 4) frequently confused words and homonyms, including contractions 5) use of apostrophes with possessive nouns 6) use of punctuation (e.g., commas in a series or in appositives and other non-essential elements, end marks, and punctuation for clause separation) 7) capitalization (e.g., beginnings of sentences, proper nouns, and titles) • Demonstrates generally correct sentence structure and sentence variation; demonstrates overall fluency and clarity with regard to the following skills: 1) correct use of subordination, coordination, and parallelism 2) avoidance of awkward sentence structures and wordiness 3) usage of transitional words, conjunctive adverbs, and other words that enhance clarity and logic 4) avoidance of run-on sentences, sentence fragments, and fused sentences 5) standard usage at a level appropriate for on-demand draft writing • May contain some errors in mechanics and conventions that do not impede comprehension
0	• Demonstrates minimal use of basic conventions with regard to skills 1–7 as listed under Trait 3, Score Point 1 • Demonstrates consistently improper sentence structure; little or no variation to the extent that meaning may be unclear; demonstrates minimal use of skills 1–5 as listed under Trait 3, Score Point 1 • Contains numerous significant errors in mechanics and conventions that impede comprehension OR • Response is insufficient to show level of proficiency involving conventions and usage
Non-scorable	• Response consists only of text copied from the prompt or source text(s) • Response shows that test taker has not read the prompt or is entirely off-topic • Response is incomprehensible • Response is not in English • No response has been attempted (has been left blank)

Sample Score 4 Essay

In the passage from Theodore Roosevelt's editorial, the former president argues against restrictions on criticizing the president for the things he does and says. Roosevelt states that it is, in fact, "morally treasonable to the American public" to try to stop people from speaking out against the president. Close to a century later, the same ideas appear in a letter to the editor by Ms. Greene, which demonstrates that this issue as it applies to freedom of speech and American civil liberties during times of crisis continues to be relevant.

The issue of American civil liberties during times of crisis has been the subject of debate since the founding of the nation. The U.S. Constitution guarantees certain rights, such as the right to freedom of speech delineated in the First Amendment. However, courts have often ruled that rights of free speech can be restricted when they interfere with the public good or general well-being of the population. One famous example of this is the right to shout "Fire!" in a crowded theater when there is no fire. Such a statement could result in panic and injury, and the person who falsely started the panic could be held accountable for the damage that results. During times of great crisis, the issue of civil liberties often comes into question. Should someone be allowed to say things during wartime that might demoralize the public or make the government look ineffective?

At the time of Theodore Roosevelt's editorial, it was almost ten years after he had left office, World War I was raging in Europe, and the U.S. government had passed laws restricting citizens from speaking out against it because of fears that public criticism could undermine the government's efforts and incite rebellion. In fact, labor leader Eugene V. Debs was imprisoned simply for speaking out publicly against U.S. participation in the war. These government actions do not reflect the U.S. Constitution and the rights of citizens detailed within it, and Roosevelt made that clear.

The September 2001 speech by George W. Bush, referenced in Ms. Greene's letter, represents a stark contrast in attitude to Roosevelt's editorial. The speech, given just weeks after the September 11th terror attacks, focused on how the United States would wage its war on terrorism. The president's stance on this battle was summed up when he stated, "Either you are with us or you are with the terrorists." Although he was speaking about American allies, this attitude, as noted by Ms. Greene, could open the door to the concept that U.S. citizens cannot use their freedom of speech to be critical of the president, and that anyone who does criticize him is automatically on the side of the terrorists.

Both Roosevelt's editorial and Ms. Greene's letter were written in times of crisis and reflect a similar viewpoint about how civil liberties should be handled during such times. The debate continues to this day, as evidenced by the recent case against Edward Snowden, who leaked information about government surveillance programs that infringed upon the civil liberties of Americans as well as foreign leaders. While some view his actions as the perfect example of why the First Amendment exists, others consider him to be a traitor who undermined the U.S. government's ability to engage in international diplomacy, and therefore harmed the public welfare.

About this essay:

This essay has earned the maximum number of points possible in each trait for a total of 4 points.

Trait 1: Creation of Arguments and Use of Evidence

This response earns 2 points in Trait 1 because it creates an argument and clearly uses evidence. The sample response presents an argument about the enduring issue of civil liberties in times of crisis and its relevance since the early 1900s. The test taker cites multiple ideas from the source texts to bolster his or her position. Additionally, the writer incorporates background knowledge about the importance of civil liberties throughout U.S. history in general and the role of civil liberties in times of crisis in particular. Taken as a whole, the response offers an argument that is closely aligned to what is directed by the prompt and is well supported by the source texts.

Trait 2: Development of Ideas and Organizational Structure

This response earns 1 point in Trait 2 because it makes clear and understandable connections between ideas and establishes a progression in which one idea logically leads to the next, starting at the very beginning: *Close to a century later, the same ideas appear in a letter to the editor by Ms. Greene, which demonstrates that this issue as it applies to freedom of speech and American civil liberties during times of crisis continues to be relevant.*

The main points are fully developed, with multiple details given in support of each. Additionally, the test taker used a formal writing style that is appropriate for communicating in either workplace or academic settings, while also keeping in mind the purpose of the task, which is to present a well-supported argument.

Trait 3: Clarity and Command of Standard English Conventions

This response earns 1 point on Trait 3 because it effectively uses standard English language rules and conventions to convey ideas with clarity. In general, the response contains minimal mechanical errors, and the errors that do exist do not impede readers' understanding. The writer uses language appropriate for expressing his or her ideas and thoughtfully composed sentences that generally avoid wordiness and awkwardness. Additionally, clarity and flow of the response are enhanced with varied sentence structure and appropriate application of transitional words and phrases to connect sentences, paragraphs, and ideas.

Remember, however, because the Extended Response question on the GED® Social Studies test asks for a draft written in approximately 25 minutes, there is no expectation that your response will be completely free of convention and usage errors.

Sample Score 2 Essay

Theodore Roosevelt speaks out in support of freedom of speech in his editorial, while Ms. Greene repeats the same support in her letter to the editor almost a century later. The issue of civil liberties during times of crisis is obviously an enduring issue in our country.

In Roosevelt's editorial, he says that the president "should be supported or opposed exactly to the degree which is warranted by his good conduct or bad conduct." He is supporting our civil liberties during time of crisis by pointing out that the president should be treated as another citizen.

In the letter to the editor, he says, "Either you are with us or you are with the terrorists." This implies that speaking out against the president or the government, will lead any person to be viewed as a terrorist, too. It implies that freedom of speech is restricted at least as far as it involves disagreeing with the president or his administration and its plans. Ms. Greene points out that the U.S. constitution gives us the right of freedom of speech.

The rights given to American citizens in the U.S. constitution were put there precisely so the government cannot take them away. Even during times of war, these rights should be protected.

About this essay:

This essay has earned 1 of 2 possible points in Trait 1, 0 points in Trait 2, and 1 point in Trait 3, for a total of 2 out of the 4 maximum points.

Trait 1: Creation of Arguments and Use of Evidence

This somewhat brief response offers an argument that demonstrates an understanding of how the enduring issue of civil liberties during times of crisis is presented in both excerpts: *Theodore Roosevelt speaks out in support of freedom of speech in his editorial, while Ms. Greene repeats the same support in her letter to the editor almost a century later.*

The writer also provides some evidence from both excerpts; for example, in the second paragraph: *In Roosevelt's editorial, he says that the president "should be supported or opposed exactly to the degree which is warranted by his good conduct or bad conduct."*

Although this brief sample response is connected to the prompt and the passages, it does not offer much information beyond what is presented in the passages about the enduring issue of civil rights during times of crisis, so it earns only 1 point in this trait.

Trait 2: Development of Ideas and Organizational Structure

This response does not earn a point in Trait 2. Although it does demonstrate an understanding of the task, the sequence of ideas is unclear, and only limited ideas are developed. For example, the test taker begins the third paragraph with *In the letter to the editor, he says, "Either you are with us or you are with the terrorists."* But he or she does not clarify who said this, which creates an unclear organization of ideas.

Trait 3: Clarity and Command of Standard English Conventions

This response earns 1 point on Trait 3. In general, the response contains minimal mechanical errors (although, glaringly, the writer does not capitalize *Constitution* throughout), however these errors do not impede readers' understanding. The writer uses appropriate language to express his or her ideas and thoughtfully composed sentences that generally avoid wordiness and awkwardness.

Sample Score 0 Essay

The quote from Roosevelt is about how you should be allowed to criticize the president if you want to. It's freedom of speach. I agree with the freedom of speech part. If I do something stupid at work, my boss never lets me hear the end of it. This is freedom of spech, and it also helps people get better at there job.

The letter has a quote from George W. Bush. The letter is about freedom of speech too. The quote talks about being with the terrorists or against thiem. I'm definately against the terrorists.

Criticism of our own government as a form of freedom of speech, and any of our civil liberties must be held sacred especially in times of crisis like this

About this essay:

This essay earns a score of 0 in each of the three traits.

Trait 1: Creation of Arguments and Use of Evidence

This sample response earns a score of 0 in Trait 1. It is extremely brief, is composed mostly of direct quotations or paraphrases from the passages, and attempts an argument that is barely connected to the ideas in the source material: *The quote from Roosevelt is about how you should be allowed to criticize the president if you want to. It's freedom of speach. I agree with the freedom of speech part.* Therefore, it does not adequately follow the prompt.

Trait 2: Development of Ideas and Organizational Structure

This sample response also earns a score of 0 in Trait 2. The organizational structure is scattered, and the progression of the one idea (Roosevelt believed in freedom of speech during wartime) is barely discernible.

Trait 3: Clarity and Command of Standard English Conventions

This sample response also earns a score of 0 in Trait 2. A chunk of the response is lifted directly from the passages, and in the sections of the response that are original writing, the test taker fails to use proper punctuation to mark quotations and makes numerous errors in sentence construction.

APPENDIX: MATHEMATICAL REASONING FORMULA SHEET

The Formulas That Will Be Supplied to You on the GED® Mathematical Reasoning Test

Area

Parallelogram: $A = bh$

Trapezoid: $A = \frac{1}{2}h(b_1 + b_2)$

Surface Area and Volume

Rectangular/right prism:	$SA = ph + 2B$	$V = Bh$
Cylinder:	$SA = 2\pi rh + 2\pi r^2$	$V = \pi r^2 h$
Pyramid:	$SA = \frac{1}{2}ps + B$	$V = \frac{1}{3}Bh$
Cone:	$SA = \pi rs + \pi r^2$	$V = \frac{1}{3}\pi r^2 h$
Sphere:	$SA = 4$	$V = \frac{4}{3}\pi r^3$

(p = perimeter of base B; $\pi \approx 3.14$)

Algebra

Slope of a line: $m = \frac{y_2 - y_1}{x_2 - x_1}$

Slope-intercept form of the equation of a line: $y = mx + b$

Point-slope form of the equation of a line: $y - y_1 = m(x - x_1)$

Standard form of a quadratic equation: $y = ax^2 + bx + c$

Quadratic formula: $x = \frac{-b \pm \sqrt{b^2 - 4ac}}{2a}$

Pythagorean Theorem: $a^2 + b^2 = c^2$

Simple interest: $I = prt$

(I = interest, p = principal, t = time)

Using the codes below, you'll be able to log in and access additional online practice materials!

Your free online practice access codes are:

FVEIH6EDMLEEW1604L54

FVEWGS11RG7X07D62VCO

FVEHV24WLBSRO1W3GQP4

FVEWX5D44IJEN28L1R11

Follow these simple steps to redeem your codes:

- Go to **www.learningexpresshub.com/affiliate** and have your access codes handy.

If you're a new user:

- Click the **New user? Register here** button and complete the registration form to create your account and access your products.
- Be sure to enter your unique access codes only once. If you have multiple access codes, you can enter them all—just use a comma to separate each code.
- The next time you visit, simply click the **Returning user? Sign in** button and enter your username and password.
- Do not re-enter previously redeemed access codes. Any products you previously accessed are saved in the **My Account** section on the site. Entering a previously redeemed access code will result in an error message.

If you're a returning user:

- Click the **Returning user? Sign in** button, enter your username and password, and click **Sign In**.
- You will automatically be brought to the **My Account** page to access your products.
- Do not re-enter previously redeemed access codes. Any products you previously accessed are saved in the **My Account** section on the site. Entering a previously redeemed access code will result in an error message.

If you're a returning user with new access codes:

- Click the **Returning user? Sign in** button, enter your username, password, and new access codes, and click **Sign In**.
- If you have multiple access codes, you can enter them all—just use a comma to separate each code.
- Do not re-enter previously redeemed access codes. Any products you previously accessed are saved in the **My Account** section on the site. Entering a previously redeemed access code will result in an error message.

If you have any questions, please contact LearningExpress Customer Support at LXHub@LearningExpressHub .com. All inquiries will be responded to within a 24-hour period during our normal business hours: 9:00 A.M.– 5:00 P.M. Eastern Time. Thank you!

NOTES

NOTES

NOTES

NOTES

NOTES

NOTES